BAD CHRISTIANS AND HANGING TOADS

BAD CHRISTIANS AND HANGING TOADS

WITCH CRAFTING IN NORTHERN SPAIN, 1525–1675

ROCHELLE ROJAS

CORNELL UNIVERSITY PRESS
Ithaca and London

First published 2025 by Cornell University Press

Library of Congress Cataloging-in-Publication Data

Names: Rojas, Rochelle, 1975– author.
Title: Bad Christians and hanging toads : witch
    crafting in northern Spain, 1525–1675 /
    Rochelle Rojas.
Description: Ithaca : Cornell University Press, 2025. |
    Includes bibliographical references and index.
Identifiers: LCCN 2024015259 (print) |
    LCCN 2024015260 (ebook) | ISBN 9781501779718
    (hardcover) | ISBN 9781501779725 (pdf) |
    ISBN 9781501779732 (epub)
Subjects: LCSH: Witchcraft—Spain—Navarre—
    History—15th century. | Witchcraft—Spain—
    Navarre—History—16th century. | Witch hunting—
    Spain—Navarre—History—15th century. | Witch
    hunting—Spain—Navarre—History—16th century.
Classification: LCC BF1584.S7 R64 2025 (print) |
    LCC BF1584.S7 (ebook) | DDC 133.4/3094652—
    dc23/eng/20240905
LC record available at https://lccn.loc.gov/2024015259
LC ebook record available at https://lccn.loc.
    gov/2024015260

In loving memory of my parents, Adolfo Luis and Cynthia Rojas

Contents

ACKNOWLEDGMENTS

I express my deepest gratitude to the late Gustavo Henningsen. The generous gifts of his time, guidance, and erudition were central to this book, and it was a great honor to be his *læring*. I extend my gratitude also to Dra. Marisa Rey Henningsen, from whom I learned much during my tenure in Sevilla.

I thank Erik Midelfort for his warm response to the note I sent to him in 2009, his encouragement to apply to study under the supervision of Tom Robisheaux, and his great advice to lean into the hanging toads. I hope my work will reflect positively on their academic legacies.

I am grateful for and honored by the funding from Duke University, the Fulbright Commission (Spain), the Charlotte W. Newcombe Foundation, and the American Association of University Women. These funding sources were crucial to the completion of this project.

There are so many wonderful people at Duke University to thank, among them Robin Ennis, Carson Holloway, Kelly Lawton, and Jehangir Malegam. Thanks to my cohort for their support, and especially Ashley Elrod. I deeply thank my mentors: Thomas Robisheaux for his constant reminder of the power of words and his attention to detail, his guidance in microhistorical methods, and his appreciation for the beautiful complexity of witchcraft beliefs; Pete Sigal for his appreciation of the peculiar, his affection for my toads, and his optimistic appraisal of the value of my work; and John Martin for his unwavering faith in me, ongoing support, and friendship.

I thank Allyson Creasman for providing succinct feedback and for kindly writing with me at the Pittsburgh public library. I am grateful to Kenneth Gowens for his mentorship and kindness, and to the anonymous readers who have provided me with invaluable feedback. I also thank Jorge Cañizares-Esguerra, Michael Ostling, and Laurel Zwissler for sharing their professional guidance.

To my friends and colleagues in Spain, especially Jim Amelang, Victoria Ruiz, and Maria Tausiet, I give thanks for their support and kindness. To my friends from the "Witches and Animals: The Animal Turn in Witchcraft Studies?" conference (Weingarten, 2019), I extend my thanks for the conviviality and conversation, especially to Wolfgang Behringer, Anders Berrojalbiz, Maria Elleby, Tommy Kuusela, Jim Sharpe, and Rita Volmer, and the sponsors, the Akademie der Diözese Rottenburg-Stuttgart/Tagungshaus Weingarten (Oberschwaben).

I must thank so many people in Navarra, starting with the amazing historian Jesús María Usunáriz for his generosity and kindness. Thanks to the late Mikel Azurmendi, to the archivists at the Archivo Dioseno de Pamplona, and to Gontzal Rubinos Artolozaga from the website TurismoVasco for letting me use one of his images. At the Archivo General de Navarra, I acknowledge the labor of all the people behind the scenes, both now and over the past five centuries, and also Berta Elcano, Peio Monteano Sorbet, and Félix Segura. A super *kaixo* goes to Miriam Etxeberria for her superb archival prowess, for rediscovering Catalina Yrañeta and the other lost witches, for her dedication to the *sorginak*, and for her extraordinariness. I also thank Mikel, las *txikis*, the familia Lara, and Carol Romera Santander for teaching me so much about Euskal Herria.

At Cornell, the encouragement of Emily Andrews and Mahinder Kingra made this book possible, and I am so humbly grateful for their support. I thank Jason Glatz for his excellent maps and David Luljak for indexing. And to Heidi Giusto I owe extra thanks for her writing and editorial support. I also thank the *Sixteenth Century Journal* for allowing some of the material on toads to reappear in this book.

Thanks to all of my friends and colleagues at Kalamazoo College who have supported me and encouraged me in this process, and especially Sandino Vargas-Perez. I also thank my students for their inspiration and brilliance, and especially Leo Kaplan and Nico Lipton for their assistance.

Finally, I am so incredibly grateful for my family and friends: the legacy of Bolivia Barquero Rojas, Adolfo, Cindy, and Roger Rojas, Liana Rojas, Daniel, Adrian, and Elisa Moreno Rojas, Barry and Flo Nielsen, and Sharon Ornstein, among other loved ones. All my love and thanks to Felix, Reyna, and Silas who shaped this book. And lastly, I thank my partner and fellow historian, Matt, for his extraordinary support of me and the stories of the witches of early modern Navarra.

Note on Translations

The various Latin terms used to describe witchcraft, *maleficium*, *sortilegium*, and *veneficium*, and their vernacular counterparts, *brujería*, *Hexerei*, *sorcellerie*, and *stregoneria*, have generated a kaleidoscopic range of definitions since the Middle Ages. Medieval understandings of the magic practitioner shifted as early modern theologians, jurists, intellectuals, and unlettered people created a set of characteristics that resulted in a cumulative stereotype of witches and witchcraft in many parts of western Europe. Some prominent themes included the notion of witches as heretics, evil deeds (*maleficia*) caused by diabolical means, attendance at witches' dances, night flight, and interaction with demons and the devil. Overall, from the middle of the fifteenth century, learned notions of witchcraft became increasingly defined by heresy and diabolism, and witches took shape as part of an anti-Christian cult. While considering the inherent limitations of any one of the many definitions promoted over the centuries, this book draws from Wolfgang Behringer's definition of witchcraft as "a generic term for all kinds of evil magic and sorcery, as perceived by contemporaries."[1] This definition reflects most closely the variegated, ephemeral, and sometimes inconsistent understandings of witchcraft in early modern Navarra.

The translations used in this book reflect the Spanish terms as presented in the records. I translate *brujería* as "witchcraft" and use the term "witch" to describe anyone that was called a *bruja* by her peers in early modern Navarra. When the records refer to *brujos y brujas*, I translate this as "male witches and female witches" so as to not render the

---

1. Wolfgang Behringer, *Witches and Witch-Hunts* (Cambridge: Polity Press, 2004), 10. I join Ronald Hutton in following "the mainstream scholarly convention" of using this definition but share his expansive understanding of its modern usages as will be discussed in the epilogue. See Hutton, *The Witch: A History of Fear, from Ancient Times to the Present* (New Haven, CT: Yale University Press, 2017), ix–x.

male witch invisible. I use the term "sorcery" for the Spanish *hechicería* and use "sorceress" to refer to anyone labeled an *hechicera* by her peers. I also do not differentiate between *hechicera* and *bruja*, as they were used interchangeably in the secular trial records.[2] It was common for villagers to describe the accused with the phrase *"bruja, hechicera,"* sometimes even supplementing the label with *"mala cristiana"* (bad Christian). Though the Inquisition differentiated between these labels according to the level of diabolical involvement, scribes, villagers, and jurists did not, so I privilege the terminology used by villagers in their reports over my own definitions of a witch or sorceress, or those proposed by other scholars. I do not place the word witch in quotations, nor do I preface it with "so-called," but rather refer to them as witches and sorceresses as did their neighbors. In doing so, I do not imply that the witches prosecuted here were genuine heretics who followed a pre-Christian, nature-based, or diabolical cult. I do not believe that the witches in these trials of early modern Navarra corporally attended witches' gatherings, interacted with or worshiped the devil, or partook in the activities of an anti-Christian cult. But it is irrelevant whether or not I believe that witch belief corresponded with a physical reality. Those who did believe in witchcraft absolutely considered it to be real.[3] The witches of Navarra were real in that villagers, magistrates, clerics, and others assumed them to be potentially dangerous members of their communities. Equally real was the devastation a witchcraft accusation brought not only to the accused but also to their families, friends, and even progeny.

Another translation choice made here retains place-names in their original Spanish. Spanish Navarra is not rendered in its French and English Navarre. As such it precludes the need to specify "Spanish Navarre" throughout, and joins other scholars who do not privilege

---

2. Cristina Tabernero and Jesús María Usunáriz Garayoa demonstrate that while the semantic range of these terms is broad and varied, their usage functioned synonymously within early modern trials in Navarra. For an analysis of these terms' histories, usages, meanings, and functions, see their "Bruja, brujo, hechicera, hechicero, sorgin como insultos en la Navarra de los siglos XVI y XVII," in *Modelos de vida y cultura en Navarra (siglos XVI y XVII)*, ed. Mariela Insúa (Pamplona: Universidad de Navarra, 2016), esp. 381–91.

3. Though the sources I engage with, specifically, witch trial records processed by the secular tribunals of Navarra from 1525 to 1675, do not support a study of the elements of reality in early modern witchcraft, I appreciate and respect the work of scholars who seek to locate actual practices and the constructions of experiences of reality. See Edward Bever, *The Realities of Witchcraft and Popular Magic in Early Modern Europe: Culture, Cognition, and Everyday Life* (New York: Palgrave Macmillan, 2008) for a compelling study of the intersections of witchcraft and the constructions of reality.

anglicized names. I use the place-names of Navarra and Castilla, as did the eminent Spanish witchcraft scholar Gustav Henningsen, but diverge from his usage of the term "Basque." While the subjects of our study no doubt spoke Basque, early moderners in this region would neither have used that term nor identified as such.[4] The only reference to a Basque identity in our records appeared when a witch from the French side of the geopolitical border was identified as being from the "pais vasco" and not Navarra. The single other reference to Basque was the term "vasgonada," meaning a speaker of the Basque tongue. Given the absence of the term "Basque" from the sources, and the fact that this book exclusively looks at Navarra and not the other three Basque provinces in Spain, this book does not use Basque as a marker of identity.

A final note of translation addresses the witches' gathering, which was referred to by the unique term *akelarre* in trials both during and after the witch panic of 1609. Trials before this date used neither *akelarre* nor the term "sabbath," rather they referred to *ayuntamientos de brujas* (witches' gatherings), *bailes* (dances), and *conventículos* (conventicles). The term "sabbath" in the context of witchcraft was not commonly used by early moderners, and never in Navarra. While a few early modern demonologists used "sabbath" and "synagogue" a handful of times (including Pierre de Lancre in reference to the French Basque trials of the early seventeenth century), it was not until the twentieth century that translators adopted this term to denote witches' gatherings. Future scholarship on early modern European witchcraft will benefit from dialogue with decolonizing methods that—among other things—advocate for privileging local, indigenous terms and avoiding anachronistic ones. As premodern scholars engage more meaningfully with diverse approaches and linguistic theories, perhaps future witchcraft studies will move away from the blanket term "witch" and treat the *bruja*, the *sorcière*, the *Hexen*, and the *strega*, allowing us to better appreciate the complexities and nuances of the captivating and provincial world of witchcraft.

---

4. The anthropologist Mikel Azurmendi (1942–2021) has written about the anachronism of using "Basque" as an identity. Azurmendi, *Las brujas de Zugarramurdi: La historia del aquelarre y la Inquisición* (Almuzara: Spain, 2013), 18–21. In a conversation with the late Dr. Azurmendi (summer 2012, Donostia), he argued that the only "identity" these Basque speakers would have had related to their villages and their animals.

Introduction
Witchcraft and Navarra

> If as historians we can take off the blinkers that
> have caused us to concentrate with unbecoming
> zeal on only the worst and most elaborate show
> trials, . . . we stand a chance of restoring magic,
> maleficium, and witchcraft to the quotidian world
> of ordinary commoners.
>
> —Erik Midelfort, 2011

During the summer of 1525, twelve-year-
old Graciana de Ezcároz occupied a position of great power and consequence. For many months, a commission from the royal tribunals of
Navarra had been touring the hills and valleys on an important security
mission "to inquire about the male witches and female witches" said
to commit diabolical deeds throughout the mountainous land.[1] Pedro
Balanza, the judge leading this inquest, solicited Graciana's expertise as
she possessed an extraordinary skill, one acquired from her experience
as a witch and inherited from her grandmother who had been burned
for witchcraft in Santesteban some years prior. Graciana knew how
to search for and discern signs of witchcraft by looking into villagers'
left eyes, a compelling technique with which to uncover the male and
female witches thought to harm neighbors, destroy crops, and fly from
windows to gather and "kiss the devil in the form of a goat under its
tail."[2] And so on the twenty-fifth of August in 1525, some four hundred villagers from the remote region of Ituren, nestled in the Pyrenean
foothills, traveled to meet Graciana and lined up before her "as if they

---

1. Archivo General de Navarra, Pamplona (hereafter AGN), TR_63825 (1533), fol. 6r.
2. Florencio Idoate Iragui, *La Brujería en Navarra y sus Documentos* (Pamplona: Institución
Príncipe de Viana, 1978), 253.

were getting indulgences."[3] Graciana examined each villager's left eye, searching for a sign that he or she may belong to the evil witch sect. Her inspection yielded a crop of twelve witches, ten women and two men. But to be certain of her judgment, she reexamined the identified witches—disguised in cloaks revealing only their left eyes—intermixed with others who were free from suspicion. Though she had been accurate on every account, out of an abundance of caution Graciana cleared two suspects, who returned to their homes undoubtedly with a great sense of relief.[4]

From this short narrative vignette emerges a complex, spacious, and often contradictory cosmology and lived experience. In many ways, this single event represents much of early modern witchcraft: it features parallels and paradoxes while simultaneously captivating its human audience, enthralling even our contemporary minds. But like their contemporaries, the commission, the villagers, and Graciana existed within a world that teemed with witches. And as people who feared and prosecuted those accused of sorcery and witchcraft, their world encompassed bad neighbors and good Christians, zealous judges and fearful villagers, peculiar witch-finding methods paired with empirical techniques, misogynous accusations and feminine agencies—paradoxical threads interwoven to form the complex web of witchcraft beliefs. This book treats this spacious and curious world of early modern sorcery and witchcraft as reflected in 150 years of surviving secular trial records from a rural, mountainous region in northern Spain.

Witchcraft in Spain calls to mind the Spanish Inquisition and its spectacular penitential ceremonies or *autos de fé*. This is not without reason as all English-language scholarship on Spanish witchcraft rests on the remnants of inquisitorial trials. Furthermore, as is the case with much European witchcraft scholarship, studies of Spain's witch trials have similarly focused on its single witch panic from 1609 to 1614 and the ample ceremonial, textual, and legal attention it generated. But a handful of years cannot be representative of nearly two centuries of beliefs and trials. Thus, this book moves in another direction and examines the typical witch trials as processed by the secular judiciary of Navarra, the royal court and council, tracing from the earliest extant witch trial records of 1525 to its final sorcery trial in 1675. Joining

---

3. Idoate, *La Brujería*, 260.
4. Witchcraft accusations could yield devastating consequences, shattering not just the lives of the accused but condemning future generations to the same infamy.

the corpus of witchcraft studies that moves away from the focus given to broad studies of witchcraft or the more spectacular witch panics, it builds upon the work of other scholars who have sought a greater understanding of common witchcraft beliefs in early modern Europe and have shown that an investigation of distinct cultural beliefs may more fruitfully be addressed via smaller scales of analyses. Accordingly, the present book does not center on spectacular and showy witch panics but attends instead to the seemingly unremarkable—but far more numerous—witch trials that yielded few deaths and did not amplify the role of the devil. As reflected in its title, *Bad Christians and Hanging Toads* argues that witches in Navarra were crafted drawing from a broad range of understandings, from people labeled as bad Christians to those who suspiciously kept chubby dead toads hanging on their doors.

A Brief History of Navarra

Nestled in the mountains of northern Spain lies Vasconia, the autonomous community of present-day Navarra. Navarra's landscapes rise to rugged peaks in the Pyrenees and span the gentle valleys in Cantabria, while vast forests and an abundance of water characterize the landscape. Multiple biogeographic areas converge in this humid northern land, including alpine systems, fluvial areas and humid zones, pastures and heaths, and extensive forests. Navarra was, and remains, a wet, mountainous land dotted with sparsely populated villages amid the rolling hills and deep valleys.[5] The inhabitants of this rural land shared greater identity with their Basque neighbors on the French geopolitical side of the Pyrenean range than with the Spanish-speaking residents of a newly formed Spain. These majestic mountains slowed the penetration of outside "civilizing" forces, and economic, legal, and religious exigencies reflected long-lived local customs and cosmologies. Fernand Braudel may well have been referring to the early modern Pyrenees when he noted "a separate religious geography seems then to emerge for the

---

5. According to the most recent census (taken in 2023), 17 percent of Navarrans live in hamlets of less than one hundred. Europa Press, "El 17% de los municipios de Navarra tiene menos de 100 habitantes," Diario de Navarra, April 7, 2023, https://www.diariodenavarra.es/noticias/navarra/2023/04/07/el-17-municipios-navarra-100-habitantes-564357-300.html. As of 2023, Navarra continues to have a low population of only 675,000. "Navarra," Expansión/Datosmacro.com, accessed September 7, 2023, https://datosmacro.expansion.com/ccaa/navarra.

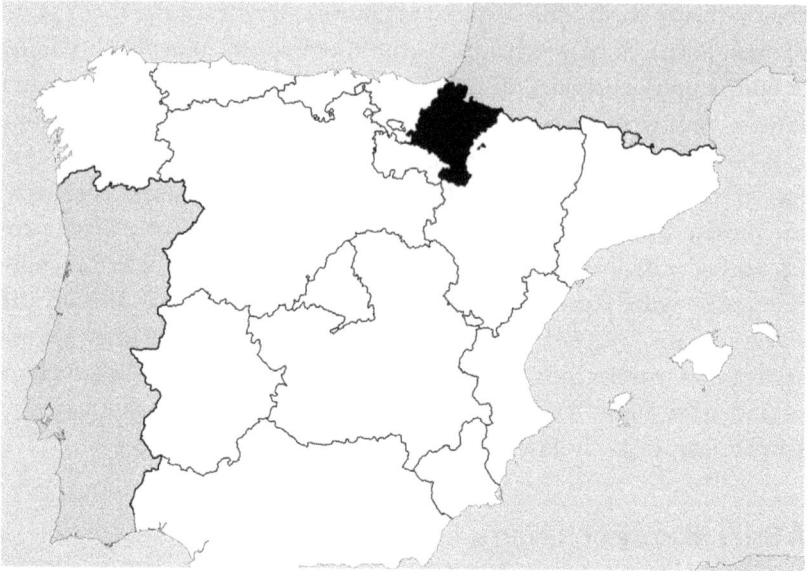

MAP 1. Location of Navarre within Spain. Source: Wikimedia Commons, CC BY-SA 3.0.

mountain world."[6] And the distinct flavor of this mountain world was infused in its trials of sorcery and witchcraft, ones that favored folkloric notions of *maleficas* (evil-doers) who used poisonous toad venoms and potent local herbs to harm fields and livestock, and bad neighbors who executed evil deeds without the devil.

The mountainous land of Vasconia has been characterized by fierce independence and semiautonomy in the face of conquest for centuries.[7] The Roman historian Livy was the first to note the Vascones' territory in his chronicle from 76 CE, and the Greek geographers Strabo (first century) and Ptolemy (second century) referred to the center of the Vascones' land as Pompaelo—modern-day Pamplona.[8] While most of Vasconia became Romanized, the mountains in the north resisted wide-scale Roman settlement and secured some amount of autonomy. Following invasions from Visigoths, and later Islamic powers, the Vascones

6. Fernand Braudel, *The Mediterranean and the Mediterranean World in the Age of Philip II*, trans. Sian Reynolds, vol. 1 (New York: Harper & Row, 1972), 35.

7. A modern history of Navarra is not discussed here, but contemporary movements for secession from Spain continue, as does the successful reintroduction of Euskera into Navarra's educational, administrative, and political systems.

8. Jesús María Usunáriz Garayoa, *Historia breve de Navarra* (Madrid: Silex S.L., 2007), 20; Julio Caro Baroja, *Con letra aguda y fina: Navarra en los textos de Julio Caro Baroja*, ed. Matias Mugica (Navarra: Gobierno de Navarra, 2014), 7.

continued to resist staunchly the interlopers' attempts at complete subjugation, as would be done in the face of future conquests.[9]

The kingdom of "Navarros and Pamploneses" was established in 803
CE following the Vascones' defeat of the Franks at the major Battle of
Roncevalles. The leader Íñigo Arista was crowned king of Pamplona and
ushered in Navarra's golden age, which would continue to flourish under the reign of Sancho III, expanding socially, politically, and economi-
cally, boasting major territorial gains throughout his eleventh-century
rule. And when the neighboring kingdom of Aragon subjugated it in
1076, again Navarra resisted, regaining its independence in 1134. The
twelfth century saw the popular Sancho "the Wise" advance Navarra
through the formation of important legal and administrative institutions, overseeing the foundation of the *consejo real* (the royal council)
and *cort general* (the general court) and intensifying the kingdom's campaign against the Moors. Significantly, Sancho the Wise transformed
his title from *Pampilonensium rex* to *Rex Navarre*, the king of Navarra, a
symbolic move signaling that Sancho was more than a noble ruler from
Pamplona—he was the king of an independent territory.[10] This bloom
was short-lived, however, and the early thirteenth century saw Navarra
depleted of its territories of Álava, Guipúzcoa, and Vizcaya by the hands
of Castilla, with the kingdom falling to French rule after the death of
an heirless King Sancho VII in 1234. The next century and a half were
characterized by instability, foreign rule, and conflicts surrounding unclear successions.[11] It was this state of internal weakness that would
linger and, eventually, be exploited by the Crown of Castilla.[12]

The expulsion of the Moors in 1492 brought Isabel of Castilla and
Fernando of Aragon dominion over every territory in Spain except for
one: the independent kingdom of Navarra.[13] Under the guise of the war
with France, the Catholic Monarchs invaded Navarra in 1512, forcing it
into subjugation that same year; though not without significant resistance. And when the Parliament of Navarra convened in 1513, Castilla
remarkably allowed the former to retain autonomy over its courts. The
new viceroy swore even to preserve Navarra's "charters, laws, freedoms,

9. Caro Baroja, *Con letra aguda y fina*, 27–29.

10. Usunáriz, *Historia breve de Navarra*, 26–50, 65.

11. Usunáriz, *Historia breve de Navarra*, 67–117.

12. For a historical overview of Navarra divided into seven major eras, see Iñaki Bazán,
dir., *De Túbal a Aitor, Historia de Vasconia* (Madrid: La Esfera de los Libros, 2006), 200–201,
Segunda Parte.

13. James Marshall-Cornwall, "An Expedition to Aquitaine, 1512," *History Today* 23, no. 9
(September 1973): 640.

exemptions, liberties, privileges."[14] This gesture had its limitations, especially as the Spanish Inquisition expanded into Navarra, subjugating its Jewish and Muslim populations and undermining Navarra's judicial autonomy. Many Navarrans remained profoundly disgruntled by the conquest, a sentiment exacerbated by the Spanish destruction of plazas, castles, and walls.[15] Following Navarra's initial resistance in 1512, two more significant efforts at liberation were made in 1516 and 1521, both backed by popular support. Navarra came closest to regaining its independence in the revolt of 1521, though this last effort was squashed at the Battle of Noáin, leaving the army in complete defeat.[16] But despite Castilla's dominance, Navarra's institutions maintained significant autonomy throughout the early modern period. The parliament, the royal court and the royal council (the royal tribunals), and the Diputación del Reino (a legal organ that supported the royal tribunals) continued to convene from the sixteenth to eighteenth centuries.[17] Whether or not this can be attributed to the "intransigence of the Vascones," as claimed by scholar María Puy Huici Goñi, or to the political prudence of the Castellano kings (including Fernando and later Charles V), it is remarkable indeed that the kingdom retained much judicial autonomy separate from royal power.[18] It is this judicial jealousy over its own trials of sorcery and witchcraft that yielded dozens of discursive witch trials processed by Navarra's secular court and council over the course of 150 years, offering a rare glimpse into quotidian witch beliefs in a region not plagued by convulsive witch panics.

Witchcraft in Early Modern Europe

Witchcraft casts a spell, attracting the attention of both scholars and the general public. In addition to inspiring myths, folktales, plays, movies, and popular imaginaries, witches have given birth to a vast scholarly literature, resulting in hundreds of treatises, books, journal articles, conference papers, edited volumes, historiographic reviews, and Internet sources devoted to witchcraft and sorcery. From madness

---

14. Usunáriz, *Historia breve de Navarra*, 139.

15. Caro Baroja, *Con letra aguda y fina*, 123–24.

16. For a thorough history of the conquest in 1512, see Peio Monteano, *La Guerra de Navarra (1512–1529): Crónica de la conquista española* (Pamplona: Pamiela, 2010).

17. Usunáriz, *Historia breve de Navarra*, 138–45.

18. María Puy Huici Goñi, *Las cortes de Navarra durante la edad moderna* (Madrid: Ediciones Rialp, 1963), 18.

to psychoanalysis, investigators of witchcraft have chosen their themes eclectically and creatively.[19] Thematic focuses range widely from studies of folklore to intellectual histories of belief, and from attention to the misogyny informing witch trials to the male witches who suffered, too, from accusations.[20] Spatial and temporal foci further nuance this complex historiography, ranging from broad overviews to microhistorical analyses, and from medieval sorcery to early modern witch-hunts.[21] Geographic breadth continues to expand as scholars have turned their studies eastward to Poland and Moscow, north toward Scandinavia, and across the Atlantic Ocean to the Americas.[22] Witchcraft lends itself to interdisciplinarity, inviting research from scholars of religion, literature, anthropology, folklore, history, and psychology. So extensive is this corpus that in addition to multiple historiographical essays addressing the witchcraft literature, two books dedicate themselves exclusively to its historiography.[23] Given the expansive witchcraft literature, it comes as no surprise that this present book has drawn eclectically from many researchers and reflects much of what other scholars of witchcraft have shown: witchcraft was diverse, variegated, and boundless.

In Navarra as elsewhere, the medieval belief in individual practitioners of evil magic evolved into a cohesive notion of the witch sect, enabling courts to find and prosecute witches with greater frequency

---

19. Erik Midelfort, *A History of Madness* (Stanford: Stanford University Press, 1999); Lyndal Roper, *Oedipus and the Devil: Witchcraft, Religion, and Sexuality in Early Modern Europe* (London: Routledge, 1994).

20. Carlo Ginzburg, *Ecstasies: Deciphering the Witches' Sabbath* (New York: Pantheon Books, 1991); Stuart Clark, *Thinking with Demons: The Idea of Witchcraft in Early Modern Europe* (Oxford: Clarendon Press, 1997); Lyndal Roper, *Witch Craze: Terror and Fantasy in Baroque Germany* (New Haven, CT: Yale University Press, 2004); Laura Apps and Andrew Gow, *Male Witches in Early Modern Europe* (Manchester: Manchester University Press, 2003); Alison Rowlands, *Witchcraft and Masculinities in Early Modern Europe* (New York: Palgrave/St. Martin's Press, 2009).

21. Brian Levack, *The Witch-Hunt in Early Modern Europe*, 4th ed. (New York: Routledge, 2016) and Wolfgang Behringer, *Witches and Witch-Hunts* (Cambridge: Polity Press, 2004) offer excellent surveys; Thomas Robisheaux, *The Last Witch of Langenburg: Murder in a German Village* (New York: W. W. Norton, 2009) provides a superb microhistory of a single witch.

22. The value of regional studies is made clear in Michael Ostling, *Between the Devil and the Host: Imagining Witchcraft in Early Modern Poland* (Oxford: Oxford University Press, 2011), Valerie Kivelson, *Desperate Magic: The Moral Economy of Witchcraft in Seventeenth-Century Russia* (Ithaca, NY: Cornell University Press, 2013), and Liv Helene Willumsen, *Witches of the North: Scotland and Finnmark* (Brill: Leiden, 2013). For novel approaches in the Americas, see Laura Lewis, *Hall of Mirrors: Power, Witchcraft, and Caste in Colonial Mexico* (Durham, NC: Duke University Press, 2003), and Emerson Baker, *A Storm of Witchcraft: The Salem Trials and the American Experience* (Oxford: Oxford University Press, 2014).

23. Jonathon Barry and Owen Davies, eds., *Witchcraft Historiography* (Basingstoke: Palgrave Macmillan, 2007); Marko Nenonen and Raisa María Toivo, eds., *Writing Witch-Hunt Histories: Challenging the Paradigm* (Leiden: Brill, 2013).

and ferocity in the sixteenth and seventeenth centuries. And as scholars have found with relative consistency, most—though by no means all—of these accused were women, often poor and unattached to a male protector. Though elite male jurists and inquisitors persecuted and prosecuted witches, unlettered neighbors and kin usually supplied denunciations to the court and contributed to legal processes. Legal systems—from ecclesiastical courts to local judiciaries to the extensive Inquisitions—supported witchcraft persecutions, wrestling frequently over the judicial right to prosecute this grave crime. Underlying these various social and legal contexts, Europe's religious cosmologies and reform projects created and supported witchcraft beliefs, often turning problematic neighbors (in Navarra, "bad Christians") into diabolical witches.

Early modern European witch trials arose from a conjunction of factors and a constellation of beliefs, and in many ways depended profoundly on local and specific contexts.[24] Centering these understandings, this book draws from scholarship that contextualizes witchcraft within its specific social and cultural relationships and advocates for the necessity of multicausal understandings. Robin Briggs turned to social contexts and networks for an understanding of witch persecutions in *Witches and Neighbors* (1996). Focusing his study on the Lorraine, Briggs demonstrated that witchcraft was dauntingly complex and could only be understood through examining multiple causations. Drawing from local sources, Briggs revealed accusations and trials to be vastly variable, leading him to conclude that "sweeping generalizations about it are either false or so banal as to lack any analytical power."[25] Stuart Clark also examined witchcraft through a manifold lens attending to the broader intellectual contexts of witch belief, situating it alongside other concerns such as religion, law, and science in his seminal work, *Thinking with Demons* (1999). Rather than casting witch belief as aberrant or ill-informed, Clark approached demonological writings with a careful analysis of language, examining witchcraft on its own terms rather than searching for external explanations for

---

24. This is seen clearly in the differences between rural and urban witchcraft, as María Tausiet has shown in *Urban Magic in Early Modern Spain: Abracadabra Omnipotens* (New York: Palgrave Macmillan, 2014), esp. 3–7. Even within the single region of Navarra, witch trials varied based on how they came to be processed, as will be argued throughout this book.

25. Robin Briggs, *Witches and Neighbors: The Social and Cultural Context of European Witchcraft* (New York: Penguin, 1996), 7.

"people's belief in things that already made sense to them."[26] Clark's work demonstrated that it made perfect sense to believe in the preternatural—and especially witches—in early modern Europe. And finally, this book makes use of the invaluable surveys of Wolfgang Behringer and Brian Levack, both of whom painstakingly compiled comprehensive witchcraft scholarship and, in combination with their own studies of witch beliefs and trials, offer extensive surveys that encompass interdisciplinary methods, regional contexts, sweeping witch-hunts, and the social, legal, religious, scientific, and cultural cosmologies that supported beliefs, fears, and prosecutions.[27]

I follow Briggs's suggestion that analyses must start at the level of the protagonists of most prosecutions—ordinary people—and accept Erik Midelfort's invitation to "learn from the small and hitherto neglected cases, including the many that resulted in exile or acquittal rather than in massive burnings at the stake."[28] This book therefore turns to the dozens of surviving witchcraft trials outside of the panic, ones that have escaped notice and that were processed under a secular court in a mountainous region in northern Spain.[29] Here I offer a brief historiographical review of the less-known but superb scholarship of Spanish witchcraft studies for two reasons: first, literature reviews tend to omit Spanish sources (beyond the customary nod to Gustav Henningsen) rendering many of these works unknown to witchcraft scholars; and second, because this book's contributions will be best understood when situated among the meager Spanish witchcraft scholarship. As shown, most scholarship has centered on the single witch panic and relied on inquisitorial sources, demonstrating clearly the need to explore witch beliefs and trials over the *longue durée*.

---

26. Clark, *Thinking with Demons*, 7.

27. Behringer, *Witches and Witch-Hunts*, which also includes contemporary witchcraft; Levack, *The Witch-Hunt*.

28. H. C. Erik Midelfort, "Witch Craze? Beyond the Legends of Panic," *Magic, Ritual, and Witchcraft* 6, no. 1 (Summer 2011): 31.

29. Two Spanish-language studies present excerpts and analyses of some of these trials; see Idoate, *La Brujería* and Jesús María Usunáriz Garayoa, ed., *Akelarre: La caza de brujas en el Pirineo (siglos XIII–XIX)*, RIEV Cuadernos 9 (Donostia: Sociedad de Estudios Vascos, 2012). None of these secular trials have appeared in English at the time of this writing in 2023. These trials have been available to scholars in various forms. While a dozen of the trials had been unlocated for several decades, some transcripts were available in Idoate's book, *La Brujería en Navarra y sus Documentos*. Two witch trials from 1576 remain missing or damaged, and thus I do not include them in my total. I also do not include slander trials due to a witchcraft label in this total.

Witchcraft in Early Modern Spain

Much scholarship on early modern witchcraft has focused dispropor-
tionately on dramatic panics and on the more explosive regions of
Europe, a trend the Spanish witchcraft literature has followed by fixat-
ing on the witch panic of 1609–14 conducted by the Inquisition.[30] And
the few studies that do not treat the witch panic still rely mostly on inquisitorial sources.[31] This combination has limited our understanding
of Spanish witchcraft, as the witch panic was a short-lived, anomalous
event, and inquisitorial reports survive only as abbreviated trial summaries.[32] Over the past six decades, few monographs in English have
focused on Spain, supporting historian William Monter's reference to
Spanish witchcraft as "the forgotten offense."[33] Monter, as other scholars have, referred to witchcraft as a crime of the Inquisition.

Unsurprisingly, multiple Spanish-language academic books have attended to the witch panic. In *The World of the Witches* (1964), the scholar
Julio Caro Baroja provided the first in-depth examination of Spanish
witchcraft through a survey of its ancient and medieval roots, and up
to modern times. The second half of the book focused entirely on the
explosive witch panic spearheaded by Spain's Inquisition.[34] Another

---

30. Here I draw from Henningsen's definition of a witch craze as "an explosive amplification caused by a temporary syncretism of the witch beliefs of the common people with those
of the more specialized or educated classes." It is also characterized by mass numbers of
denunciations and confessions, a break in the "functional" role of witch belief, and the indictments of atypical people (such as people of wealth and power, men, and children). See Gustav Henningsen, *The Witches' Advocate: Basque Witchcraft and the Spanish Inquisition, 1609–1614*,
Basque Series (Reno: University of Nevada Press, 1980), 392.

31. For a comparison of Spanish Inquisition cases of witchcraft and sorcery (*Supersticiones*) in northern and southern Spain, see Gunnar Knutsen, *Servants of Satan and Masters of
Demons: The Spanish Inquisition Trials for Superstition, Valencia and Barcelona* (Turnhout: Brepols,
2009). And for an illuminating analysis of witchcraft in Saragossa, see María Tausiet, *Ponzoña
en los Ojos: Brujería y superstición en Aragón en el sigo XVI* (Madrid: Turner, 2004), and *Urban Magic
in Early Modern Spain* (2014).

32. All witch trial records from the inquisitorial tribunal of Logroño were destroyed following Napoleon's 1808 invasion during the Peninsular War; therefore, the only materials
available to scholars are the *Relaciones de las causas*, abbreviated summaries of the trials sent to
the Suprema in Madrid. Lu Ann Homza, *Village Infernos and Witches' Advocates: Witch-Hunting in
Navarre, 1608–1614* (University Park: Pennsylvania State University Press, 2022), 8.

33. E. William Monter, *Frontiers of Heresy: The Spanish Inquisition from the Basque Lands to
Sicily*, Cambridge Studies in Early Modern History (Cambridge: Cambridge University Press,
1990), 255.

34. At the time of this monograph's publication, the trial documents from the panic had
yet to be relocated after their usage by Henry Charles Lea, but Caro Baroja was fascinated by
the conclusions drawn by the inquisitor Alonso Salazar y Frías. Julio Caro Baroja, *The World of
the Witches*, trans. O. N. V. Glendinning (Chicago: University of Chicago Press, 1964).

prolific author of Navarran institutions and culture, Florencio Idoate, combined over one hundred excerpts from royal court records (some of which are no longer legible or available) with his analyses of the witch panic and other trials in *La Brujería en Navarra y sus Documentos* (1978). Indebted to Idoate's work as the former archivist of the Archivo General de Navarra (AGN) and for his introduction to these unpublished sources, this book expands upon this source base by more deeply engaging with the trial excerpts and adding a dozen trials not included in his publication. Yet another prominent scholar of Basque studies, the anthropologist Mikel Azurmendi, explored the witch panic and the dominant power held by inquisitors in *Las brujas de Zugarramurdi* (2013). Azurmendi meticulously examined the power relationships among villagers and between the inquisitorial interlopers, making clear that witchcraft as understood by villagers "had nothing to do with . . . the three inquisitors who persecuted the witchcraft of the people who spoke Basque."[35] And more recently, the eminent historian of Navarra, Jesús María Usunáriz, brought together a dozen scholars in *Akelarre: La caza de brujas en el Pirineo (siglos XIII–XIX)* (2012).[36] This edited volume examined various components of Spanish witch trials such as their medieval underpinnings, demonic possessions, and the French experiences of the Pyrenean witch panic.[37] One contribution that stood out in its attention to secular trials was Usunáriz's "La caza de brujas en la Navarra moderna," which laid out the patterns among the various jurisdictions of witchcraft throughout the sixteenth and seventeenth centuries in Navarra. Drawing from trial records of the royal tribunals, Inquisition records, and the work of Idoate, Usunáriz succinctly captured the various patterns, trial stages, and judicial contexts, and argued for sophisticated cultural and social investigations of witchcraft at the regional level.[38]

In English, four of the six books on Spanish witchcraft published by academic presses center on the witch panic. Gustav Henningsen's exhaustive investigations in both *The Witches' Advocate: Basque Witchcraft and the Spanish Inquisition, 1609–1614* (1980) and the subsequent *The*

---

35. Mikel Azurmendi, *Las brujas de Zugarramurdi: La historia del aquelarre y la Inquisición* (Córdoba: Almuzara, 2013), 13–14.

36. Usunáriz, *Akelarre*. This excellent collection of essays is dedicated to Henningsen.

37. Historians of witchcraft should all look forward to Jan Machielsen's *The Basque Witch-Hunt: A Secret History*, forthcoming from Bloomsbury in 2024.

38. Usunáriz provides illuminating maps that track the various witch trials throughout the sixteenth century. "La caza de brujas en la Navarra moderna (siglos XVI–XVII)," in Usunáriz, *Akelarre*, 309–18.

Salazar Documents (2004) drew from the Inquisition's surviving trial summaries (*Relaciones de las causas*) and correspondences to explore the witch panic. Henningsen's work attended to ethnographic and folkloric beliefs, the development of the witch panic, the social dynamics of the panic, and the crucial role of the Spanish Inquisition. These tomes, coupled with the scarcity of English-language studies, resulted in Spanish witchcraft's nearly exclusive association with this singular panic.[39] Forty years later, historian of British witchcraft Emma Wilby turned to the Basque witch panic in *Invoking the Akelarre: Voices of the Accused in the Basque Witch-Craze, 1609–1614* (2019), seeking to uncover popular practices or folkloric beliefs that villagers may have "mined" in their witchcraft testimonies. Drawing from previously translated documents emerging from the panic and situating them within a broader European folkloric context, Wilby yielded a provocative, "thematic analysis" of the Basque witch panic.[40] Most recently, the historian Lu Ann Homza has reexamined the famous witch-hunt in *Village Infernos and Witches' Advocates: Witch-Hunting in Navarre, 1608–1614* (2022). Homza's meticulous research revealed that villagers' slander lawsuits and unchecked notarial derelictions contributed to the Suprema's disapproval of the Inquisition's handling of the matter, leading to its new, strict guidelines beyond the efforts of the inquisitor Alonso Salazar.[41] Homza's book enriches our understandings of the witch panic by revealing the crucial roles of women, children, and collective village action throughout this momentous event.

Only two studies among the scholarship of Spanish witchcraft published in English have looked beyond the witch panic. In *Servants of Satan and Masters of Demons* (2009), Gunnar Knutsen examined the differences between inquisitorial witch trials in Barcelona and Valencia drawing from the Inquisition's cases of *Supersticiones*. Knutsen showed that witchcraft in Valencia was free from diabolism, while Barcelona's trials emphasized the diabolical aspects of witchcraft, demonstrating that differing cultural influences shaped witch beliefs in each region. Turning toward Aragon, María Tausiet's *Urban Magic in Early Modern Spain* (2014) examined the types of magical practices within the trials of Saragossa, arguing that magic in urban Saragossa rested upon

---

39. Before Henningsen, Henry Charles Lea addressed the witch panic in *A History of the Inquisition of Spain* (New York: MacMillan, 1906), 4:222–39.

40. Emma Wilby, *Invoking the Akelarre: Voices of the Accused in the Basque Witch-Craze, 1609–1614* (Brighton: Sussex Academic Press, 2019), 3.

41. Homza, *Village Infernos*, 165–79. The Suprema is the main office of the Inquisition.

conjurations, invocations, and spells, and thus differed from rural magic's greater association with diabolism. Tausiet endeavored to incorporate source material from all three justice systems in Saragossa: the Inquisition's tribunal, Saragossa's secular "Chapter and Council," and the episcopal court, but the Inquisition held a virtual monopoly over trials of the crimes it labeled *Supersticiones*.[42]

Focused on the witch panic and Spain's Inquisition, the Spanish literature has left the nature of quotidian witchcraft at the village level largely unexplored. This book, by contrast, explores witchcraft beliefs outside of the single panic by turning toward the unremarkable, regular witch trials that yielded few deaths and did not draw widespread attention, but produced over a thousand folios of testimonies. By shifting its attention toward a century and a half of witch trials processed by the secular tribunals of Navarra, this book seeks to enrich our understanding of early modern witchcraft by examining the discursive testimonies of suspected witches, their neighbors who accused them, and the jurists who judged them.

Sources and Language

The remarkable range of trials adjudicated by the secular court in early modern Navarra has been overshadowed by the witch panic's scholarship, resulting in the oversight of these sources, some which have never before appeared in print.[43] These regional sources challenge assumptions about the dominance of the Inquisition and upend the narrative of Navarra's witch-crazed reputation. Housed in the AGN, the records emerge from the courts of Navarra (the royal court and council, also called the royal tribunals) that tried a remarkable number of witchcraft cases compared to other regions in Spain (as per the current scholarship). To highlight the exceptional nature of these sources, the secular court of the neighboring kingdom of Aragon, for example, only tried

---

42. For example, the ecclesiastical court treated only eight trials focused on charlatans and deceivers, while the secular court treated a single case throughout the early modern period. Tausiet, *Urban Magic in Early Modern Spain*, chap. 1. Her exceptional first book on witchcraft in Aragon, *Ponzoña en los Ojos* (2004), investigated witch trials in Aragon as tried by the Inquisition, the ecclesiastical court, and the single witch trial by the secular court, though regrettably, this work remains untranslated from Spanish.

43. Roughly a dozen trials presented here have not appeared in print. About a dozen others had parts that appeared in Idoate's work. Some of the trials had not been located from around 1978 to 2014 when they were rediscovered by the tireless labor of the extraordinary employees at the AGN.

one case of witchcraft during the entire early modern period![44] This fact illuminates the extraordinary nature of witch trials conducted by Navarra's royal tribunals. Free from the Inquisition's filter, these dense sources constitute a superb source-base for researching Navarra's cauldron of witch beliefs since the tribunals' legal procedures differed from the more standardized process favored by the Inquisition. The depositions were produced under an interrogation procedure that invited open-ended statements from villagers, generating thousands of folios of discursive depositions from farmers, fishermen, net-makers, parents, children, healers, cobblers, clerics, judges, and accused witches, permitting an intimate exploration of everyday witch belief at the village level.[45] Though certainly not virginal imprints of early modern Navarrans' declarations, these mediated records nonetheless represent a dialogue and created a narrative.[46]

Beyond the secular witch trials, this book draws from documentary materials found in the AGN and elsewhere. Fiscal records from the medieval treasury registers attest to the medieval heritage of persecution of sorcery in Navarra and show, for example, that women were burned as witches in the early fourteenth century as reflected in brief accounting ledgers tallying costs for chains, wood, and executioners' salaries.[47] Another supplementary source, an inheritance petition brought forth by the prosecuting magistrate's heirs seeking their share of the witches' confiscated goods, fills in some gaps created by missing and deteriorated records from the early 1525 prosecutions.[48] This legal suit provides the names of accused witches, their villages, inventories of their material goods, and some testimonial records. Bringing this event even closer into focus are surviving correspondences

---

44. See Tausiet, *Urban Magic in Early Modern Spain*, chap. 1.

45. To offer a point of comparison, in the trials of two witches in 1647 appearing in both the inquisitorial and royal courts, the file from the Inquisition's records on both sorceresses covers only eight folios total whereas the royal tribunals' offer 222 folios of reports. Archivo Histórico Nacional, Madrid (hereafter AHN), Inq., Lib. 838, fols. 19v–23r, and AGN, TR_17176 (1675).

46. This informs the lengthy, dialogic trial excerpts that appear throughout this book. Carlo Ginzburg proposes this approach to witch trials in *Clues, Myths, and the Historical Method*, trans. John Tedeschi and Anne Tedeschi (Baltimore: Johns Hopkins University Press, 1989), 159. To support this approach, the reader will notice direct quotes throughout to allow the records to speak.

47. Here, again, I restrict the study to the region of Navarra and not the other three Basque provinces. But Ander Berrojalbiz offers other early sources from Basque regions in *Sources from the Dawn of the Great Witch Hunt in Lower Navarre, 1370* (Cham: Palgrave Macmillan, 2023).

48. AGN, 1525-Caja 113512, AP_Rena, Caja 94, N. 13.

including letters between the magistrates of the court and council, communication between these judges and the Spanish inquisitors, and grievances from the vicar general of Navarra. These surviving letters involved a wide range of intermediaries such as the Council of Castilla, the inquisitor general in Madrid, and the vicar general of Pamplona. These letters are found in the AGN, the Archivo General de Simancas (AGS), and the Archivo Histórico Nacional (AHN) in Madrid. Finally, though this study moves away from the Spanish Inquisition, I have examined all records of those witches who were tried by both judicial arms by comparing *procesos* (trial records) from the royal tribunals with the Inquisition's *Relaciones de las causas* housed in the AHN.[49] To these records I add a single developed witch trial processed by Navarra's episcopal court and housed in the Archivo Diocesano de Pamplona (ADP).[50]

Though not produced by the Spanish Inquisition, these early modern sources present their own challenges as the influence of magistrates, scribes, and translators inherently shaped them. Court records reflect a specific institutional context and the manners in which people navigated the power asymmetries within legal settings. Much was omitted, misrecorded, and lost in translation as their testimonies were noted within the overall goals of a courtroom or trial. Still, the open-ended interrogation processes allowed for diverse and discursive depositions. And while suspicious conformity and repetition of exact phrases among the witnesses appeared in several trials (usually chain trials), most villagers' denunciations differed from one another, allowing me to approach those varying sources with greater confidence that villagers were not merely replicating suggestive statements from their interrogators. Furthermore, the royal tribunals' trial records made clear from the onset when accusations were not initiated by the villagers, as the limited variability of the accusations in these particular trials reflected the denunciations that were furthered by a specific person or family. It is with the cautionary tales of other scholars that I approach these sources critically, but also with the appreciation that within these

---

49. In this case, the examination pertains solely to cases treated by the tribunal with oversight of Navarra. Thanks to a personal gift from Gustav Henningsen, many of the Inquisition sources from the AHN have been given to me digitally. I do not, however, attend to the slander trials treated by the royal tribunals that emerged from the witch panic.

50. Archivo Diocesano de Pamplona (hereafter ADP), Proceso de 1569, Aguinaga, Cartón 13.

records, as Carlo Ginzburg has suggested, the voices of villagers can be approached.[51]

A final note on the sources is that of language: the people of Navarra did not speak Castellano or Spanish, but rather Euskera or Basque, which they referred to as *vascuence*.[52] Though Castellano had been used in official matters since the medieval period, it was not until the conquest of Navarra in 1512 that the Spanish tongue began to force itself into the kingdom and the surrounding Basque regions (Guipúzcoa, Álava, Vizcaya).[53] Very few villagers in early modern Navarra spoke Spanish, but all spoke Euskera, a language isolate ancestral to the Vascones (ancestors to current Basque peoples).[54] Though geographically surrounded by Romance languages (those that evolved from Vulgar Latin between the sixth and ninth centuries), Euskera is not related to them. Its origins and history remain uncertain, causing scholars to argue that an early form of the Basque tongue predated the arrival of the Indo-European languages to the area,[55] while others have sought to prove its Indo-European roots.[56] As Peio Monteano has shown in his work on Navarra in the sixteenth century, the majority of inhabitants spoke Euskera, a language that nobody wrote. Conversely, few Navarrans spoke Castellano, the language of official documents, and even fewer could read and write it.[57] The dominance of Castellano in written sources does not reflect the fact that Euskera remained the culturally dominant language in Navarra even a century after the Spanish conquest. Because it does not resemble Spanish in any way whatsoever, magistrates and villagers relied upon interpreters, introducing yet

---

51. See Natalie Zemon Davis's critical review of Emmanuel LeRoy Ladurie's *Montaillou: The Promised Land of Error* in "Les Conteurs de Montaillou," *Annales. Histoire, Sciences Sociales* 34, no. 1 (1979): 68–70; Ginzburg, *Clues, Myths, and the Historical Method*, 159–64.

52. For more on the Basque language, see Jose Ignacio Hualde, Joseba A. Lakarra, and R. L. Trask, eds., *Towards a History of the Basque Language* (Philadelphia: John Benjamins, 1995), and Peio Monteano, *El iceberg Navarro: Euskera y castellano en la Navarra del siglo XVI* (Pamplona: Pamiela, 2017).

53. Caro Baroja, *Con letra aguda y fina*, 353–54.

54. Name given to the pre-Roman tribe that inhabited the region known as present-day Navarra.

55. Joaquin Gorrochatequi and Joseba A. Lakarra, "Why Basque Cannot Be, Unfortunately, an Indo-European Language," *Journal of Indo-European Studies* 41, nos. 1/2 (2013): 203–37.

56. Gianfranco Forni, "Evidence for Basque as an Indo-European Language," *Journal of Indo-European Studies* 41, nos. 1/2 (2013): 39–180.

57. In his excellent study on the lasting pervasiveness of Euskera and its importance in Navarra's history, Monteano also makes provocative connections between Euskera and witchcraft beliefs. See *El iceberg Navarro*, 97–104.

another layer of mitigation between the words expressed by the villagers and the text appearing in the documents.

Methods and Structure

This book analyzes the lengthy testimonies of witnesses, the accused, the judges, and litigators in witch trials, examining each one through a historical lens and close reading, unpacking historical clues as they elucidate how witch beliefs reflected early modern religion and society. It builds on the work of other historians who have sought to make sense of alternative systems of beliefs that might strike modern readers as irrational. Inspired by these scholars, I approach my documents with the understanding that the villagers' words and the tribunals' records reflected a world that made sense to them within their cultural systems and cannot be disregarded as irrational or superstitious beliefs.

Historians of the early modern world often depend upon written records of oral speech, and the judicial proceedings "might be comparable to the notebooks of anthropologists, recording fieldwork performed centuries ago."[58] In his *Night Battles*, Ginzburg approached his sources of inquisitorial interrogations as narratives, using these records to draw out the folkloric traditions and evolution of popular beliefs of the *benandanti*, a group of special villagers in the Friuli region who were crafted into witches by the Inquisition's imagination.[59] Ginzburg treated these records, not just as interrogations, but as mitigated dialogues that represented a conversation, an exchange of ideas, and potentially held the voices of the villagers themselves. Fortunately for this study, the villagers of Navarra were very talkative. The judges, like me, were trying to elicit information from the villagers. They wanted to know who the witches were, why they were suspects, what crimes they had committed, and so forth. In many ways, they shared the same questions that interest us, inviting us to treat these records as a "transcript."[60] While Ginzburg lamented the repetitive and "monologic" quality often encountered in Inquisition sources, he offered hope for "some exceptional cases where we have a real dialogue: we can hear distinct voices, we can detect a clash

---

58. Ginzburg, *Clues, Myths, and the Historical Method*, 141.

59. Carlo Ginzburg, *The Night Battles: Witchcraft and Agrarian Cults in the Sixteenth and Seventeenth Centuries*, trans. John Tedeschi and Anne Tedeschi (Baltimore: Johns Hopkins University Press, 1983).

60. Ginzburg, *Clues, Myths, and the Historical Method*, 160.

between different, even conflicting voices."[61] Remarkably, the sources of Navarra evidence "different, even conflicting" depositions as the norm, encouraging their use as "dialogic texts" toward an understanding of village witchcraft beliefs. To be sure, suggestive questioning was present, though usually implicit, but the responses provided by the villagers of Navarra were variable, diverse, and often contrary, suggesting that the villagers navigated how they chose to respond to the inquiries. These dialogues reveal a "particular way of talking about and understanding the world," and thus I turn to these discourses to better understand the nature of witch belief in Navarra.[62]

To unpack these dialogues, this study draws from the literary method of discourse analysis that views the function of language beyond the sentence. This approach encompasses a series of interdisciplinary methods that can be used to explore distinctive social features in different types of studies. It recognizes that words are not neutral but play an active role in creating that which they are used to describe. Thus, our knowledge of the world is not objective truth. No such "truth" exists. The ways in which the villagers understood the world were historically and culturally specific and contingent and reflected in their language. So, to understand the reality of witch belief in early modern Europe, we must turn to the words and categories that villagers used to represent their world. Informed by this framework, I have analyzed the importance and contexts of specific words and phrases in an attempt to elucidate witch beliefs, attending closely to what words and signifiers people used to designate witches. Their wordy discourses reveal how witches were crafted, what factors led to accusations, what sorts of behaviors exonerated witches from suspicion, and what kinds of feelings these witches emoted in their neighbors.

One of the most crucial implications of this study is that when we as scholars can move away from extraordinary people and events, specific contexts and nuances come more sharply into view. For example, one of the first observations emerging from these nonpanic trials made clear that power was brokered and shared by villagers. Of course, the elite magistrates of the royal tribunals and the inquisitors at Logroño held significant roles, but the shared language of witchcraft, used by elites and commoners alike, was largely predicated on village-level

---

61. Marianne Jorgensen and Louise J. Phillips, *Discourse Analysis as Theory and Method* (London: Sage, 2002), 1.

62. Ginzburg, "Morelli, Freud, and Sherlock Holmes," 5–36.

occurrences. To illustrate, from a more distant view, two older women accused in 1576 could be seen as classic, tidy tales of two old widows who may have been eccentric or beggars. But a closer examination of the vitriol used against them quickly made clear that the accusations were immensely personal and levied by interrelated individuals. This led me to search for previous cases within the families, and it emerged that neither woman had the *mala fama* (bad reputation) of being a witch in the least. And neither woman was poor or powerless; rather they were wealthy and respected matriarchs. This was no case of heterodox behaviors; this was pure revenge. Another reward of a close investigation at the regional level was the realization of the crucial role religious behaviors and expectations held in the crafting of Navarra's secular witch trials. While those with weak religious actions may have been largely ignored, in times of Catholic reforms and witchcraft trials, people scanned themselves (and others) in search of shortcomings. So, examining the language of witchcraft, the words that emerged repeatedly—*malas cristianas*, bad Christians—offered great clues. Most of these villagers had not endured lifelong accusations, but suddenly they appeared, accused of being a *mala cristiana*. An examination of how this term was used suggests that it was a shorthand for a witch and had little to do with theological heresies. But depending on the time period (such as during the chain trials), who a witch was and what she or he was accused of doing were shaped by the type of trial that processed witches and sorceresses. The judicial context of each witchcraft accusation influenced who was crafted as a witch and what types of *maleficia* (evil deeds) were said to be committed.

This book has followed Ginzburg's proposed model for "construction of knowledge" inspired by the art historian Giovanni Morelli.[63] Ginzburg argued that small details yielded large discoveries. The cultural histories of witchcraft have seen the value in the small, uneventful aspects of witchcraft over the spectacular and episodic witch-hunts. This has inspired my research to attend to the "thick descriptions" of the seemingly insignificant, the odd.[64] Hanging toads, for example, may appear extraneous, but a close investigation of toads using both a broad lens (toads in natural philosophy and religion) and a narrow lens (toads within Navarra and the Inquisition's reports) yielded rich insights for

---

63. Ginzburg, "Morelli, Freud, and Sherlock Holmes," 7.

64. Clifford Geertz, "Thick Description: Towards an Interpretive Theory of Culture," in *The Interpretation of Cultures: Selected Essays* (New York: Basic Books, 1973), 5.

this project. This book seeks to reassert the value of microhistorical lenses and to reorient our understanding of the past by contextualizing the witch, not only in terms of extending and complicating the story of witches and their persecution in Navarra beyond the popular events of 1609–14, but also by adding nuance to understanding the roles of competing courts, how different trials unfolded, and the reforming campaigns north of the Pyrenees and elsewhere.[65]

Bad Christians and Hanging Toads dedicates each of its five chapters to a particular aspect of Navarra's witch beliefs and witch trials, reflecting a close examination of witchcraft within its legal, religious, and cultural contexts. The first chapter, "The Witches of Sixteenth- and Seventeenth-Century Navarra," sketches an overview of the witch trials under the secular tribunals of Navarra beginning with its medieval inheritance and concluding with the last sorcery trial in 1675. Crucially, it introduces the three different patterns of witchcraft persecutions (isolated, chain trials, and the witch panic) in Navarra. It then guides the reader through the judicial procedures from accusations through to sentencing, situating the legal and institutional contexts of the early modern trials. Following this, "The Struggle for Souls" attends to the entangled relationship between the Spanish Inquisition's tribunal in Navarra and its secular court, analyzing the tense relationship between the two competing jurisdictions. The ambiguous nature of the mixed crime of witchcraft contributed to a constant battle over witches, while many accused witches and their defense attorneys (*procuradores*) sought actively to be judged by the inquisitorial arm. After these legal contexts, "The Christian Crux" situates witch belief within its religious contexts, examining the centrality of Christianity in defining witches, and the notion of a "bad Christian" (*mala cristiana*) as synonymous with witch. Though not all *malas cristianas* were witches, all witches were *malas cristianas*, reflecting the Catholic reforms influencing witchcraft's prosecution. Chapter 4, "The Testament of Toads," elucidates the diverse ways toads were used to understand how witches committed their acts of *maleficia*. This section intersects with the scientific supports of witch belief, as toads' bufotoxins yielded visible effects in the real world. The metamorphosis of the toad's roles also demonstrates the changing

---

65. Scholarship has shown the incredibly diverse manifestations of the Protestant and Catholic Reformations and the effects of reforms on witchcraft, gender, and law. For an overview, see the edited volume by Peter Marshall, *The Oxford Illustrated History of the Reformation* (Oxford: Oxford University Press, 2015). For the roles of reform in witch trials, I recommend Levack, *The Witch-Hunt*, 100–118.

nature of witchcraft beliefs and the negotiations between elite judges and unlettered villagers. "The Cauldron of Witch Beliefs" concludes the study and turns to the detailed villagers' reports at the heart of the witch trials and of this book. Rich and variable, these depositions reflect the vast and deep cauldron of belief from which villagers and jurists drew to craft their witches. Taken together these chapters illuminate how witchcraft was forged and informed by an amalgamation of legal, religious, and social forces over the course of the sixteenth and seventeenth centuries.

As its primary focus, this book uncovers the inner logic that imbued witchcraft belief with meaning and illuminates the coherence of systems of witchcraft beliefs. It joins the work of others who have turned to regional sources to promote an understanding of alternative systems of belief that might strike modern readers as irrational or absurd. Witchcraft understandings were natural and part of the "magical universe" in which these people dwelled.[66] The cauldron of witch beliefs allowed elite judges and unlettered villagers to draw from various ingredients to craft witches. But we must not conflate witchcraft *beliefs* with witchcraft *accusations and trials*. Witchcraft beliefs reflected a world in which magic appeared as an indispensable technology for navigating life, while a witchcraft accusation could permanently stigmatize and traumatize not just the accused, but also their family and progeny.[67] To be sure, witchcraft accusations and trials represented tragedy and sometimes death for those on the receiving end, as legal, gender, and witchcraft scholars have argued for decades.[68] However, to put the witchcraft trials of Navarra's royal tribunals into context, I must clarify that an accusation outside of the witch panic was extremely rare (though no less tragic

---

66. I borrow this term from the ambitious work of Stephen Wilson who describes the early modern European world as a "magical universe" where magic was infused into everything. While sustaining engagement with his work is beyond the scope of this book, his treatment of the wider context of witchcraft beliefs that "were in turn part of a much wider system of magical belief and practice" offers compelling insights into the magical universe. See *The Magical Universe: Everyday Ritual and Magic in Pre-Modern Europe* (London: Hambledon, 2000), throughout but esp. xvii–xxx for his introduction.

67. The psychological and physical toll ruined lives permanently. For a palpable and noteworthy depiction of the consequences of an accusation, see Robisheaux, *Last Witch of Langenburg*, 191–227, 302–27.

68. Though not specific to tragic outcomes, an interdisciplinary volume dedicated to witchcraft and emotions is Laura Kounine and Michael Ostling, eds., *Emotions in the History of Witchcraft* (London: Palgrave Macmillan, 2016).

for the accused).[69] As a final note, the chapters that follow introduce the reader to many fellow humans from the sixteenth and seventeenth centuries, people who will reappear throughout the chapters. It is my hope that my research demonstrates that "a close reading of a relatively small number of texts . . . can be more rewarding than the massive accumulation of repetitive evidence," and that these early moderners will inspire within the reader a greater appreciation, understanding, and even empathy for those who lived with and as witches.[70]

---

69. Here I draw from archivist Peio Monteo's estimate of nearly one hundred thousand trials in the AGN from the sixteenth century. *El iceberg Navarra*, 48. Of these, only approximately three dozen processed accused witches.

70. Ginzburg, "Morelli, Freud, and Sherlock Holmes," 7.

CHAPTER 1

The Witches of Sixteenth- and Seventeenth-Century Navarra

> Notice has come that in parts and places in the
> mountains of Navarra . . . there are many people,
> men and women alike, who are witches.
>
> —Royal tribunals, Pamplona, 1576

In 1510, the theologian Martín de Arlés y Andosilla, canon of the Cathedral of Pamplona, composed a treatise aimed at extirpating the superstitious practices persisting in the kingdom of Navarra. In his *De superstitionibus*, Andosilla underscored the connection between the region and a widespread belief in witchcraft and sorcery, lamenting that locals "falsely believe in witches and sorceresses and this is most prominent in the Basque region to the north side of the Pyrenees mountains, [where they are] commonly called *brujas* (witches)."[1] But Andosilla was not the first to initiate reforming efforts of the "superstitious" Basque-speaking people. In 1323 a synod convened in Logroño had decreed that "diviners, enchanters, augers, sorceresses, and those who commit other types of *maleficia*, whoever they may be" would receive excommunication.[2] So intense was this effort, the punishment extended to "all those who go to them, and believe in their words and acts, and take advice from them, and use them."[3]

---

1. Martín de Arles y Andosilla, *El tratado "De Superstitionibus" de Martin de Andosilla*, trans. José Goñi Gaztambide (Gobierno de Navarra: Institution Principe de Viana, 1971), 276.

2. Fernando Bujanda, "Documentos para la historia de la diócesis de Calahorra: Constituciones o casos del obispo don Miguel," *Berceo* 1 (1946): 121.

3. Bujanda, "Documentos para la historia," 121.

Synodal records, Andosilla's treatise, and multiple medieval ledgers documenting the execution of sorceresses reveal the long-standing connection between magic, sorcery, and witchcraft and the mountainous land of "Vasconia."

Spanning 150 years, these cases reveal a variety of trial patterns and a deep cauldron of beliefs. This chapter explores Navarra and its unique royal tribunals, examining the legal processes of crafting a witch or sorceress, and follows the various stages from denunciation to sentencing. Together these sections reveal that the remarkable privileges of Navarra's royal courts, combined with the specific manner in which each trial unfolded (isolated, chain, or panic), shaped not only the legal processes used but the accusations against and profiles of the accused.

Legislating Medieval Magic

Surviving fiscal reports from the fourteenth century bear witness to the fact that the secular courts tried and executed those, mostly women, accused of magical arts.[4] Penal proceedings of sorcery predating Navarra's surviving trial records emerge in accounting ledgers that documented annual expenditures from districts in Navarra submitted to the treasury of the kingdom.[5] Though records from only thirty-seven years of the fourteenth century remain, significant evidence reveals that the court of Navarra was no stranger to the prosecution of magic.[6]

The medieval fiscal records mention a dozen women charged with *maleficia* by virtue of their herbal craft. A report from 1314 offers the first account of the punishment of maleficent magic by the secular court when two women from the village of Ziga (thirty miles north of Pamplona) were accused of "killing women with bad herbs," imprisoned for two weeks, and burned for "the *maleficia* they had done." The payments solicited for the "logs and chains and cut sticks" and the labor "of the men who burned them and with their expenses in the prison" are all that remain of their stories, haunting murmurs tucked away in

---

4. I extend my gratitude to Félix Segura Urra, chief archivist at the AGN, for his generous assistance in pointing me to these special sources.

5. Félix Segura Urra, "Hechicería y brujería en la Navarra medieval: De la superstición al castigo," in *Akelarre: La caza de brujas en el Pirineo (siglos XIII–XIX)*, ed. Jesús María Usunáriz Garayoa, RIEV Cuadernos 9 (Donostia: Sociedad de Estudios Vascos, 2012), 287.

6. Segura Urra, "Hechicería y brujería en la Navarra medieval," 288. This is also made clear in Ander Berrojalbiz, *Sources from the Dawn of the Great Witch Hunt in Lower Navarra, 1370* (Cham: Palgrave Macmillan, 2023).

archival receipts.[7] Over a decade later, Joana la Christiana and several other "sorceresses and herbalists" were sent to the stake for "poisoning the people and being herbalists and doing much *maleficia*."[8] Their trial and execution cost the court thirty-four *sueldos*, the value of more than twenty lambs, or five weeks' salary for a laborer.[9] A record from the following year reports that "Jordana de Irissari, herbalist" was burned in San Juan Pie de Puerto, the capital of lower Navarra at that time.[10] In 1336 another unnumbered group of "*sortilegiis* . . . [were] brought to justice," while two years later Condesa de Urritzaga was "accused by her neighbors in Lasso that she had done sorceries," for which she was burned publicly in the marketplace of San Juan Pie de Puerto.[11] The capital hosted another burning in 1342 when two women, Alamana de Sara and Montanya de Vasques, "were killed according to their confession for being 'herbalists=*hechiceras*.'"[12] The fiscal demands from their execution offer some clues about their deaths, which generated expenditures for "the salary for the men who strangled them, the salary for the town crier who trumpeted their sentence, the cost of the rope to take them . . . the cost of the firewood to burn them."[13] It is noteworthy that this procedure of a public notification, and death by the garrote before public burning in the capital, mirrors the only surviving execution sentences of two witches in 1575.[14] The same year of 1342, the "lady of Aroztegui and a woman from Gabat" were burned in the market of Garriz for being "herbalists and *hechiceras*." The request for payment included the "costs of each one of their loads of firewood, and a beam on which they were tied and burned."[15] Unfortunately, the kingdom changed its accounting procedures in 1360, and these ledgers came to a halt.[16]

---

7. AGN, Comptos, Reg. 43 (1314), fol. 168v.

8. AGN, Comptos, Reg. 25 (1329), fol. 244r.

9. Florencio Idoate Iragui, *La Brujería en Navarra y sus Documentos* (Pamplona: Institución Príncipe de Viana, 1978), 11.

10. AGN, Comptos, Reg. 26 (1330), fol. 214v. San Juan Pie de Puerto (Saint-Jean-Pied-de-Port) was the old capital until the conquest by Castilla in 1512.

11. AGN, Comptos, Reg. 36 (1336), fol. 104r; Reg. 40 (1338), fol. 222r.

12. This quote appears as it was written in the archival source. AGN, Comptos, Reg. 47 (1342), fol. 231.

13. AGN, Comptos, Reg. 47 (1342), fol. 231.

14. Though executions for witchcraft occurred in 1525, those records do not survive, leaving the death sentences of 1575 as the only extant records of an execution in Navarra by the secular court. See AGN, TR_699853 (1575).

15. AGN, Comptos, Reg. 47 (1342), fol. 251r.

16. This does not mean that sorcery trials came to an end, however. For example, the 1370 sorcery trials of Pes de Guoythie and Condesse de Beheythie in Lower Navarra reveal

From these medieval records emerges a pattern: women, accused of using herbs for *maleficia*, were sentenced and burned in public spaces. Like most of medieval Europe, Navarra had not yet developed the full stereotype of the witch sect complete with cannibalism and the devil. But the cumulative concept of the diabolical witch emerging in the late fifteenth century led to a proliferation of legislation on how to deal with the threat these evildoers posed to early modern Christian society.[17] Thus as the cohesive notion of witchcraft took shape, the courts were better prepared to identify, persecute, and prosecute this great evil.

Patterns of Witch Trials

Navarra's trials of witchcraft and sorcery assumed multiple forms, and their patterns shaped the testimonies and foci of both witnesses and magistrates. Scholars have constructed helpful categorizations to describe witchcraft persecution patterns in early modern Europe. William Monter, for example, classified "small panics" as "groups of four, five, six, perhaps ten people arrested, tortured, and often killed . . . in one tiny jurisdiction over a span of eight to fourteen months."[18] Erik Midelfort defined large-scale witch-hunts as more than twenty executions in one year,[19] while Wolfgang Behringer classified "*witch trials* with up to three executions, *panic trials* with 4–19 victims, *large-scale witch-hunts* with 20–99 executions, *major persecutions* with 100–249 executions, and . . . *massive witch-hunts* with more than 250 victims within less than five years" in a territory.[20] Brian Levack categorized witch-hunting quantitatively but included qualitative characteristics. "Small hunts" comprised of individual prosecutions and groups of one to three people; "medium-sized hunts" claimed between five and ten victims and included torture and often stopped there "because the supply of stereotypical witches had dried up"; and "large hunts" included ten to hundreds of victims

---

for us sophisticated, developed notions of witchcraft that would later be reflected in early modern Basque trials. See Berrojalbiz, *Sources from the Dawn of the Great Witch Hunt in Lower Navarra, 1370.*

17. For an understanding of this shift from its "prehistory" to the early modern concept of witchcraft through the writings of Johannes Nider, see Michael Bailey, *Battling Demons: Witchcraft, Heresy, and Reform in the Late Middle Ages* (University Park: University of Pennsylvania Press, 2003).

18. E. William Monter, *Witchcraft in France and Switzerland: The Borderlands during the Reformation* (Ithaca, NY: Cornell University Press, 1976), 89.

19. H. C. Erik Midelfort, *Witch-Hunting in Southwestern Germany, 1582–1684: The Social and Intellectual Foundations* (Stanford: Stanford University Press, 1972), 9.

20. Wolfgang Behringer, *Witches and Witch-Hunts* (Cambridge: Polity Press, 2004), 49.

and "were characterized by a high degree of panic."[21] Henningsen identified qualitive criteria (the connection with the devil, who became suspects, and the percentage of the local population accused) to define a witch craze as "an explosive amplification caused by a temporary syncretism of the witch beliefs of the common people with those of the more specialized or educated classes."[22] While this definition succinctly described a "witch craze" or "panic," it did not address other, nonpanic patterns in Navarra's trials of witchcraft and sorcery under any tribunal, including the Inquisition.

While useful, general categorizations, often predicated on executions, offer a limited application to Navarra's secular witch trials. In fact, one of the largest witch panics in early modern Europe would fall short of being labeled a "large-scale witch-hunt" under Behringer's classification. The scheme I propose for Navarra's secular trials of witchcraft and sorcery draws from qualitative criteria to categorize the data. Informed by the run of surviving documents, from 1525 to 1675, three patterns of witch trials emerge defined not by the number of executions, but by the manner in which the prosecution unfolded (table 1). "Isolated trials" were instigated and treated in a single location with a single person, or single group of people. These included one—or more—accused witches but did not extend beyond that one moment in time and space. This pattern appeared in the various trials of solitary witches and sorceresses, a group of accused witches in 1595, and the few trials of the seventeenth century following the witch panic. These trials differed from instances of "chain trials," cases that extended beyond one village and instigated a search for other witches. The number of accused varied among chain trials, and it is difficult to determine exactly how many people were ultimately tried, but generally they tended to encompass more than twenty villagers. Three examples of chain trials emerge from the records in 1525, 1539–40, and 1575–76. The third and least common pattern is that of a "witch panic" characterized by mass numbers of denunciations and confessions, a break in the "functional" role of witch belief, and the indictments of atypical people.[23] The magnitude

---

21. Brian Levack, *The Witch-Hunt in Early Modern Europe*, 4th ed. (New York: Routledge, 2016), 171–73.

22. He distinguished between witchcraft and witch panics in his table of "aspects" toward a "dynamic theory of witchcraft." Gustav Henningsen, *The Witches' Advocate: Basque Witchcraft and the Spanish Inquisition, 1609–1614*, Basque Series (Reno: University of Nevada Press, 1980), 391–92, table 15.

23. Henningsen, *The Witches' Advocate*, 391–92.

Table 1. Overview of witchcraft and sorcery trial types in early modern Navarra

ISOLATED TRIALS		CHAIN TRIALS		WITCH PANIC	
YEAR	ACCUSED	YEAR	ACCUSED	YEAR	ACCUSED
1535	1	1525	56	1609–14	2,000+
1551	3	1539–40	21		
1561	2	1575–76	46		
1590	1				
1595	17				
1647	2				
1661	1				
1672	3				
1675	2				

Source: The numbers are drawn from Usunáriz, "La caza de brujas," 342.

of confessions and hundreds of accusations that occurred in Navarra in 1609–14 is a clear example of a witch panic. More importantly, these three patterns of prosecution enable us to see the regional trends of witch trials in early modern Navarra and attest to their great variability. These patterns also demonstrate that the method of a witch's prosecution related directly to the profile of and accusations against her. That is, the manner in which the case unfolded (individual trial, chain trial, witch panic) influenced who was accused (usual suspects with notoriety or atypical ones, such as wealthy men), how they had come to the court's notice (personal denunciation or judicial inquest), and how the accused was sentenced (absolution or execution).

Isolated Trials

Isolated trials appear as singular people or a single group in one village that did not generate an increased pursuit within the village or elsewhere. Isolated trials of solitary individuals tended to focus on women, while those that featured a group of suspects included men. The first isolated trial, appearing in 1535, provides an example of the solitary sorcery and witchcraft trials peppered throughout Navarra's records. María Sagardoy from the village of Aezcoa was denounced as a "bad Christian and poisoner."[24] This accusation, coupled with the

24. AGN, TR_209502 (1535), fol. 3r.

reputation that she kept a fat, dead toad on her porch, proved suf-
ficient for her arrest and imprisonment in Pamplona's royal jails. The
sorceress belief here was established: she was female, performed her *maleficia* alone, and concocted poisons to harm neighbors and society at
large. The devil, the witches' gatherings, night flight, and preternatural
powers made no appearance. Trials of solitary sorceresses and witches
relied heavily on the accused's reputation or *fama* in the village without dipping into diabolical ideologies.[25] At this time, in the autumn of
1535, the royal tribunals did not zealously pursue a conviction, nor did
María's denunciation generate a search for other witches, or a hunt for
every other "bad Christian" in Aezcoa. This would not be the case, however, when this same valley would experience chain trials five years later.

Another isolated trial appeared in 1561 with the energetic prosecution of sixty-eight-year-old Graciana Belza from the Valley of Roncal.
A robust list of accusations over three folios in length suggests that
every ill experienced by the villagers of Vidángoz was attributed to this
notorious neighbor. Her reputation as "a *mala cristiana*, a sorceress, a
witch" was substantial, as multiple villagers reported that her threaten-
ing behaviors left the whole village "terrified."[26] The village's terror testifies to the crucial role of the perceived intent to harm that informed
people's fear and willingness to denounce their neighbors. This isolated
trial featured a notorious town witch with established *mala fama* and
numerous denunciations. Yet despite the multiple and diverse accusations against her, there was a complete absence of diabolism, fantastical
elements (such as therianthropy), or accounts of witches' gatherings.
Diabolical tropes *usually* did not emerge in the isolated witch trials
of Navarra. Similarly, in the summer of 1590, Milia de Otano was denounced by a dozen villagers as "a person of bad opinion, a sorceress,
a charlatan, and full of superstitions."[27] Witnesses both in support of
and against Milia described the rituals she used to improve women's
fertility, help babies and livestock nurse, and unbind spells impeding
procreation.[28] But Milia also suffered from "the reputation that if she
was not content with her payment, she would hold back cures from her

---

25. This is not always the case as will be seen in 1595. *Fama* was one of the five main tropes
emerging in Navarra's cauldron of witch beliefs.

26. AGN, TR_211115 (1561), fol. 22r. While Graciana was tried alongside another accused witch, María Lopez, only Graciana was pursued so harshly while María was fined and
exiled for one year.

27. AGN, TR_148294 (1590), fol. 15r.

28. As Guido Ruggiero has shown in *Binding Passion: Tales of Magic, Marriage, and Power
at the End of the Renaissance* (New York: Oxford University Press, 1993), the magical powers of

clients. And if she had already unbound them, she would undo it and make it even worse until she was satisfied with the payment."[29] Even so, despite the ample reports of heterodox behaviors and illicit healing by a woman using rituals and countersorcery, no one used the term "witch." These charges did not devolve into a quest for denunciations or accusations of diabolism. The devil seemed to materialize only when larger groups of individuals were accused of witchcraft.

This occurred in an isolated trial from 1595 when an extended family from the village of Inza was accused of witchcraft by the alcalde (municipal magistrate), Fermín Andueza. Under coercive interrogation by Andueza and his son, the imprisoned group supplied confessions diverging sharply from the more typical concerns of witchcraft in Navarra (such as destroyed crops or bad neighbors), reflecting instead diabolical anxieties. Confessing to renouncing God and engaging in unnatural sex with the devil and one another, this level of diabolism transcended that of any other isolated witch trial in the tribunals' records. Within a month of their transfer to the royal jails, many of the accused villagers recanted their confessions, reporting tales of violent coercion by the Andueza clan. This unfortunate case came to its end when the court scribe traveled to Inza to receive testimony about the alleged perjuries and discovered that the original scribe deposing the accused witches had told many people, including his daughter, mother-in-law, and neighbors, that the accused "were not witches, nor were those they in turn denounced as witches."[30] Instead of *fama* at the village level, these "witches" were crafted by the hands of a very select group of people (Andueza's family and some unnamed clerics). Though this trial included seventeen villagers, comprising an extended family and children, it remained isolated in both scope (no other witches were sought) and time (no further arrests were made).

From 1595 until 1647, no crimes of sorcery or witchcraft fell to the royal tribunals. And following the Inquisition-led witch panic of 1609–14, the four trials of the secular court processed in the seventeenth century all reflected an isolated trial pattern.[31] But this absence of trials

---

women to bind men both in their fidelity and their (im)potence threatened patriarchal and church control.

29. AGN, TR_148294 (1590), fol. 20r.

30. AGN, TR_71319 (1595), unnumbered.

31. None of these sources appear in Idoate's book, while two of them are mentioned in Jesús María Usunáriz Garayoa, "La caza de brujas en la Navarra moderna (siglos XVI–XVII)," in Usunáriz, *Akelarre*, 337. Given this, this section dedicates some details to the untreated sources.

does not indicate an absence of belief. The dozens of crimes that fell under the Inquisition's label of *Supersticiones* between the witch panic and the royal tribunal's sorcery trial of 1647, and the four trials of sorcery that fell to the royal tribunals, all testify to the continued belief in magic and sorcery throughout the seventeenth century.[32]

In 1647, María Yrisarri and María de Ollo, two healers from Pamplona, were denounced to the royal court for witchcraft and sorcery and "diabolical arts" that brought about "much harm in the republic."[33] As their *procurador* argued for their referral to the Inquisition, the court's *fiscal* (prosecutor) fought to retain their case, highlighting the presence of *maleficia* and the lack of any solid proof of heresy. Ultimately, they were remitted to the Inquisition. About a decade later, the court charged fifty-three-year-old María Brigante with sorcery following the accusation of murdering a jurist, Bartolome Ximénez, by means of spells and a bewitched doll. Two dozen villagers from her native town of Lumbier reported María's *mala fama* and notorious reputation for sorcery, while her *procurador*'s defense argued that the testimony was brought forth with bad intentions and could "not be proven by the witnesses" being no more than "illusion and fantasy."[34] The court nonetheless attributed Bartolome's death to María's spells. This late isolated trial featured medical, clerical, and legal arguments of bewitchment, demonstrating the continuity of belief despite the slimming number of judicial persecutions. A decade later, in 1672, another isolated trial appeared before the royal tribunals when Pedro de Badostain and María de Sarasa were charged with *maleficia* and sorcery. Their *mala fama* in the town of Burlada had reached its crescendo when a newborn died in his mother's arms, distorted and black, following a visit from María. The court sentenced María harshly to four years of exile, testifying further to a continuity in strong belief of the magical universe despite the reduction of trials of magic.[35]

The last isolated trial under the royal tribunals offers a paradoxical conclusion to Navarra's history of sorcery and witchcraft prosecutions. The 1675 trial of María Esparza features sophisticated investigative

32. I draw this data from Henningsen's unpublished *Supersticiones* log given to me in 2012 and 2016. Recall that the category of *Supersticiones* encompassed healing, superstitious prayers, and other superstitions, and that the Logroño tribunal oversaw the three Basque provinces in addition to Navarra.

33. AGN, TR_16058 (1647), fol. 6v.

34. AGN, TR_59308 (1661), fol. 99v.

35. AGN, TR_299756 (1672), fol. 123r.

techniques fused with faulty reasoning. Many villagers in Esquiroz attested to fifty-year-old María's effective powers of healing, while ten witnesses spoke of her *mala fama*. But the most curious component—one that had not been used before in Navarra's witchcraft and sorcery trials—was the presence of and reliance on medical experts. This investigative process transcended the bounds of the magistrates and enlisted four *medicos* to discern if the source of María's healing "could possibly be natural" or if the various ills ascribed to her were the result of "supernatural effects."[36] Based on a reading of the accusations, these four educated medical men concluded sorcery was the source of her healing powers. Despite the procedural change, the continuity in belief was palpable, and María received a harsh sentence of exile. Following this isolated trial, never again did the royal tribunals adjudicate a trial for sorcery or witchcraft. This final case provides an opportunity to observe how the court had changed over the 150 years as it phased out chain trials, while simultaneously challenging arguments that credit an era of "rational" thought with the end of early modernity's witch trials.

Chain Trials

Chain trials—defined here as cases that extend beyond one village and instigate a search for other witches—occurred in 1525, 1539–40, and 1575–76. Various patterns in chain trials emerge: in situ investigations were often begun by officials, neighboring villages generated accusations, interrogations and accusations centered on diabolical tropes, "new" suspects cropped up among the accused, and larger numbers of villagers—including males—were accused. The record of witch trials under the royal tribunals began with a series of chain trials in 1525 involving a zealous judge, his traveling entourage of assistants, and a young witchfinder.[37]

In January 1525 the royal council dispatched the magistrate Pedro Balanza to "inquire, learn, correct, punish, and sentence the diabolical sect and the crimes committed by these witches who are said to be

---

36. AGN, TR_17176 (1675), fol. 26v.

37. Idoate, *La Brujería*, 34. Since the records from the judge, Pedro Balanza, and his activities are scant, it is impossible to categorize this event with certainty. Relying on numerical data alone, the witchcraft prosecutions of 1525 could fall into the category of a "witch panic." But given the absence of complete documentation it is most appropriate to label it a chain trial.

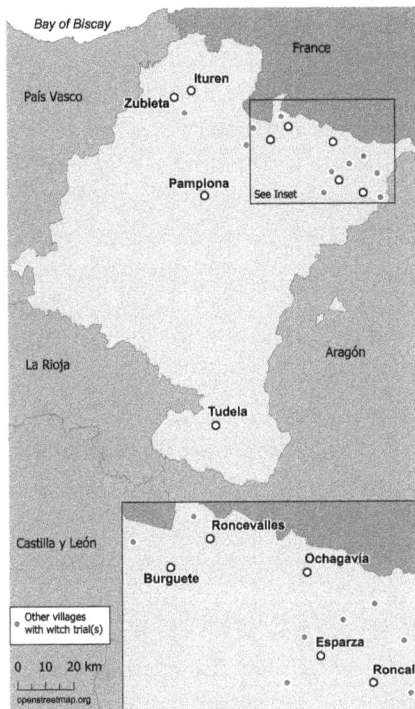

MAP 2. Witch trials held by the royal tribunals, 1525

in this Kingdom of Navarra."[38] Balanza began an energetic campaign against the witches in the Valleys of Roncal and Salazar, working diligently alongside a dozen various assistants (see map 2). The results were swift and dramatic, and within a few months the first mass execution was held.[39] But these anomalous, decentralized executions did not occur in Pamplona; instead, a traveling judiciary toured villages, and "the executions were made in the same villages where they had committed their crimes."[40] This diverged from the tribunals' customary judicial procedures that typically saw the justices dispatch the accused to Pamplona. These chain trials occurred in multiple valleys and lasted over six months, involving one to two hundred witchcraft accusations (not all were further processed by the court) and yielding approximately fifty

---

38. AGN, TR_63825 (1533), fol. 6r.
39. Idoate, *La Brujería*, 24.
40. Idoate, *La Brujería*, doc. 7.

executions.[41] The judicial power concentrated in a single magistrate's hand, and the search for witches (based on young Graciana de Ezcároz's examination of villagers' pupils), lent itself to a careless execution of justice. The chain trials under Balanza heightened tensions between the royal tribunals and the Inquisition and would serve as a cautionary tale against overzealous persecutions of witchcraft.

Fifteen years later in 1540, the same valleys experienced another episode of chain trials (see map 3). The tribunals charged a large group of villagers with being "witches [and] poisoners" who met at night to gather "filth and powders and burnt toads and other poisons" with which to kill their neighbors.[42] The accused villagers included the town's alcalde, Lope Esparza, a denunciation triggered perhaps by suspicion of negligence as the authorities claimed witches remained in the valley following the trials of 1525.[43] The indictments against the accused detailed diabolical, antisocial, and heretical activities at witches' gatherings, but interestingly lacked specificity (for example, no one was specifically charged with drying up the milk of their neighbor's best cow). This mirrors the general and diabolical accusations generated in other chain trials, revealing that the more people who were accused, the more generalized—and diabolical—accusations became. In total, the royal tribunals arrested nearly thirty people in these chain trials but acquitted most, handing out only four sentences, while transferring dozens of the remaining accused witches to the inquisitorial tribunal.[44] These chain trials ended at that point, and Navarra remained relatively free from witchcraft prosecutions until the latter quarter of the century when the bulk of the secular court's witch trials would occur in less than one year's time.

The final momentous chain of trials began in 1575 in the tiny village of Anocíbar with a priest, the unfortunate María Johan afflicted by unexplained fits, and two young boys. The vigilant priest Pedro de Anocíbar reported that two brothers, ten-year-old Miguel and eight-year-old Martín, had been taken to the witches' gatherings by their aunt, sixty-year-old María Johan.[45] The priest himself had prepared the

41. Usunáriz, "La caza de brujas," 311. Idoate offers higher estimates of 80 and 110 executions, Idoate, *La Brujería*, 40–41.

42. AGN, TR_63994 (1540), fols. 59r–60r.

43. As suggested by Usunáriz in "La caza de brujas," 312.

44. The names of the accused appear in the *auto de fé* of 1540. The Inquisition ended up processing forty-nine accused witches, thirty of whom were children.

45. AGN, TR_69853 (1575).

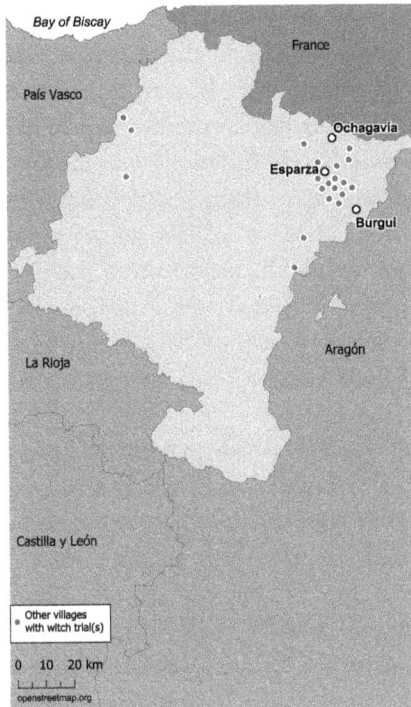

MAP 3.   Witch trials held by the royal tribunals, 1539–40

questions and interrogated the boys, presenting this material to the royal court in late August 1575. After being summoned by the *fiscal* and denying her guilt, María Johan was subjected to three sessions of inter-rogative torture, convicted, and sentenced to be "burned in the Plaza de la Taconera" in Pamplona on October 25, 1575. The two boys also accused Miguel Zubiri of witchcraft, and he received the same sentence, his execution held at the same site the following month.[46]

The first executions for witchcraft in five decades instigated a chain reaction of witch fears and a search for witches throughout Navarra.[47] As village authorities launched investigations into their regions' witches, more were crafted and found.[48] In only seven months, the

46. AGN, TR_69853 (1575), fol. 94r

47. E. William Monter briefly mentions this "outbreak of witch hunting" in *Frontiers of Heresy: The Spanish Inquisition from the Basque Lands to Sicily*, Cambridge Studies in Early Modern History (Cambridge: Cambridge University Press, 1990), 268-69.

48. This phenomenon would later be astutely characterized by Alonso Salazar y Frías, an inquisitor involved in the witch panic, who remarked: "There were neither witches nor

royal tribunals processed more than half of its total documented witch trials![49] A detailed treatment of all the trials and accused witches lies outside the scope of this section, but an overview of the chain trials will serve to highlight their features and commonalities.[50] These trials began to unfold immediately following the discovery of the witches of Anocíbar, as commissaries from the tribunals toured throughout the valleys of northern Navarra, collecting information.[51] A blend of established town witches, fresh suspects, and the ease of using a witchcraft denunciation to settle old scores supplied witches in every town where they were sought (see map 4). And within ten days of the aforementioned María Johan's execution, a new group of witches had been discovered.

Villagers throughout Navarra immediately began to find and denounce witches to the tribunals, who reported: "We have been informed that in the village of Huarte and its jurisdiction there are many people who have done much harm with spells and other maleficent arts."[52] This report produced four witches accused of a diabolical definition of witchcraft used often in 1575-76 that featured the witches' gatherings, night flight, relationships with toads, poisoning with deadly powders, and occasionally, sexual deviance and the presence of the devil.[53] By the end of 1575, an inquest spread to the village of Urdiain where five villagers denounced eighty-year-old Graciana Martínez for witchcraft, accusing her of raising a herd of toads to poison crops, animals, and children. But countering these accusations, seventeen villagers testified on her behalf, including the vicar, an abbot, and even one of the prosecution's witnesses. The *fiscal* nonetheless sentenced the bedridden Graciana to "perpetual exile."[54] This harsh punishment, despite the weakness of her case, demonstrates that in times of chain trials the procedures of an energetic court often broke from typical patterns of jurisprudence resulting in hyperaggressive sentencing. It also reveals the devastation

---

bewitched in a village until they were talked about and written about." Henningsen, *The Salazar Documents*, 342.

49. Of the existing known secular witch trial records, 54 percent occurred from November 1575 until March 1576, at which time the Inquisition assumed jurisdiction.

50. See Levack, *The Witch-Hunt*, 171–75 for some general trends in larger accusations.

51. These towns were Oricáin, Ostiz, Burutáin, Etuláin, and Esáin, in the Valleys of Ezcabarte, Olaibar, and Anué.

52. AGN, TR_327213 (1576), fol. 1r.

53. AGN, TR_327213 (1576), fols. 78r–80v. Diabolical dimensions emerged as one of the five main tropes in Navarra's cauldron of witch beliefs.

54. AGN, TR_327215 (1576), fol. 63r.

an accusation could bring. Meanwhile, another village in the Valley of Araquil launched an inquest of those "suspected to be witches sorceresses" resulting in the arrest of seven women and three men, all charged with the stereotyped, diabolical notions of witchcraft so prevalent during this pattern of witch trial.[55] Along with many others from the chain of witch trials, all the accused ended up in the arms of the Spanish Inquisition, where most received penances or absolutions.

In January 1576, the village of Burguete hunted for its witches and five were found: one with established *mala fama*, along with two other women and two men. Villagers' reports centered on the most notorious witch, Graciana Loizu and her toad familiars.[56] The magistrates sentenced Graciana to exile while freeing the appended accused witches demonstrating a trend found within chain trials: villagers free from long-standing witch reputations found themselves arrested alongside persons with established *mala fama*. In Navarra's secular trials, these accompanying witches were usually released, and sentencing was reserved for the primary suspects.

January's searches continued into February as the court dispatched a commissary to the villages of Ostiz, Burutain, and Esáin. The language found in the villagers' reports makes strikingly clear the impact Pamplona's executions had on these chain trials, as multiple witnesses alluded to the "accused witches from the village of Anocíbar."[57] Sixty-six-year-old Peruzqui de Yráizoz was not alone when he admitted he did "not know who in the place of Burutain and its neighbors have the *fama* and reputation and are witches . . . because before those from Anocíbar were imprisoned and killed as witches, he never saw any [witches]."[58] Similarly, fifty-year-old Martín Joan Torena's testimony reveals much about the crucial importance of Anocíbar and its repercussions, noting "it had never come to his notice that any person at all in his town had the *fama* of being a witch until the ones from Anocíbar were imprisoned and burned. And from that moment on, he heard . . . of those who are *brujos* and *brujas* in the said land."[59] This villager reveals for us the importance of publicly created *fama* and elucidates that witch fears were sensitive to and dependent upon collective discussions. Witch crafting and designations did not reflect an occult label doled out in private.

---

55. AGN, TR_327295 (1576), fol. 1r.
56. AGN, TR_98192 (1576), fols. 17r, 19r.
57. AGN, TR_11219 (1576), fols. 9v–10v.
58. AGN, TR_11219 (1576), fol. 9v.
59. AGN, TR_11219 (1576), fol. 10r–v.

As news of the burnings in Pamplona reached villagers, they in turn became primed to find witches among their neighbors, leading to more searches and suspects.

In the same month of February, the villages of Legarda and Urtega also began inquiries into "who have been or are in the opinion of being witches or sorcerers."[60] This yielded two very unlikely suspects in Navarra: Teresa de Ollo, a *hidalga* (noblewoman) with an impeccable reputation, and Juanes Isturiz, a man of great wealth. The familial connections among all the former's accusers made clear that hers was the unmistakable case of a witchcraft accusation utilized for vengeance. The denunciation of this well-respected, wealthy woman illustrates how suspects in chain trials often broke with traditional witch stereotypes. While Juanes was released, which happened often for male witches, Teresa perished in prison within a month of her arrest.[61] A similar situation occurred in March as the tribunals dispatched commissaries to the village of Muez "to inquire and discover who are male witches and female witches in the Valley of the Berrueca."[62] Though the village did not have any witches to report, one clever family of aristocrats seized this opportune time to avenge their father's death and settle decades' worth of animosities by denouncing another prominent family's matriarch, the wealthy María Perez de Olalde, for witchcraft. María, a *hidalga*, died within a month of incarceration.[63]

The chain trials of 1575–76 illuminate that when witches were actively sought in a legal context, they were found easily. Accusations were used to create a "roll" of suspects drawing from those with *mala fama*, as well as the newly accused villagers who appeared during chain trials. So tangible was this roll that several cases used the term *rolde* or the "roll of" witches. The curious use of the word *rolde* offers us some clues as to when broad searches for witches were occurring. Within the archives of Navarra, the use of *rolde* is reserved for accounting, fiscal, and administrative purposes. In inheritance cases, it sometimes appears as "*rolde* and memorial" of a list of belongings on the contents of coffers. Out of 150 *procesos* in the AGN from 1475 to 1675 that use the term *rolde*, none employed *rolde* to list people, only goods.[64] Yet, during the chain

---

60. AGN, TR_327744 (1576), fol. 1r.
61. AGN, TR_327744 (1576), fols. 166r–168r.
62. AGN, TR_294640 (1576), fol. 1r.
63. AGN, TR_294640 (1576), fol. 67r.
64. For example, in an inheritance dispute in 1537, a woman petitioned the court to aid in restitution of her possessions and presented the "*rolde* of her mother's goods" (AGN,

MAP 4. Witch trials held by the royal tribunals, 1575–76

trials, the word *rolde* applied toward humans appeared multiple times as investigators inquired in villages for names on the *rolde de brujas*, the roll of witches.

Fortunately, the royal tribunals did not follow the pattern of witch-hunting in more volatile regions where a routine line of the interrogation process dedicated itself to seeking accomplices, multiplying the number of accused.[65] The vast majority of witches crafted in the chain trials of 1575–76 ultimately arrived at the Inquisition's court where they either received absolution or were processed in the *auto de*

TR_197088). Some examples include a payment for a *"rolde* of wheat sacks" removed from the house of Jeronimo de Sarasa who died of plague (AGN, TR, 329815, 1600); a request for a payment of 458 *ducados* owed for the *"rolde* of cargo" delivered by Sancho from Pamplona (AGN, TR, 202345, 1638); and an inheritance sought from the *"rolde* and memorial of his parents' goods" sought by a son (AGN, TR, 227747, 1656).

65. For a useful explanation and map, see Behringer, *Witches and Witch-Hunts*, 105, and chap. 4 more broadly. Also Levack, *The Witch-Hunt*, 69–81, and chap. 6.

fé (penitential ceremony) of 1577. While the Inquisition's intervention broke the chain reaction of trials at this time, this same judiciary would fan the flames of Navarra's witch panic three decades later.

Witch Panic

The infamous witch panic began with the confession of a young woman who had recently returned to her home in a northern village of Navarra from the French Pyrenees where she had been working. While living on the French side of the border, the now-reformed witch, María de Ximildegui, had attended witches' gatherings called *akelarres*, which occurred also in Zugarramurdi on Spanish soil. María soon denounced several of her neighbors, and within a month, nearly a dozen villagers supplied witchcraft confessions to the parish church.[66] The confessions soon reached the tribunal's ears in Logroño, and by late January of 1609, the inquisitors had summoned several suspects for questioning. Meanwhile, some of those who had confessed to witchcraft locally sought out the inquisitors to recant their confessions. At the same time, fearful parents and officials pleaded with the tribunal to prosecute these witches who reportedly continued to kidnap children, taking them to the *akelarres*. Within six months, the Inquisition had collected evidence of at least three hundred accused witches and an even greater number of bewitched children.[67] Through combined results of voluntary and involuntary confessions, the crucial roles of children, mass denunciations, procedural irregularities, and preaching to exhort clemency, hundreds of confessions and accusations poured in, morphing into the extraordinary witch panic of the early seventeenth century (see map 5). As much excellent scholarship has already treated this event, this study restricts itself to a brief overview.[68]

---

66. Lu Ann Homza, *Village Infernos and Witches' Advocates: Witch-Hunting in Navarre, 1608–1614* (University Park: Pennsylvania State University Press, 2022), 1–2.

67. Homza, *Village Infernos*, 40.

68. For English speakers, I suggest Lu Ann Homza's *Village Infernos and Witches' Advocates*, which addresses the roles of parents, children, derelict notaries, and external influences in the witch panic and its resolution. See Henningsen's *The Witches Advocate* for full accounts and detailed ethnographic data, and *The Salazar Documents: Inquisitor Alonso de Salazar Frías and Others on the Basque Witch Persecution* (Leiden: Brill, 2004) for complete inquisitorial transcriptions. And for a provocative (though slimly cited) analysis, see the classic by Julio Caro Baroja, *The World of the Witches*, trans. O. N. V. Glendinning (Chicago: University of Chicago Press, 1964). In Spanish, see Usunáriz's edited volume, *Akelarre*. For an anthropological treatment of the panic, see Mikel Azurmendi's *Las brujas de Zugarramurdi: La historia del aquelarre y la Inquisición*

Thirty-one accused witches received formal sentences meted out at the Inquisition's *auto de fé* on November 7 and 8, 1610. These punishments, which included the burning of eleven unconfessed witches, served as both a public warning for transgressions and as entertainment for many people who traveled great lengths to witness this elaborate ritual of penance and punishment.[69] But instead of resolving the witch problem, this dramatic ceremony intensified witch concerns. As children continued to report kidnappings by witches, parents took matters into their own hands leading to "wide-spread, village-based torture."[70] Following these continued reports of witches plaguing the region, the Suprema dispatched one of the Logroño tribunal's inquisitors, Alonso Salazar y Frías, to the area in May 1611, where he began an eight-month-long visitation throughout the tribunal's territory.[71] Salazar noted judicial misdeeds and expressed his concerns and recommendations to the Suprema. Further, he noted the oversized role of children in the panic.[72] He thus advocated complete silence and discretion with the shrewd observation that "In my experience I have seen that there were neither witches nor bewitched in a village until they were talked about and written about."[73] While Salazar no doubt influenced the Suprema, Lu Ann Homza has recently shown that villagers, women, and families *also* shaped inquisitorial policy by bringing their accusers and torturers to the secular court for slander.[74] Notarial derelictions further influenced inquisitorial policy as the Suprema lost faith in the reliability of these witch trials.[75] This resulted in new instructions issued by the Suprema in August 1614 that drew from the 1526 witchcraft

---

(Córdoba: Almuzara, 2013). Idoate offers useful analyses and transcriptions in *La Brujería*, 175–216, 372–420.

69. Canonist Francisco Peña said of the nature of the *auto de fé*: "the main purpose of the trial and the execution is not to save the soul of the accused but to achieve the public good and put fear into others." From his *Manual de los Inquisidores* (1578), as cited in Monter, *Frontiers of Heresy*, 174.

70. Homza, *Village Infernos*, 47.

71. AHN, Inq., Leg. 1679, Exp. 2.1, No. 2[a], fol. 16r.

72. Homza centers the roles of children, referring to the witch panic as "fundamentally a children's event," *Village Infernos*, 29–35, 120, 185–87. While Henningsen highlighted children as the central aspect of what he called the second "stage to the witch craze," Homza has shown that children played central roles before the *auto de fé* of 1610. See Henningsen, *The Witches' Advocate*, 210–11, and Homza, *Village Infernos*, 30.

73. Henningsen, *The Salazar Documents*, 342.

74. Homza, *Village Infernos*, 21–23.

75. Homza, *Village Infernos*, 165–79.

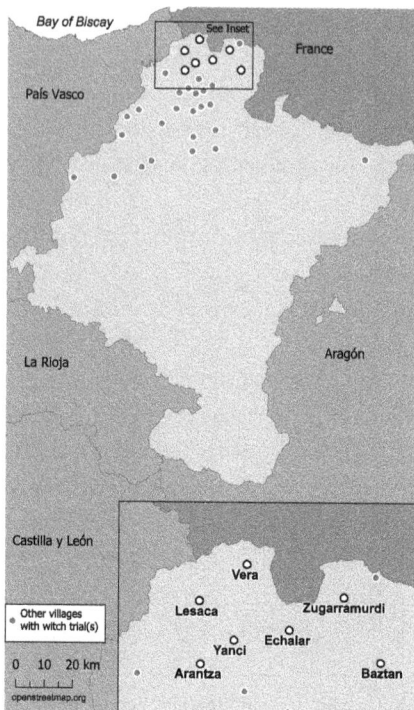

MAP 5. Witch panic under the Inquisition at Logroño, 1609–14

regulations while adding sixteen clauses taken from Salazar's own recommendations.[76]

The Inquisition's dramatic public penitential ceremony had intensified the witch panic. While *autos de fé* sought to attract and captivate spectators, this one featuring the infamous witch sect would prove to be extraordinarily well attended. After preparing stages and stands for observers (including a wooden structure eighty-four feet long, eleven levels of stands to accommodate one thousand people, portable benches, and a stage), the *auto* began on November 7, 1610.[77] Among the thirty-one accused witches dressed in *sanbenitos* (penitential smocks) and caps covered with flames and devils, eleven were sentenced to execution. The public ritual—including processions, lengthy readings of accusations and confessions, ceremonies of penance and forgiveness, scenes of

---

76. For the new list of instructions, see Homza, *Village Infernos*, 175–80; Henningsen, *The Witches' Advocate*, 370–77.

77. Homza, *Village Infernos*, 40–41. See Henningsen, *The Witches' Advocate*, 181–93 for a full description of this event.

contrite tears, and burnings of neighbor-witches—affected immensely all those present, which was said to number thirty thousand. So impactful was this *auto de fé* with its accompanying capital punishments, the printer Juan Mongastón reported: "Having listened to so many ghastly monstrosities for the space of two whole days . . . we all returned to our several homes, crossing ourselves the while."[78]

The witch panic represented a pivotal event in the history of witchcraft in Navarra. It is clear this mutation in witch belief was caused by a constellation of influences, including rumors from France, sermons preached by local priests, the persistence of villagers in eliciting confessions from family members, the extreme reliance on children, the composition of Logroño's tribunal, gross derelictions of duty, and the unintentional effects of preaching, visitations, and published edicts. The Inquisition's eagerness to solve this problem had only made it worse. As this section has shown, it is crucial to situate how villagers came to be prosecuted and the legal processes shaping each trial.

The Royal Tribunals of Pamplona

The roots of Navarra's royal court and council reach back to 1329 when Queen Juana II instituted the judiciary to improve and streamline legal procedures.[79] The establishment of this legal arm concentrated power in the hands of a single court and weakened noble authority. After the Spanish conquest, the royal court and council was reorganized with the court serving as the lower tribunal and the council as the appellate court. This restructuring included the appointment of a regent and six judges but reserved for the king the right to appoint the regent and two of the councilors, thus ensuring a Castellano regent would preside over the council.[80] Councilors serving in these positions required a law degree and an "Old Christian" lineage, yielding a tribunal composed of nobles and relatives. Additionally, four secretaries took declarations from witnesses, drafted agreements, recorded the trials, and carried out sentencing, including corporal punishments.

The *fiscal* oversaw the royal tribunals, supervising the discipline of the officials in the lower court and appearing as the official accuser

---

78. Henningsen, *The Witches' Advocate*, 193.

79. María Puy Huici Goñi, *Las cortes de Navarra durante la edad moderna* (Madrid: Ediciones Rialp, 1963).

80. Jesús María Usunáriz Garayoa, "Las instituciones del reino de Navarra durante la Edad Moderna (1512–1808)," *Revista Internacional Estudios Vascos* 46, no. 2 (2001): 691.

in all cases of serious matters, such as murder, sedition, and as the records reveal, trials of sorcery and witchcraft. As such, summaries and sentences in the trials often emerge from the *fiscal*. Opposing him, the *procurador* or "lawyer of the poor," served as the defense attorney for the accused. This included both those too poor to afford legal representation as well as wealthy individuals. To obtain their positions, *procuradores* had to complete a minimum of five years of legal training, fulfill an internship, and pass the council's aptitude test.[81]

The court and council functioned independently from the episcopal court (*curia diocesana de Pamplona*) and the Inquisition, and somewhat separately from the king and the viceroy. As noted by historian Jesús María Usunáriz, "it was the royal council, not the viceroy . . . who was charged with administering justice in the kingdom."[82] These special provisions no doubt strengthened the royal tribunals' sense of entitlement to the prosecution of witches and sorceresses, and it is within this early modern context—just a few years after Navarra's final revolt—that the royal court and council adjudicated its first witch trials in 1525.

As with other regions throughout early modern Europe, Navarra's legal jurisdictions were messy and overlapping. Not only did witchcraft prosecution fall to three judicial courts—the secular royal court and council, the Spanish Inquisition's tribunal in Navarra, and the episcopal *curia diocesana de Pamplona*—but Navarra's legal codes contained no explicit legislation on how to treat cases of witchcraft and sorcery. Its laws, extending back to its medieval *fueros* (local, foundational charters), simply did not address the crimes of witchcraft and sorcery.[83] This ambiguity nurtured a battle between the royal tribunals and the Inquisition's tribunal lasting over a century, and though the Inquisition oversaw the majority of trials of witchcraft and sorcery, the secular court approached approximately 150 accused witches and sorceresses from 1525 to 1675.[84] The *curia diocesana de Pamplona* did not stake high claims to witchcraft persecution, and only one significant witch trial

---

81. Usunáriz, "Las instituciones del reino de Navarra," 691–92.

82. Usunáriz, "Las instituciones del reino de Navarra," 694.

83. This stands in contrast to the secular court in neighboring Aragon, who promulgated witchcraft laws in 1584 and 1586. In Saragossa, most trials of sorcery and witchcraft fell to the Inquisition. María Tausiet, *Urban Magic in Early Modern Spain: Abracadabra Omnipotens* (New York: Palgrave Macmillan, 2014), 17.

84. These accused are distributed among the thirty-five *procesos* of witchcraft in the AGN on which this study focuses.

came to its court.[85] And while local alcaldes wielded power in civil matters and often initiated inquiries into *maleficia*, the records suggest they
usually surrendered suspected heretical evildoers to higher judiciaries.
But in the absence of explicit legislation regulating sorcery and witchcraft, it is not possible to define with certainty the exact criteria the
tribunals drew from in their initiation of trials.

Trials of witchcraft and sorcery in Navarra were produced under a
local inquisitorial judicial process. Introduced into continental European jurisprudence by the sixteenth century, the inquisitorial system
replaced the accusatorial one throughout most of Europe and significantly facilitated the conviction of accused witches. Inquisitorial
elements relied on formal initiation and prosecution and were biased
toward opinions informed by legal and theological doctrines featured
in demonologies.[86] Courts operating under the inquisitorial system
tended to be more likely to use severe punishments as a deterrence
against the crime of witchcraft. Though not all of Europe adopted the
inquisitorial process (England and Scandinavia, for example, persisted
in accusatorial procedures), Spain and other major legal systems adopted a general form of inquisitorial processes that focused on official prosecution and the search for "objective truth."[87] Inquisitorial
procedures, though somewhat varying according to local contexts,
established the initiation of prosecutions and the manner in which
magistrates determined guilt. Navarra's records reflect inquisitorial
methods, but as the historian Rita Voltmer has shown in the case of
the Holy Roman Empire, the courts combined inquisitorial and accusatorial procedures until the mid-seventeenth century—an observation
reflected clearly in Navarra's nuanced court records.[88]

Navarra's interrogation processes were not tightly scripted but rather
encouraged villagers to share freely the social drama, the gossip, and
the *fama*. Initial interrogations tended to be open-ended, many simply

85. This stands in contrast to the noninquisitorial witch trials in Aragon that were treated
by the episcopal court instead of the secular court. See Tausiet, *Urban Magic in Early Modern
Spain*, 23.

86. Bengt Ankarloo and Stuart Clark, "The Rise of Government and the Judicial Revolu-
tion," in *Witchcraft and Magic in Europe: The Period of the Witch Trials* (London: Athlone Press,
2002), 68; John Langbein, *Prosecuting Crime in the Renaissance* (Cambridge, MA: Harvard University Press, 1974), 131.

87. Ankarloo and Clark, "The Rise of Government," 66.

88. Rita Voltmer, "The Witch in the Courtroom: Torture and the Representations of Emotion," in *Emotions in the History of Witchcraft*, ed. Laura Kounine and Michael Ostling (London:
Palgrave Macmillan, 2016), 99.

inquiring as to whether there were any witches in the area. Testimonial transcripts reveal, too, that commissioners and judges posed different questions to different witnesses. In several trials, for example, children were pressed about magical elements while adults' interrogations centered on *fama*.[89] Most questions tended to be general and not focused on a particular act of *maleficia* or charge. The magistrates compiled these testimonies, while adding their own list of charges that sometimes did not emanate from the testimonies, most frequently during times of chain trials.

From Villager to Witch

Accusations of witchcraft and sorcery began often by villagers at the local level. While several trials suggest a cleric or alcalde instigated a denunciation himself, accused witches came to the authorities' attention usually via the murmurs of *mala fama* supported by numerous neighbors. This occurred, for example, when villagers denounced a "bad Christian" to a parish priest, or a bad neighbor to the local alcalde. Other times witches came to be crafted by vengeful neighbors.[90] And some witches, especially during the chain trials and the witch panic, were simply "caught up" in the net of witch-hunting. Once an accusation came to the notice of the alcalde, it is probable that he would conduct his own preliminary inquest (called "the first instance") before transferring the denunciation to Pamplona. When the magistrates of the royal court received the denunciation, a commissioner, scribe, and translator would conduct in situ their own interrogations of the accusers and, sometimes, of the accused. If the *fiscal* decided to move forward with the case, a functionary from the tribunals would escort the

---

89. Children did participate as witnesses and, sometimes, as witchfinders (1525, 1595). However, from my research examining the testimonies from all the witnesses taken together, seldom did children hold a stand-alone role. For example, while it can be disconcerting to identify three child witnesses (aged eleven, twelve, and fourteen) who testified in the early trial of Fortuno and the deceased bulls in 1539, recall "that in all the town of Ochagavía it is published publicly among the neighbors that Fortuno Legaz is a witch" (AGN, TR_36180 (1539), 9r, 13r). It was not children's testimonies alone, nor even mostly, that convicted Fortuno. The data shifts significantly, however, if we include the witch panic during which 1,384 children under the age of fourteen confessed to witchcraft. For an analysis of children and parental fear, see Homza, *Village Infernos*, 74–75, 102–4, 185–86.

90. *Mala fama* and vengeance are two of the main tropes that bubble forth in the cauldron of witch beliefs.

accused to the royal jails (*cárceles reales*) adjacent to the royal tribunal.[91] While court records portray the walk from the outskirts of Navarra to Pamplona in barren terms of hours and receipts for the use of mules, men, and minutes required to bring the accused securely to the tribunals, it takes little imagination to envision the terror women and men experienced as they scaled the steep passage upward toward the imposing judicial complex, along the ramparts, and approaching the walled city of Pamplona. Plucked from their rural spaces and deposited within an inhospitable penal system, accused villagers faced the harsh conditions of imprisonment and intimidating interrogations produced in the Spanish language of legal text, a tongue few (if any) of the accused understood.

Upon imprisonment, a functionary inventoried the accused's goods, as the sale of these possessions covered the debts incurred while in prison. This included the charges for arrest and transport, court costs, travel expenditures for scribes and interrogations, litigating fees, and room and board. Their material goods were usually minimal; a typical "list of goods" (*lista de bienes*) including only well-worn clothing, old bedding, pots and pans, and a meager supply of grains, hardly enough to occupy a single folio. And while several notable exceptions appear in the trials—surprising lists of multiple houses, vineyards, plots of land, livestock, furnishings, and other household goods—each of these emerged from revenge accusations in the chain trials of 1575–76.[92] The poverty of most witches prompted their *procuradores* to petition for poor relief to fund their basic sustenance. While we cannot conclude with certainty that the court condemned its prisoners to endure hunger from meager rations, it is safe to assume that provisions lacked severely, and harsh conditions threatened the very lives of the accused. And while in 1567 an official public policy sought to provide rations for destitute inmates who could "prove" their poverty, reports of starvation and death among prisoners continued to appear throughout the witch trials.[93]

---

91. The prison began in 1308 as a tower-prison housed within the royal castle, though the judicial-penal space of the trials treated here was not constructed until 1541 where it remained in Pamplona's center throughout the early modern period. This is the present-day *Casco viejo* or "old town" where the Archivo General de Navarra is situated on the original foundations of the royal castle. Pedro Oliver Olmo, *Cárcel y Sociedad Represora: La criminalización del desorden en Navarra (siglos XVI–XIX)* (Gipuzkoa: Universidad del País Vasco, 2001), 93.

92. AGN, TR_327744 (1576), fols. 21r–24v.

93. Oliver Olmo, *Cárcel y Sociedad Represora*, 123–24.

With the accused in custody, the tribunals issued a summary complaint against the accused announcing the witch's name, hometown, residence, and a generalized accusation. A typical pronouncement began: "The Supreme Court of this Kingdom of Navarra received notice that María de Arguello . . . of the town of Senosiain . . . bewitched a child. . . . She is securely imprisoned in the jail, accused of sorcery."[94] María's denunciation—prompted by a bad reputation (*mala fama*), in turn reported by the town alcalde, and then transferred to the royal court—reflects the common trajectory for average trials. The trial records, or *procesos*, began with the testimonies against the accused, as translated and recorded by one of the scribes. Commissioners of the court interviewed witnesses for the *fiscal*, encouraging them to share freely about the social drama. It is these lengthy interrogations and testimonies reported by a motley crew of villagers—clerics, town officials, men, women, and children alike—that occupy the bulk of the *procesos*. While *procesos* sometimes included the interrogations of the accused, this remained an inconsistent feature in the trials, obscuring a clear view of the accused's agency. This does not imply, however, that accused witches did not navigate the interview process by choosing what to say and what to omit, thus shaping their narratives and defense. Formal declarations of innocence and arguments of defense, however, were conducted to the court through their *procuradores*. The defense sought to disprove accusations by establishing that their clients, as *buenas cristianas*, enjoyed *buena fama*. The striking contrast in the arguments set forth by *procuradores* and contemporary legal defenses lay bare the core differences in modern understandings of witchcraft and those of the villagers of Navarra. Defense attorneys did not dispute the reality of sorcery and witchcraft, the ability to fly, or the use of toads, listing instead articles, most of which addressed *fama* or reputation, that they would prove or counter as part of their defense through the interrogations of their own sets of witnesses.

Though the articles of defense varied throughout the trials, several themes emerge consistently. The first line of defense—in every single trial of witchcraft and sorcery—argued that the accused was a *buena cristiana* (a good Christian) and focused on their Catholic acts, Christian reputation, and/or legitimate marital status. The villagers' reports on behalf of the accused likewise focused on the *buena cristianidad* of the witch and her good reputation. In cases involving accusations of

---

94. AGN, TR_333121 (1576), fol. 1r.

murder by *maleficia*, *procuradores* argued that the deaths were by "natural means" and presented substantiating reports from villagers. For example, when in 1576 María de Aniz was accused of witchcraft and blamed for the murder of her husband and two other men, her *procurador* Martín de Aragon argued that the latter died from "natural causes" and her husband died due to a fall.[95] He then presented eleven testimonies from a range of witnesses testifying to her husband's unfortunate accident and the well-known illnesses of the two men.[96] Another frequent line of defense centered on enmities that often drove witchcraft accusations. The importance of this defense is reflected in the 1576 trial of María de Olagüe in which her *procurador* countered accusations of therianthropy with arguments that her accuser harbored ill will to her family, and not by questioning the reality of her transformation into domesticated animals.[97] Defense statements varied throughout the trials, and each case brought its own matrix of circumstances, but generally speaking, a witch's defense concentrated on proofs of proper religious behavior, refutations of specific acts of *maleficia* (especially those involving murder), and arguments pointing to feuds among accusers and the accused.

Sentencing the Witch

Sentences handed down to accused witches by the royal tribunals relied less on deliberate executions and more on banishments, though executions did occur in 1525 and again in 1575. The trial records do not reveal the decision-making processes of the magistrates, and sentences appeared without legal justifications or arguments. Presented as short, simple sentences from the *fiscal*, punishments ranged from public humiliation to banishment to absolution. And while orders for torture and execution are not absent from the trial record, records documenting these corporal punishments appeared sparingly.[98]

---

95. AGN, TR_69260 (1576), fol. 43r–v.

96. In response to this solid defense, the *fiscal* oddly introduced child witnesses and the vicar of Olagüe who introduced the witches' gatherings to the accusations, including reverence to the devil. AGN, TR_69260 (1576), fols. 66–68r.

97. AGN, TR_69260 (1576), fol. 22r.

98. Torture was always recommended by the *fiscal*, even if it did not come to fruition. Thanks to a generous peer reviewer for clarifying this and to Jesús María Usunáriz Garayoa for clarifying this for me in a personal correspondence, September 26, 2023.

Public Humiliation

Humiliation within the public sphere aimed to impact both the sentenced and the audience. Observable penal rituals helped define sanctioned and unsanctioned behaviors and, like *fama*, established norms. The exhibition of the sentence expanded its effect and warned the public against engaging in the crimes of the accused. As Michel Foucault analyzed: "The body of the condemned man was once again an essential element in the ceremonial of public punishment . . . it served as the public support of a procedure that had hitherto remained in the shade; in him, on him, the sentence had to be legible for all."[99] These public rituals both reinforced the accepted social order and demonstrated the tangible power of the secular court. While the Inquisition's tribunal held its elaborate penitential ceremony, the *auto de fé*, the royal tribunals used their public penal displays "to project an image of the council as a divinely sanctioned magistrate, with the God-given duty and power to punish."[100]

The public humiliation of the carpenter Juan de Jenda in 1576 offers a view of the royal tribunal's public rituals. Accused of witchcraft and meeting with "a large number of men and women that made reverence to the devil," Juan was sentenced by the *fiscal* "to be taken from the prison where he is, riding horseback on a beast of burden, nude from the waist up, with the sound of the trumpet and the voice of the town crier publishing his crimes . . . and one hundred lashings . . . [and] ten years' of exile."[101] The court drew attention to this ritual through the theatrics of partial nudity and loud pronouncements of guilt, used to publicly warn against the taint of witchcraft. Four months later, Juan's sentence was reduced "to the humiliation only."[102] Juan's sentence—the only surviving one composed solely of public humiliation—calls into question whether the magistrates' main concern was his guilt, or the opportunity to warn against the practice of, or accusations of, witchcraft. So crucial was public penitence, the tribunals relied on this punitive measure up until its final trial of witchcraft and sorcery. In the final sorcery trial in 1675, María Esparza was sentenced: "To be mounted on a beast of burden, nude from the waist up, with a penitential cone hat

99. Michel Foucault, *Discipline and Punish: The Birth of the Prison*, trans. Alan Sheridan, 2nd ed. (New York: Vintage Books, 1995), 43.

100. Jason P. Coy, *Strangers and Misfits: Banishment, Social Control, and Authority in Early Modern Germany* (Leiden: Brill, 2008), 126.

101. AGN, TR_11219 (1576), fols. 24r, 79r.

102. AGN, TR_11219 (1576), fol. 80r.

on her head, and brought through the public streets and announced with the sound of trumpets and the voice of the town crier publishing her crimes, to two hundred lashings, and to ten years of exile."[103] Though the records suggest her humiliation was not carried out, it is noteworthy that public humiliation continued to hold legal weight and cultural significance.

Banishment

Banishment—from the village, the greater region or valley, or the entire kingdom of Navarra—served as the most frequent sentence for accused witches. The tribunals utilized banishment to cleanse the community by purging itself of unwanted people, a common practice serving a therapeutic and restorative purpose throughout the early modern period.[104] The official expulsion of Navarra's convicted witches ranged from three months to perpetual exile, with some twenty sentences handed out. Bureaucratic records dispassionately note the process of transporting the sentenced witch on horseback, under "secure guard," to the outskirts of Navarra. In the abovementioned trial of María Esparza, her warden reported it took six days to lead María by horseback out of Navarra. Taking her hand, Juan Saturtegui led her across the border and into Aragon, and warned her to never again return to her kingdom, her land, or her life.[105]

While not as immediately final as physical death, exile resulted in a social death for the sentenced witch. And social death led frequently to physical death as stigmatized witches lost access to resources and their unsavory label deterred people from providing charity. With little or no possessions, the lack of support from kin or neighbors, and their *fama* commanded by a witchcraft conviction, few prospects existed for these sentenced witches and sorceresses, most of whom were older, widowed women. Their experience after exile is hard to ascertain, as the *fiscal*'s final sentence usually concluded the case and any information about the accused. But one banished witch did reemerge in the trial records of the royal tribunals when she reappeared in Pamplona, permitting a serendipitous glance at the gravitas of banishment.

---

103. AGN, TR_17176 (1675), fol. 31r.

104. In his study of banishment in early modern Germany, Coy has shown the crucial role of expulsion rituals in establishing communal roles as well as the power (and limitations) of central authority. See Coy, *Strangers and Misfits*, 1-10.

105. AGN, TR_17176 (1675), unnumbered.

Graciana Belza, harshly sentenced to five years' exile in 1561, returned to Navarra in the dead of winter several months after her sentencing. The *procurador* pleaded for the magistrates' mercy on her behalf, pointing out that she was an elderly woman and that it was the court's torture that had left her crippled and unable to work. He elucidated the terribly real consequence of exile by adding that "she cannot vouch for herself, and with the *fama* she has that she is a witch, no one has wanted to take her in their house." Graciana, "terribly lost, dying of hunger" and driven to desperation by "the extreme necessity that she was in," had returned to her village, her children, and her home.[106] So perilous was banishment, Graciana had returned to petition the court for mercy, as she faced death by cold and starvation. But the court, understanding well the exile's intended effect, denied her request and doubled her original sentence, condemning Graciana to two hundred whippings and ten years of exile.

Absolution

Unlike the Inquisition, which promoted penance and absolution, the royal tribunals did not absolve accused witches and sorceresses with frequency, though they did dismiss cases or transfer them to the Inquisition.[107] The *fiscal* pardoned only ten witches throughout the trial records: eight during the chain witch trials in 1575–76, one from the isolated trial of 1595 that left nine villagers from Inza dead, and an accused sorceress from 1675.[108] In most of these cases it is unclear why the accused witch was pardoned, as many of the trial reports' contours appeared no different than those of convicted witches. For example, in the case of three accused witches from Piedramillera in 1575—all named María—two Marías were absolved while one María was sentenced. Several other trials featured absolutions for some of the accused but not others, despite their similarities, with no clear explanations or fruitful clues as to how the jurists reached their sentencing.

In contrast, the solid defense for María Arguello in 1675 offers a clue of what may have influenced her favorable absolution. Accused of using "evil sorcery" to kill a boy, her *procurador* insisted that the magistrates

---

106. AGN, TR_211115 (1561), fol. 83r.

107. Penance was the most common sentence handed out by the Spanish Inquisition throughout its jurisdictions. Homza, *Village Infernos*, 17.

108. María Arguello is accused of sorcery in 1675, but unlike María Esparza accused along with her, she is absolved. AGN, TR_333121 (1675), fol. 79v.

dispatch botanists and apothecaries from Pamplona to examine the bowls that reportedly contained illicit unguents. In a detailed procedural description narrating the transfer of the bowls from the alcalde to the court under official supervision, the records offer a glimpse of something resembling a modern-day dossier. The various phases of the investigation were controlled, annotated, and signed. And after much deliberation, the apothecaries declared that "there is no unguent at all," rather, "some mixture of oil" in one of the bowls and "some little bit of grease or fat" in another.[109] They concluded with assurances that she could neither harm nor heal with these materials; they were completely innocuous. Still, we cannot entirely attribute her absolution to the investigative techniques, and doubtless there existed other nuances outside of our limited view.

Torture

In the Roman law, "full proof" appeared only in the form of the testimony of two eyewitnesses or confession by the accused.[110] Navarra's courts also considered the accused's confession to be *regina probationum*: the "queen of proofs."[111] No other form of proof—aside from the firsthand testimony of two unimpeachable witnesses—offered such close proximity to the "truth." From the late medieval and throughout the early modern periods, torture served as a form of judicial investigation that sought to uncover the truth by yielding a confession. But torture was not free from criticism, and intellectuals and theologians raised frequent concerns about false confessions induced by physical pain. As with us, many early modern minds found judicial torture to be fraught with issues, but they would have disapproved equally of our burden—or lack thereof—of proof. They would struggle to understand how modern Western juries, lawyers, and judges rely comfortably on interpretations drawn from circumstantial evidence as "proof" beyond a reasonable doubt. Circumstantial evidence was often considered an inadequate standard of truth, and as such counted as a "half proof." And

---

109. AGN, TR_333121 (1675), fol. 75r+v.

110. Richard M. Frather, "Conviction According to Conscience: The Medieval Jurists' Debate Concerning Judicial Discretion and the Law of Proof," *Law and History Review* 7, no. 1 (Spring 1989): 23–88.

111. For more on confession in witchcraft trials, see Thomas Robisheaux, "'The Queen of Evidence': The Witchcraft Confession in the Age of Confessionalism," in *Confessionalization in Europe, 1555–1700: Essays in Honor and Memory of Bodo Nischan*, ed. John M. Headley, Hans S. Hildebrand, and Anthony J. Papalas (Aldershot: Ashgate, 2004).

so, the royal tribunals, operating within a legal system that thought it possible to attain the truth through regulated coercion, turned to judicial torture.[112]

Scholars have credited the laxity of Spanish witchcraft persecutions to restrictions placed on torture by its Inquisition, which used judicial torture in only 1 percent of its cases.[113] Though it is impossible to state with certainty the number of torture sentences total (as missing data from the trials of 1525 may skew these results), surviving records document around 4 percent of accused witches' interrogations under torture.[114] This does not mean, however, that the *fiscal* did not call for defendants to be put to the question of torture with greater frequency.

The understandings informing judicial torture suggest that certain crimes—such as witchcraft and sorcery—required torture to uncover the truth. Passionate arguments made by the *fiscal* in the early witchcraft and poisoning trial of Fortuno Legaz in 1539 reveal that judges felt torture provided a crucial tool as witchcraft was "difficult to prove" and that conjectures and *fama* alone were insufficient proofs "within the ordinary law." He drew explicitly from conventional legal precedent arguing: "Most importantly, according to the law, crimes committed with poison are often made in secret and seldom can you find and know the *truth*, without torment."[115] Since no known secular legislation for early modern witchcraft in Navarra survives, it is not possible to assert that it was considered a *crimen exceptum* in Navarra.[116] But the *fiscal* certainly envisioned the use of torture in witchcraft cases as essential, as *maleficia* was usually committed clandestinely, prohibiting the court access to eyewitnesses and rendering confession the only viable option. No tool elicited confessions, "the truth," as effectively as torture. And so the *fiscal* appealed to the court's desire for effective judicial

---

112. For a helpful discussion of torture, alongside other facets of Navarra's criminal processes, see Daniel Sánchez Aguirreola, *Salteadores y Picotas: Aproximación histórica al estudio de la justicia penal en la Navarra de la Edad Moderna el caso del bandolerismo* (Pamplona: Gobierno de Navarra, 2008), 125–35. For example, of the 269 highway assaults he examined, the *fiscal* asked for torture in forty of those cases, and followed through with seventeen (134).

113. Henry Kamen, *The Spanish Inquisition: A Historical Revision* (London: Weidenfeld & Nicolson, 1997), 188. Monter, however, claims the Inquisition used torture in "slightly over one fourth of all prisoners charged with major heresies" while suggesting the rate of torture was lower for those charged with sorcery, *Frontiers of Heresy*, 74.

114. Within the surviving royal tribunals' witch trial records, six documented judicial interrogations under torture survive, those for five women and one man.

115. AGN, TR_36180 (1539), fol. 67r. Italics mine.

116. Witchcraft's status as a *crimen exceptum* not only relaxed laws regulating torture techniques, it simultaneously encouraged and intensified them. Levack, *The Witch-Hunt*, 78–80.

proceedings, promoting torture as the correct judicial tool to make it "quicker and easier to convict."[117] But despite this reasoning, the court denied Fortuno's torture. Twenty years later, however, the same *fiscal* would have greater success in his request. The surviving transcripts present a haunting depiction of this order that illustrates the intimate relationship between torture and a search for the truth in early modern witch trials.

In the summer of 1561, in the "chamber of torment," Graciana Belza received her first interrogation under torture. But before this she had been warned that "if she did not tell the truth, they would put her to the question of torture and they would administer it very sternly, until she declared the truth."[118] Keeping in mind the *fiscal*'s order for a "robust" search for "the truth," the judicial torture was carried out as follows, recorded carefully by the scribe:

> They ordered the sticks tightened, and having been tightened, the magistrates told her to tell the truth. . . . Asked if she knows the manner in which the spells and witchcraft is usually done, she said that she does not know. And so, the magistrates seeing her negativity, ordered to have the sticks tightened even more, and having been tightened, they told her to tell the truth in all she had been asked. She said she knows nothing. . . . And then, the magistrates ordered to give [her] a jug of water, and after giving the jug of water, they asked her to tell the truth in all she has been asked. . . . And she always responded that she did not know anything.[119]

By inflicting pain on her body, the court sought to coax her conscience to free itself of its guilty burden and admit her wrongdoing. Torture served as a tool to get at the truth, though a modern observer may question (as did many early moderners) whether that truth was "true" or merely pain's by-product. But defining truth as a collective production situated in a specific cultural-historical context demonstrates how and why confession was accepted as truth and "full proof."[120] Graciana's refusal to confess, to give the truth, resulted in a second torture session

117. AGN, TR_36180 (1539), fol. 67r.

118. AGN, TR_211115 (1561), fol. 65r.

119. AGN, TR_211115 (1561), fols. 65r–66r.

120. And at the heart of the "truth" lies systems of belief. Steven Shapin, *A Social History of Truth: Civility and Science in Seventeenth-Century England* (Chicago: University of Chicago Press, 1994), 4.

that broke both arms and crippled her. Graciana remained steadfast in her innocence and refused to confess despite the unfathomable pain she no doubt endured. Despite their lack of a confession, the magistrates found her guilty and sentenced her to one hundred lashings and five years' banishment (later extended to ten after she returned to her village, described above). This trial demonstrates that sometimes, even when torture failed to yield a confession, a generous number of witnesses implicating a witch and extensive *mala fama*, combined with an adamant *fiscal*, could override its absence. And it reminds us of the devastation of a witchcraft denunciation.

Graciana Belza was the only accused witch whose judicial torture was documented outside of the chain trials of 1525 and 1575-76. During the latter, the royal court ordered torture in almost 50 percent of the cases (seven of sixteen trials total) but followed through in only three cases.[121] While acknowledging the egregious physical and psychological effects torture no doubt brought upon the accused, it can be argued that while the *fiscal* ordered it with frequency, the court of Navarra did not rely heavily on orders of interrogative torture.

Death

The royal tribunals of Pamplona rarely actively sentenced witches to death, though many died in their prison. While surviving records suggest approximately thirty to fifty accused witches were executed in 1525 under the magistrate Pedro Balanza, without extant records from these trials it is not possible to examine how the death sentences were discussed, decided upon, and executed.[122] What is most important to note is that it was an anomalous event, and such in situ executions were not repeated in the history of Navarra's secular witch trials. Only three sentences of execution survive in the tribunals' records, and only two were carried out: those of María Johan on October 25, and Miguel Zubiri on November 28, 1575. María Johan and Miguel were to be "taken through the main streets of this city and to the Campo de la

---

121. AGN, TR_69853 (1575); AGN, TR_327295 (1576). There is always the possibility, however, that records of judicial torture no longer exist, especially since the *fiscal* was *always* expected to advocate for the strictest approach, including torture. This may have been due to his duty to balance leniency with rigor, or perhaps, to play the Devil's advocate. I extended my gratitude to one of the book's peer reviewers for sharing these thoughts with me.

122. Idoate offers a full discussion of Balanza and these events in *La Brujería*, 23-67.AGN, 1525-Caja 113512, AP_Rena, Caja 94, N. 13.

Taconera of this city" where an erected stake awaited. They were to be hanged first, and their bodies burned in open flames until they "returned to ash."[123] These executions impacted Navarra profoundly and set off a chain reaction of witch concerns and trials not seen in half a century. But despite these executions in 1525 and again in 1575, most of Navarra's deceased witches did not perish by means of burning, but rather by the deadly prison conditions.

Prison conditions in early modern Navarra mirrored those throughout Europe as cold, dark, dank, and generally unsanitary spaces. Prison deaths occurred with frequency, as reflected by the fact that the majority of deaths of accused witches (setting aside the first witch persecution of 1525 and the single panic) occurred within the royal prisons' walls. The first recorded prison death of an accused witch was that of Teresa de Ollo, a *hidalga* detained in the royal prisons on a witchcraft charge. Within two months of her arrival to the prisons in February 1576, she was dead.[124] Her speedy death reflects poor prison conditions while suggesting her privileged lifestyle rendered her ill-prepared for the cold dampness public jails offered. This suspicion is strengthened by the similar fate met by another *hidalga*, María Perez de Olalde, shortly thereafter. Weeks before Teresa's death, eighty-year-old María was brought to the royal prisons on ambiguous charges of witchcraft emanating from a rival family. Her wealth afforded her an aggressive defense and allowed her the uncommon luxury of a medical examination by a doctor who visited her in the prison, declaring her to be in "mortal danger" and recommending her immediate release if she were to survive.[125] The council denied her freedom, and within the month María was dead.

The most disturbing string of prison deaths took the lives of nine accused witches from Inza in 1595. Seventeen villagers—ranging in age from nine to sixty—were transferred to the royal prisons in Pamplona. Within two months of their imprisonment, the prisoners complained of deplorable conditions in which they were starving to death. They petitioned the court for their release, explaining they were poor with no goods to support themselves, and begged for mercy, claiming "they are suffering with dire need, so great that they have had to pawn their coats and other garments in order to eat."[126] It is not unheard of to find petitions from prisoners proclaiming their poverty, invoking the expression

---

123. AGN, TR_69853 (1575), fol. 117r.
124. AGN, TR_327744 (1576), fol. 166r.
125. AGN, TR_294640 (1576), fol. 65r.
126. AGN, TR_71319 (1595), fol. 108v.

"they are dying of hunger," but the notable language used to describe their intense deprivation, their pawning of their coats off their backs (thus their source of warmth), and their claims that the food rations were insufficient to sustain their lives stand out among all the recorded claims of poverty. By mid-March at least four accused witches had died, as evidenced within this petition for release: "what the *fiscal* gives them for food is not enough to sustain them, especially for the diseases that are present, and from which four of them have died and now three are in danger of dying."[127] Their *procurador* concluded by begging for their release lest they perish in that prison.

Tragically, nine villagers perished due to the royal prison conditions in Pamplona, including nine-year-old María Johan Chorro and her sixteen-year-old sister. They were all women and girls, and all died "Christian" deaths according to their cellmates. In total, more than half of the accused witches from Inza died within the walls of Pamplona's royal prison. These deaths, though not caused by a direct execution, illustrate that the business of crafting, persecuting, and prosecuting suspected witches yielded much tragedy and many deaths, mostly of women.

Navarra's independent spirit and its unified, established, and powerful tribunals shaped its witchcraft and sorcery trials of the early modern period. Unlike less centralized legal systems found in some parts of early modern Europe, Navarra's strong and structured courts prevented local alcaldes and territorial lords from prosecuting accused witches and sorceresses. The legal systems that guided witch trials in Navarra leaned heavily toward the reports given by villagers, not learned ideas of diabolism, while the presence of the Inquisition also provided a means of checks and balances at times. But patterns varied, and during times of chain trials or the witch panic, diabolism emerged as a focal point and the Inquisition proved to be inconsistently restrained. Even so, Navarra's judicial processes relied on testimony that was attentive to *fama* and other localized concerns. Further, when the royal tribunals did actually follow through with an order for judicial torture, seeking accomplices was not a central part of the interrogation, thus keeping the net from widening too far, too often. Together, these factors helped shape a relatively restrained approach to witchcraft prosecution under the remarkable royal court and council of Navarra (1484–1841).

---

127. AGN, TR_71319 (1595), fol. 111r.

CHAPTER 2

The Struggle for Souls

The witches are heretics, apostates, and have
renounced God and worshipped the devil . . . and
thus pertain to the Holy Office. . . . The council
[of Navarra] should not have ignorance of the
form and order of the law.

—The *Fiscal* of the Holy Inquisition, 1575

In Pamplona's torture chamber in Octo-
ber 1525, María de Ituren confessed to being a witch. On Wednesday
and Friday nights, she traveled to the mountains in the form of a horse
and there met with other witches to eat meat, drink wine, and kiss
the devil's backside. Remaining until cockcrow, the heretical María
disavowed God and the Virgin Mary and all the saints, while simultaneously committing *maleficia* and destroying crops through various
powders and unguents made from toads.[1] María also confessed to the
murder of the shoemaker's baby, a death she induced by rubbing an unguent on his unfortunate wife's pregnant belly. Worse yet, María used
the disinterred baby's heart to work her magic. Later in the same month
of October, María found herself before a commissary of the Inquisition.
Though she ratified her previous confessions before the inquisitorial
agent, she made certain to caveat that her heretical renunciation was
not "from the heart."

María was among dozens of accused witches prosecuted in 1525
by Navarra's royal tribunals. But what of the Inquisition's tribunal?
How had María also come to its attention and examination? Though

---

1. Florencio Idoate Iragui, *La Brujería en Navarra y sus Documentos* (Pamplona: Institución Príncipe de Viana, 1978), 258.

Navarra's inquisitorial tribunal had been established in Calahorra some four years earlier, the royal court and council of Navarra retained significant autonomy following its recent conquest by Castilla. Yet even at this nascent stage of coexistence the two judicial arms wrestled over the region's accused witches, and María was but one of the dozens of witches who found herself at the center of this struggle for the soul, that is, the early modern seat of the human intellect and spirit. The royal tribunals drew from early modern philosophical understandings of the soul as housing self-awareness, a defining characteristic of being human, while the Inquisition argued for the correction of the spiritual soul and its eternal salvation.[2] Given the ambiguous understandings of the soul, judicial boundaries, and the very definition of witchcraft, there is little wonder this struggle over witches would persist for well over a century.

This chapter explores the contentious relationship between Navarra's inquisitorial tribunal and its royal tribunals through an examination of instances where the same accused witches were tried by *both* courts.[3] As a *crimen mixti*, a crime that fused secular with heretical concerns, both judicial systems could, and did, lay claims to witchcraft's oversight. And while accused witches attracted the attention of both the secular and inquisitorial courts—generating much debate and spilled ink in search of an explicit legal or intellectual characterization—the ambiguous definition of witchcraft became no clearer. Taken together, the trials of the secular tribunals and the Inquisition's summaries of cases, as well as contentious letters between the two judiciaries and the Council of Castilla, show that witchcraft's complicated legal categorization and the continued confusion over what defined a witch only complicated the jurisdictional difficulties further between the

---

2. From Aristotle to Hobbes, premodern intellectuals disputed vigorously the soul and its relationship to being human. It is this duality of the soul's site of the spirit *and* human intellect and free will that I use to describe these jurisdictional disputes as a "struggle for the soul." For more on the early modern soul and its debates, see Richard Serjeantson, "The Soul," chap. 6 of *The Oxford Handbook of Philosophy in Early Modern Europe*, ed. Desmond M. Clarke and Catherine Wilson, online edition (Oxford Academic, May 2, 2011), https://doi.org/10.1093/oxfordhb/9780199556137.003.0007. For a shorter definition of the soul as the seat of intelligence, see Michael Edwards, *Time and the Science of the Soul in Early Modern Philosophy* (Leiden: Brill, 2013), 65–68.

3. The cases of judicial overlap are found in the Spanish Inquisition's *Relaciones de las causas*, cases submitted by each inquisitorial tribunal to the Suprema, the supreme seat of the Inquisition in Madrid. As this chapter treats only witches tried by both the royal tribunals and the Inquisition's tribunal with oversight of Navarra, it only briefly examines the witch panic as it related to shaping inquisitorial policy toward witchcraft.

competing courts. While the messiness of early modern legal systems led to juridical contests throughout Europe, the newly conquered kingdom of Navarra held on even more tightly to its judicial power as it resisted the foreign interlopers from Castilla.[4] Navarra's strong courts and jealous protection of its long-standing powers created a particular set of circumstances that affected not just how witch trials progressed, but who villagers crafted as witches and under which circumstances. These power dynamics invite us to narrow our focus from large panics held by centralized powers and to examine regional rivalries, debates, and contexts that may more brightly illuminate how witches came to be accused and how magistrates defined their crimes across the borders of the sacred and the profane.

The Legal Landscapes

Early modern Spanish legal culture consisted of ambiguous laws, inconstant codes, and special juridical privileges. In short, it was a messy patchwork of competing powers ranging from local ecclesiastic courts to the emerging early modern state.[5] And as the legal profession and therefore legal systems grew, savvy early modern Europeans exploited the complicated jurisdictions to their own advantages, even becoming quite litigious.[6] While the wealthy tended to invoke court systems to settle disputes over estates, inheritances, and seignorial duties and rights, the peasantry turned to the courts, too, for their own justice regarding dowries, contracts, and other personal matters.[7] As the courts increased in popularity, legal procedures and criminal prosecutions became increasingly complicated. The inquisitorial system, judicial

---

4. Peio Monteano brings into focus how strongly Navarra resisted Castilla's 1512 conquest in his thorough analysis of it; see *La Guerra de Navarra (1512–1529): Crónica de la conquista española* (Pamplona: Pamiela, 2010).

5. In his description of sixteenth- and seventeenth-century legal systems in Castilla, Richard Kagan described the administration of justice as "plagued by a bewildering array of lesser courts and tribunals, the jurisdictions of which were often poorly defined." See *Lawsuits and Litigants in Castile 1500–1700* (Chapel Hill: University of North Carolina Press, 1981), 35.

6. Neither Navarra nor Spain was unique in this, as litigiousness characterized much of early modern Europe. For example, in his studies of Venice, Jonathan Seitz has shown how litigants frequently sought justice in a wide array of courts. See *Witchcraft and Inquisition in Early Modern Venice* (Cambridge: Cambridge University Press, 2011), 1 and throughout.

7. Besides individuals, larger entities also used the courts to settle disputes. Mid-sixteenth-century Sevilla offers a tantalizing example of this when, at one point, it was engaged in eighty-five lawsuits against the high court of Granada! See Kagan, *Lawsuits and Litigants*, 16.

torture, and a search for other suspects converged to provide a mechanism with which to prosecute those crafted as witches.[8]

In Navarra, disputes usually appeared before a village alcalde, priest, or seignorial figure, offering villagers several means of settling their disputes in the *primera instancia* ("first instance").[9] These tribunals resided within local municipalities consisting of the alcalde (municipal magistrate), *regidores* (council members) and the *sindico procurador* (city attorney).[10] If the alcalde decided he could not address the situation properly at the *primera instancia*—in crimes such as witchcraft— he would transfer it to another court for adjudication. Navarra's royal courts, though reorganized by Castilla in the early sixteenth century, drew from the medieval *fueros* that allowed them to draw from traditional preeminence.[11] The royal tribunals included the royal court, which served as the regular court, and the council, which oversaw appeals. Alongside the tribunals, the Diputación (standing judicial committee) supported the courts, and the Cámera de Comptos attended to economic and financial matters, while the ecclesiastical and military courts functioned independently, retaining immunity from interference at the hands of the royal tribunals.[12]

The episcopal tribunal, the *curia diocesana*, held jurisdiction over the diocese, adjudicating a wide range of issues as they pertained to clerics and members of the orders, as well as those of the secular orders. Cases handled by Navarra's episcopal court included matters of benefices and offices, civil processes over debts, and criminal cases of violation

---

8. For more on the evolution of legal procedures and the roles of different courts, see Brian Levack, *The Witch-Hunt in Early Modern Europe*, 4th ed. (New York: Routledge, 2016), 68–78, 81–95.

9. Cases of the first instance tended to be smaller issues, such as local business practices or clarification of property lines, disputes that could be settled privately or informally in smaller tribunals. See José María Imízcoz Beunza, *Elites, Poder y Red Social: Las élites del País Vasco y Navarra en la Edad Moderna* (Bilbao: Universidad del País Vasco, 1996), 120. While its focus lies in the eighteenth-century seignorial powers, see Jesús María Usunáriz Garayoa, *Nobleza y señoríos en la Navarra Moderna: Entre la solvencia y las crisis económica* (Navarra: EUNSA, 1997), 3–6 for an introduction to early jurisdictional issues.

10. Imízcoz Beunza, *Elites, Poder y Red Social*, 120–22.

11. Rafael García Pérez, *Antes Leyes que reyes: Cultura Jurídica y Constitución Política en la Edad Moderna (Navarra, 1512–1808)* (Milan: Giuffrè Editores, 2008), 101 and 113 for examples of instances where the *fueros* and *ius comune* (common laws) informed penalties.

12. For more on the functions of the royal courts of early modern Navarra, see chap. 1 in María Dolores Martínez Arce, *Aproximación a la Justicia en Navarra durante la edad moderna: Jueces del Consejo Real en el siglo XVII* (Pamplona: Ediciones Fecit, 2005). For a complete list of the royal courts' members, activities, and resolutions, see the comprehensive studies of Rocío García Bourrellier, María Dolores Martínez, and Sergio Solbes Ferri, vols. 1–2 (1513–1829) of *Las Cortes de Navarra desde su Incorporación a la Corona de Castilla* (Pamplona: EUNSA, 1993).

Table 2. Judicial courts in Navarra and trials of sorcery or witchcraft

JUDICIAL SPHERE	SECULAR	INQUISITORIAL	EPISCOPAL
Court name	Royal court: Civil and criminal cases Royal council: Appellate and Supreme Court	Tribunal in Navarra	Curia diocesana
Period of witchcraft/ sorcery trials	1525–1675	1520–1681[1]	1569[2]
Cases of witchcraft[3]	Approximately 35	Variable[4]	1

[1]These dates emerge from the unpublished database of Gustav Henningsen and do not represent other inquisitorial tribunals outside the one with oversight of Navarra. There was a witch trial in 1507, though likely in Durango and not in Navarra. For an excellent analysis of this unclearly documented event, see Iñaki Bazán, "Superstición y brujería en el Duranguesado a fines de la Edad Media: ¿Amboto 1507?," *Clio & Crimen* 8 (2011): 191–224.

[2]Here I categorize a witch trial as one where the court sustains a primary focus on the defendants' alleged practice of sorcery or witchcraft. Other trials involving issues of sorcery, witchcraft, or the fallout from the witch panic exist in the ADP, but I omit them as they do not align with the criteria I define. An example of an episcopal court trial related to witchcraft that does not fit into the definition of a witch trial is that of accused witches from the village of Erratzu who brought forth complaints of an abusive priest who forced their confessions of witchcraft. For this related trial, see Homza, *Village Infernos,* 144–46.

[3]These figures are in dialogue with data from the scholarship of Usunáriz which lists fifty-three cases of witchcraft in the royal tribunals, while this study draws from approximately thirty-five. See Usunáriz, "La caza de brujas," 316, 320.

[4]I defer to the Inquisition figures offered by Henningsen (unpublished database, 2016) and Usunáriz ("La caza de brujas," 316, 320) in their scholarship.

of ecclesiastical discipline. It also held authority over some laity in relation to execution of testaments, graves, religious foundations, and above all, issues surrounding marriage (promises and nullity).[13] Still, as with other early modern regions, the delimitations of each jurisdiction could be blurred. The nature of the issue at hand could be called into question, as the spiritual and temporal realms overlapped often.[14] Throughout Europe, the judicial lines between secular and ecclesiastical courts were tested, but Spain possessed yet another arm wrestling for power: that of its Inquisition.

13. García Pérez, *Antes Leyes que Reyes,* 318. Defendants were represented by lawyers who were employed by the bishop and held in a jail called the bishop's tower. Lu Ann Homza, *Village Infernos and Witches' Advocates: Witch-Hunting in Navarre, 1608–1614* (University Park: Pennsylvania State University Press, 2022), 17.

14. For example, in 1693 an accused murderer escaped secular justice by seeking refuge in a church. The royal courts ordered him removed by force from the church, provoking the bishop's ire. So angered by this perceived imposition on his jurisdiction, the bishop excommunicated all the magistrates of the court and council of Navarra and sentenced them to exile from the diocese. This action caused the courts to be suspended as it left only two magistrates unaffected by the excommunication despite the invention of the viceroy and the Cámara de Castilla. See García Pérez, *Antes Leyes que reyes,* 322.

Established in 1478 by Isabel and Fernando, the Inquisition merged spiritual concerns with political imperatives. Its original aims addressed concerns of *conversos* (converted Jewish populations) but extended to all forms of heresy.[15] Reaching throughout Spain, its peripheries, and across the Atlantic, this exceptional judicial arm prosecuted numerous heresies against European, *mestizo*, and African descendants until its final abolition in 1834. Its tribunals prosecuted multiple crimes including crypto-Judaism, Lutheranism, bigamy, blasphemy, bestiality, homosexuality, and witchcraft, assuming that these crimes included heretical acts. The Inquisition functioned through a complex combination of its own ministries, intelligence agencies (composed of commissioners and lay agents), and, of course, the participation of parishioners during Spain's reformation.[16] Navarra's tribunal was initially seated in Pamplona, then moved to Estella, later to Tudela, and then to Calahorra in 1540 where it remained for three decades. The tribunal ultimately settled in Logroño in 1570, a town some eighty kilometers southwest of Pamplona (see table 2).[17]

The Inquisition and Witchcraft

Throughout the Inquisition's three centuries of existence, thousands of people accused of witchcraft and sorcery fell to its prosecution under the category of *Supersticiones*. Despite this, the Inquisition's role in prosecuting witchcraft was less energetic than is sometimes assumed, and relatively few were handed over to secular authorities for execution.[18] It has also been argued that the Holy Office was more temperate toward accusations of witchcraft than many secular and ecclesiastical courts in Europe as witchcraft was not the most important crime it sought

---

15. See Henry Kamen's *The Spanish Inquisition: A Historical Revision* (London: Weidenfeld & Nicolson, 1997), "The Coming of the Inquisition" for more on its original foundations.

16. Born from an international Inquisition symposium, Ángel Álcalá et al.'s *Inquisición española y mentalidad inquisitorial* (Barcelona: Editorial Ariel, 1984) provides a useful overview of the structure, organization, and functions of the Inquisition. See especially "La infraestructura social de la Inquisición" (123–46) for the importance of networks of commissaries and familiars.

17. Henry Charles Lea, *A History of the Inquisition of Spain* (New York: MacMillan, 1907), 1:368.

18. Execution was not performed by the Inquisition; rather, heretics with death sentences were released or *relajado* ("relaxed") to secular authorities. See Gustav Henningsen and John A. Tedeschi, eds., in association with Charles Amiel, *The Inquisition in Early Modern Europe: Studies on Sources and Methods* (Dekalb: Northern Illinois University Press, 1986).

to punish.[19] Owing to the relatively small number of those sentenced to death, the heresy of witchcraft has been referred to as the Inquisition's "forgotten crime."[20] Still, nearly five thousand trials fell under *Supersticiones* from 1540 to 1700, which included crimes ranging from witchcraft to sorcery to unsanctioned prayers.[21] The Inquisition's tribunal in Navarra alone processed hundreds of cases of *Supersticiones*. While perhaps less persecuted than other crimes, sorcery and witchcraft were of concern to the Inquisition, and it sought jurisdiction over these transgressions with vigor.

Maleficent magic since antiquity had been tried by secular courts, but the establishment of the papal Inquisition in the early thirteenth century challenged this prosecutorial control.[22] Laws in Castilla from 1370 and 1387 confirmed the heretical nature of sorcery and its punishment by the secular court if committed by the laity and by the ecclesiastical judiciary if clergy were involved. A royal decree in 1500 ordered secular justices to seek diviners and arrest and punish them, thereby reinforcing secular control of the crime. Thus, at the time of the Spanish Inquisition's creation, witchcraft and sorcery remained mostly in the hands of the secular courts though in some regions episcopal courts tried witches. While a few inquisitorial tribunals prosecuted several witches, such as Saragossa (1498–1500), Toledo (1513), and Cuenca (1515),[23] the early Inquisition did not actively pursue crimes of witchcraft, sorcery, and other "superstitions."[24] This did not mean the Inquisition was disinterested, as reflected in an agreement reached between the tribunals of Aragon and the king in 1512, which allowed for inquisitorial jurisdiction over witchcraft in cases where heresy was involved.[25] As a *crimen mixti*, the secular component of witchcraft precluded the

---

19. Kamen suggests that two important reasons for this were that some inquisitors were skeptical of the reality of diabolical witchcraft and that the tribunal made no claims to exclusive jurisdiction. Furthermore, the Inquisition's goal focused on confessions and penance more so than punishments. Kamen, *The Spanish Inquisition*, 193, 270–71.

20. E. William Monter, *Frontiers of Heresy: The Spanish Inquisition from the Basque Lands to Sicily*, Cambridge Studies in Early Modern History (Cambridge: Cambridge University Press, 1990), 255.

21. Gustav Henningsen and Jaime Contreras, "The Database of the Inquisition," in Henningsen and Tedeschi, *The Inquisition in Early Modern Europe*, 58.

22. Richard Kieckhefer, *Magic in the Middle Ages*, Cambridge Medieval Textbooks (Cambridge: Cambridge University Press, 1989), 41.

23. Kamen, *The Spanish Inquisition*, 270.

24. There was a witchcraft event that occurred in 1507 likely in Durango.

25. This accord also included the crimes of usury, blasphemy, and bigamy. Kamen, *The Spanish Inquisition*, 75.

Inquisition's exclusive control of witch trials. Doubts also remained as to whether heresy was an immutable component of witchcraft. Furthermore, the Inquisition, influenced by the tenth-century *Canon episcopi* that attributed witchcraft to demonic illusions, maintained its skepticism of the reality of diabolical witchcraft.[26] If the diabolical pact and witches' gatherings did not occur in reality, was heresy even involved? But the increased centrality of the diabolical pact shifted the vision of witchcraft and, as the Inquisition would argue, placed the crime in its hands. A pact with the devil, of course, was inherently heretical.

Regional differences shaped each tribunal's vigor for certain crimes.[27] Navarra's inquisitorial tribunal would in its life-span process hundreds of witch trials, fight fiercely for its judicial rights over this bedeviling crime, and sponsor one of the largest witch panics in the early modern period.[28] Influenced by both its sprawling and mountainous geography and demography of rustic Basque-speakers, the volume of witch trials treated by the tribunal of Logroño was remarkably robust. Navarra, and other regions of northern Spain, experienced notably larger numbers of trials featuring diabolism and *maleficia* than southern Spain.[29] The Muslim influence in southern Spain largely shaped this trend, as Islamic cosmologies allowed for magical practices that did not necessitate a diabolical pact. Northern Spain, however, consisted mostly of Old Christian populations, which tended to be better acquainted with demonological thought and seemed more inclined to utilize and support the local courts, both factors that generated a greater number of witchcraft denunciations than in areas with higher

---

26. The *Canon* concluded it was heretical to believe that people, mostly women, held preternatural powers. For a deeper analysis of this often-cited canon, see Chris Halsted, "'They Ride on the Backs of Certain Beasts': The Night Rides, the *Canon episcopi*, and Regino of Prüm's Historical Method," *Magic, Ritual, and Witchcraft* 15, no. 3 (Winter 2021): 361–85.

27. As William Monter has shown, the priorities and punishments among the Inquisition's various tribunals differed from one another. The chapters of *Frontiers of Heresy* reflect the regional and temporal differences among crimes of focus and punishments among several tribunals. See p. vii for the book's contents, and p. x for a list of useful tables of comparison.

28. Separating the thousands of trials by region is beyond the scope of this project, thus general information and overall numbers regarding witchcraft under the Logroño tribunal inherently include witches in Guipúzcoa, Álava, and Vizcaya. The witches I examine closely, however, are restricted to trials that pertain specifically to Navarra.

29. Henningsen referred to this difference between the southern and northern portions of Spain as "the geography of witchcraft." Gunnar Knutsen examines this difference between northern and southern Spain in *Servants of Satan and Masters of Demons: The Spanish Inquisition Trials for Superstition, Valencia and Barcelona* (Turnhout: Brepols, 2009), xi.

Muslim populations. Old Christian populations, such as Navarra's majority, also tended to resist the Inquisition's judicial intrusion.[30]

The stronger the secular court, the more influence it had over the prosecution of witches. Weak inquisitorial tribunals, therefore, had a constricted range of influence to take the witches as their own, while tribunals in a position of strength easily wrestled suspected witches from local courts. It was not uncommon for the Inquisition to try witches that were initially arrested by secular courts, and even within the strong royal tribunals of Navarra this occurred, usually during the chain trials. While the royal judges of Navarra were often forced or chose to surrender witches to inquisitors, they nonetheless tried more witches than most (if not all) secular courts in Spain.[31]

Navarra's inquisitorial tribunal navigated several inconvenient factors. Its vast oversight included the entire Basque-speaking region of Spain, an expansive and mountainous territory that in addition to Navarra, included Guipúzcoa, Álava, and Vizcaya. The unique Basque tongue presented great linguistic challenges to the inquisitors, as few villagers spoke Castellano and even fewer inquisitors spoke Basque. Further, this newly conquered kingdom persevered in its strong and proud identity and conspicuously resented the Inquisition and its loss of judicial power to the foreign interlopers. The amphibious definition of witchcraft and its ambiguous legal classification only complicated matters further. It is within this setting, soon after its creation, that the tribunal in Navarra engaged in its first jurisdictional battle with the royal court over the crime of witchcraft, testing the limits of both courts in a contest over who would retain control of this witch project over the next century.[32]

---

30. Knutsen, *Servants of Satan and Masters of Demons*, 176.

31. Few studies have been conducted on secular witch trials in early modern Spain, thus it is possible Navarra's royal tribunals tried more than all others. For example, the meticulous work done by María Tausiet shows the neighboring kingdom of Aragon's secular court tried two witches. See *Urban Magic in Early Modern Spain: Abracadabra Omnipotens* (New York: Palgrave Macmillan, 2014) and *Ponzoña en los ojos: Brujería y superstición en Aragón en el sigo XVI* (Madrid: Turner, 2004).

32. This differs sharply from witchcraft cases in the Republic of Venice where the Inquisition had free exclusive jurisdiction over Venetian witch trials. Only cases that were seen to impinge governmental authority, such as trials with prominent male defendants, were sometimes contested. Seitz, *Witchcraft and Inquisition*, 2, 33.

The First Battle, 1525

Thirteen years after the 1512 *concordia* declared the Inquisition could prosecute witchcraft and related matters of heresy, the Inquisition tested Navarra's royal tribunals following the swift actions taken by one of its magistrates. In 1525, the many small villages dotting the Valleys of Roncesvalles and Salazar teemed with brujos and brujas gathering in the fields to concoct poisons made from toads, ruin crops and wheat fields, and engage in unnatural and diabolical sex.[33] These scandalous reports spread throughout the Pyrenean valleys, prompting Navarra's council to dispatch one of its magistrates, Pedro Balanza, to investigate the horrors of "the *brujos* and *brujas* of the valley of Roncal" and other parts.[34] Beginning in January, Balanza and his retinue of some twenty assistants interrogated and arrested dozens of accused witches, executing an unknown number without first bringing the accused to Pamplona. The council had directed Balanza to take this immediate action, an unusual order that invited criticism—and the Inquisition—to its door. And by May, after his colleagues received a report claiming some eighteen witches had been executed, fellow jurists Dr. Redín and Dr. Artega implored Balanza to refrain from ordering any further executions without consulting with the rest of the council. At the heart of their concern lay the ire—and unwanted attention—additional actions might elicit from the Inquisition. Their reinvigorated interest in procedure became clear as their letter underscored "especially with this difference that the inquisitors have with us . . . we beg you, that before you sentence or execute anyone, you share the cases you had concluded with us."[35] The imprudence of Balanza and the council of Navarra intensified the animosities between them and the Inquisition, provoking even episcopal disapproval.

Pedro Balanza's expeditious executions elicited the attention of Pamplona's vicar general, Juan de Rena. Rena wrote to the council in June 1525 citing a "certain altercation" between the inquisitorial and

---

33. The complete trial records of this witch event do not survive, but surviving archival records, letters from the royal council, complaints from the vicar general, an inheritance petition regarding the accused witches' confiscated goods, and allusions to this episode by both courts—and the Council of Castilla in Madrid—provide an approximation. Idoate's transcriptions in *La Brujería* supply crucial archival records that have since deteriorated and are no longer legible. See AGN, TR_35728 (1525); AGN, 1525_CO_PS1.1, Leg. 66, N. 4; Idoate, *La Brujería*, 249–75.

34. Idoate, *La Brujería*, 25.

35. Idoate, *La Brujería*, 252.

secular courts, which in turn brought the inquisitor Fresneda to Pamplona where he met with Rena. Together they approached the council and petitioned to review the cases, a request that resulted in an "altercation of sorts."[36] But the council stood firmly by its right to judge this evil sect, exposing the limitations of the Inquisition's ability to force cooperation. Given this "unfortunate situation," the Inquisition then turned to yet another judiciary for reinforcement: the royal council of Castilla in Madrid. The vicar continued in his letter to warn Pamplona's obstinate judges that Inquisitor Fresneda was now forced to turn "to the Court of Castilla and inform Your Majesty, asking *him* to decide to whom pertained the knowledge of this issue."[37] In the meantime, however, so that "such evil was not left unpunished," the council of Navarra had and would continue to proceed with the cases.

The witches of Navarra, amplified by Balanza's aggressiveness, had attracted the attention of the Inquisition, the vicar general, and, ultimately, the king of Spain, Charles V. Aware of the many watchful eyes, the council continued to urge circumspection, admonishing Balanza to act with restraint and awareness, and reminding him "there are many jurisdictions, and if we do not do things judicially, the kingdom could have reason to complain about us."[38] The council sought, through caution and discretion, to remain autonomous and free from inquisitorial interference. And though the Inquisition would later complain that "this business of the witches causes much work," it was not a "business" it sought to relinquish. Still, the Inquisition did not successfully intervene in this first battle over Navarra's witches, its impotence revealing its own lack of clear protocols on witchcraft and making obvious its need for an official approach if it was to be effective in the future.

Within a year of this judicial battle, Inquisitor General Alonso Manrique called a meeting to deliberate on the Inquisition's approach to the prosecution of witchcraft. Gathering in Granada, the council—consisting of ten inquisitors and elite men—deliberated on questions regarding witchcraft ranging from basic definitions to procedural guidelines.[39] One question they considered was whether witches actually committed the crimes to which they confessed or not. They debated also if those

36. AGN, 1525_CO_PS1.1, Leg. 66, N. 4, fol. 1r.

37. AGN, 1525_CO_PS1.1, Leg. 66, N. 4, fol. 3r–v. Italics mine.

38. Idoate, *La Brujería*, 257.

39. See Lu Ann Homza, *The Spanish Inquisition, 1478–1614: An Anthology of Sources* (Indianapolis: Hackett, 2006), 153–63, for a thorough transcription of this meeting.

who did commit these crimes should be exiled, "relaxed" (sentenced to death), or handed over to a secular court after their reconciliation so they may be punished further for their actions. Also in question was whether knowledge of these evil deeds and their punishments should even concern inquisitors at all.[40] Their deliberations and determinations, though by no means unanimous or unequivocal, shaped the Inquisition's attitude and approaches to witchcraft for the remainder of the sixteenth century and into the seventeenth.[41]

A unanimous understanding of whether witchcraft occurred in reality eluded the council. While a majority of six decided that witches did attend witches' gatherings, four maintained that their attendance was imagined. If the witches had not physically engaged in the witches' gathering and its accompanying *maleficia*, there was no secular crime, only spiritual transgression. Yet more than half of the group believed these acts occurred on the physical plane, thus maintaining blurred jurisdictional lines concerning witchcraft and complicating the manner of its prosecution.[42] Regardless of the witches' crimes, all in attendance agreed that the Inquisition should maintain involvement with the prosecution of witchcraft.[43] Some argued that inquisitors should punish witches for crimes related to matters of faith, while a secular judge should punish them for their temporal crimes. Another participant suggested that the matter should be left up to the inquisitors according to each case but agreed the Inquisition could turn the accused over to the secular justices once it concluded with the case.[44] Another participant voted that witches condemned to the Inquisition's perpetual

---

40. AHN, Inq., Lib. 1231, fol. 634r.

41. One main constraint for Spain's Inquisition was that heresy was supposed to be a component of witchcraft for the Inquisition to hold jurisdiction over it. See Kamen, *The Spanish Inquisition*, 270–76, for a discussion on the Inquisition's uncertainties regarding the realities and thus heresies of witchcraft. See also Gustav Henningsen, "La Inquisición y las Brujas," *Ehumanista: Journal of Iberian Studies* 26 (2014): 133–52.

42. To be sure, this confusion over the definition of witchcraft was not only a problem with which Spain's Inquisition and its secular courts grappled, as legislating an unclear, but grave, crime proved difficult. Spain's Inquisition discussed its roles in witchcraft trials repeatedly from 1525 through 1610 trying to settle who held jurisdiction, while the Papal Inquisition in Venice did not struggle with this, holding on firmly to its understanding of witchcraft as inherently heretical. See Homza, *Village Infernos*, 89–91; Seitz, *Witchcraft and Inquisition*, 35.

43. Edward Peters, *Inquisition* (New York: Free Press, 1988), 101.

44. In canon law, perpetual imprisonments were often handed down to reconciled heretics. In the early years of the Inquisition, it was not uncommon for this sentence to be served in local jails or individual homes, and not in the Inquisition's secret jails. Stephen Haliczer, *Inquisition and Society in the Kingdom of Valencia, 1478–1834* (Berkeley: University of California Press, 1990), 82–83.

prison should never be released to secular authorities, regardless of their temporal crimes. Asserting inquisitorial dominance, two others decreed that under *no* circumstances should witches ever be referred to secular judges.[45]

The sophisticated conclusion reached by one inquisitor, the *licenciado* Valdes, underscores the difficulty of proof in cases of witchcraft. Noting the struggle in determining whether witches *actually* committed the crimes to which they confessed, Valdes encouraged improved sophistication in investigations, such as an inspection of the unguents witches claimed to use for their *maleficia*. If these investigations confirmed that the witches had in fact committed the crimes, the inquisitors should then consider the pact made with the devil and the heresy entailed by such an act. And as heretics, they "must be given the ordinary penalty that is usually given, which the laws provide."[46] Mercy was to be shown in exchange for confession, the willingness and sincerity of the confession reducing the severity of the punishment. Valdes privileged the Inquisition's authority, concluding "once the witches have completed the penance from the inquisitors, the secular judges can proceed to punish them for the deaths, damages, and other crimes they have committed."[47]

The council of Granada thus produced an official order of operations for judicial procedures. The Inquisition was to be afforded the right to decide if heretical acts were involved, and if they were indeed present, inquisitors would mete out justice first and then pass along the witches to answer for their secular crimes. Though the Inquisition now armed itself with an official set of protocols, this by no means guaranteed that the secular courts—especially those as fiercely independent as the royal court and council of Navarra—would accept or respect it. And remaining at the very center of this limited resolution was the inherent ambiguity of the very definition of witchcraft.

Castilla's Ruling on Witches, 1530

Several years after Balanza from Navarra's council executed multiple accused witches, Castilla's council weighed in on the ongoing judicial battle between the inquisitorial and secular courts in Navarra. Recall

45. AHN, Inq., Lib. 1231, fol. 634v.
46. AHN, Inq., Lib. 1231, fol. 635r.
47. AHN, Inq., Lib. 1231, fol. 635r.

that the *licenciado* Fresneda had assured Castilla's council he would
keep it abreast of Navarra's witch issues, a promise that prompted its
judicial opinion. Referring to certain accused "poisoners" being held
by the royal tribunals, the *licenciado* Aguirre from the council of Castilla reminded Navarra that "this business of the witches is not new,
yet another time the royal council proceeded in other similar cases and
had the same altercation it is having now with the inquisitors of that
kingdom."[48] He stressed that after much deliberation during the previous dispute, it had been determined that imprisoned witches and their
cases were to be remitted to the Inquisition for examination, and assuming they had qualities pertaining to heresy or apostasy, they would
remain under that jurisdiction. He accepted, however, that "those who
do not have heretical qualities shall be remitted to the royal council
and to the other secular judges of this kingdom, even though there has
been much doubt as to whether these homicides and other crimes had
actually been confirmed."[49] This, along with the porous definition of
witchcraft, provided the Inquisition with the autonomy to select the
cases over which it sought oversight and discard the ones it did not.
Castilla's conclusions reinforced those reached by the Inquisition in
Granada a few years prior.

The council of Castilla based its decisions heavily on the procedural
irregularities and questionable executions of the secular court in 1525.
These hasty actions informed its conclusions that Navarra's judges
"should not have jurisdiction over these cases, rather they should turn
over these cases to the inquisitors of that kingdom" so that they can
determine what applies to them.[50] Castilla's distrust of Navarra's royal
tribunals had prompted their support of the Inquisition's right to determine "what is theirs" and what should remain with the royal council. While Castilla's judicial power over the royal tribunals was limited,
its interest in the issue of Navarra's witchcraft was palpable. Still, their
involvement and clarifications did little to resolve the issues between
the battling jurisdictions, or articulate a clearer definition of witchcraft, and thus the next group of witches brought with it another skir-
mish between the two courts.

48. AGN, TR_AS.Titulo.9, Faja 1, No. 8, fol. 2r.
49. AGN, Tr AS.Titulo.9, Faja 1, No. 8, fol. 2r.
50. AGN, Tr AS.Titulo.9, Faja 1, No. 8, fol. 2r.

Inquisition Triumphant, 1539–40

Following a decade of respite from the witch trials of 1525, dozens of witchcraft accusations throughout the Valley of Salazar emerged in the spring of 1539, reigniting the battle over prosecutorial rights between the royal tribunals and the Inquisition. These witches, including the town's alcalde Lope Esparza, were said to attend gatherings where they made poisons with toads and dead infants to destroy crops and livestock.[51] They also allegedly engaged in profane sex and disavowed God, the saints, and the holy mother church.[52] These secular *and* spiritual crimes invited a legal challenge between the two competing interests. The secular magistrates arrested and imprisoned the alcalde, along with a dozen others, for witchcraft. Alerted to this situation, the Inquisition wrote to Navarra's council immediately, making clear its intent to examine "what appears to be information pertaining to the Holy Office . . . in this matter of the witches."[53] The inquisitors argued the material within the charges belonged to them, as some of the accused had confessed to renouncing God "and things of this nature rightfully should be determined by [the Holy Office]." Highlighting the reports of heresy and apostasy, the inquisitors fought for their legitimate power and promised to deal with the witches in a manner "conforming to justice and according to their rights." And they informed the council of their forthcoming visit to Pamplona.[54]

The inquisitors arrived at Pamplona's royal tribunals with support from the Crown. In a letter to the Inquisition's tribunal, the inquisitor Dr. Olivan reported: "We received a letter from Your Majesty sending us to Pamplona to deal with this business of the witches imprisoned in the royal jails; we were diligent in doing so, conforming to Your Majesty's mandate."[55] By aligning inquisitorial activity with the will of the king, Dr. Olivan justified his intervention and preemptively prevented defiance by the judges from Navarra. He further substantiated his role with mention of the "lettered men, theologians, and jurists" with whom he consulted about the cases. As a result of his investigations, and in consulting with the viceroy and the judges of the royal council, it was

---

51. Idoate provides analyses and primary source excerpts from the witches of the Valleys of Salazar and Roncal in *La Brujería*, 61–67, 283–97.
52. AGN, TR_63994 (1540), fols. 1r–3r.
53. AHN, Inq., Lib. 322, fol. 258v.
54. AHN, Inq., Lib. 322, fol. 259r.
55. AHN, Inq., Lib. 785, fol. 220r. The tribunal was situated in Calahorra at this date of December 1539.

concluded that many witches indeed had characteristics that fell under the Inquisition's purview and that it would "see justice in these cases."[56] Following this show of power, dozens of witches were processed by the Holy Office, despite their confessions to multiple secular crimes including murder and crop destruction. Navarra's secular court remained in possession of only four.

In addition to sentencing forty-nine witches, the Inquisition hosted its public *auto de fé* in Pamplona and not Calahorra where its tribunal stood. It boasted that these witches had been adjudicated by the most "zealous and experienced" lawyers in existence.[57] Though the Inquisition argued it was better served to proceed with witch trials due to its meticulous attention to the quality of its cases, it nevertheless penanced and reconciled thirty children under fourteen for witchcraft and apostasy.[58] Eight witches over the age of fourteen were abjured *de levi* (slight suspicion of heresy) and two *de vehementi* (strong suspicion), while nine adult female witches were reconciled. By drawing from the ambiguous nature of witchcraft and highlighting the witches' apostasy and heresy, the Inquisition had triumphed in its intervention.

Within a week following the *auto de fé*, Inquisitor Olivan took care to communicate the Inquisition's actions to the Council of Castilla while simultaneously justifying its right to legal oversight. He wrote to Madrid: "I have already written the king [about] how we concluded the cases of these witches and others *that pertained to us*, decided upon by the consultants who were the best lawyers in the city and people with experience and jealous of our holy Catholic faith," and it was determined they should be processed by the Inquisition and thus an *auto de fé* was held.[59] Within six months of its initial inquiries, the witch situation in the Valley of Salazar concluded. The bulk of the witches landed in the Inquisition's tribunal, while four (including the town alcalde), received punishment from the secular tribunals.[60] This event demonstrated inquisitorial power, while also revealing that the royal court was sometimes a natural place for witch trials to begin, though

---

56. AHN, Inq., Lib. 785, fol. 220v.

57. AHN, Inq., Lib. 833, fols. 11r, 13r–15r.

58. Sentences handed out by the Inquisition varied from absolutions (uncommon) to relaxations (executions handled by secular authorities). Penance required defendants to renounce their offenses and receive punishments such as fines, banishment, or wearing a sanbenito. Reconciliation incurred heavier penalties such as flogging, confiscation of belongings, and long prison or galley work sentences. See Kamen, *The Spanish Inquisition*, 199–200.

59. AHN, Inq., Lib. 833, fol. 11r. Italics mine.

60. AHN, Inq., Lib. 833, fol. 13r; AGN, TR_63994 (1540).

not always conclude. Though unevenly, the witches in these chain trials were shared between the courts, and sentences were handed down on both sides of the judicial divide.

For nearly two decades following this "business of the witches," few accusations of witchcraft and sorcery reached judicial ears, and neither tribunal processed many trials for these crimes. The royal tribunals prosecuted two isolated trials (1551 and 1561), and the Inquisition's tribunal sentenced seven people charged with *Supersticiones*.[61] But this peace would be ruptured by a chain of witch trials that rattled villages throughout the valleys, resulting in the accusation of dozens of witches, the deaths of several accused witches in the secular judges' hands, and the Spanish Inquisition's decisive intervention.

The Clash Continues, 1575–76

In August 1575, two young boys from the village of Anocíbar accused their aunt María Johan of taking them to the witches' gatherings. These brothers, aged eight and ten, also implicated two other villagers, María Xandua and Miguel Zubiri. The children alleged their aunt had renounced her faith, made a pact with the devil, and poisoned the wheat fields. Charged with diabolism, heresy, apostasy, and *maleficia*, María Johan, María Xandua, and Miguel Zubiri were arrested by the royal court.[62] These accused witches, imprisoned in Pamplona, inspired officials and town alcaldes to search for—and find—other witches throughout the region. While the potential for a repeat from 1525 lingered, there were differences from fifty years prior. Situated against a backdrop of established contentions regarding jurisdiction over witches' secular and spiritual crimes were the directions of the council in Granada, support from Castilla, and legal precedent from 1540.

Following notice of these imprisoned witches, the Inquisition issued strong reminders to the royal council of the protocol surrounding witchcraft and its ultimate authority. But the secular authorities had already executed María Johan on October 25, only two months following her accusation, and within a month, Miguel Zubiri was executed as well at the Taconera within Pamplona's city walls. These public executions triggered a chain of witch trials as they inspired officials in other

61. Henningsen, unpublished *Relaciones de las causas* data for all *Supersticiones* in the Logroño tribunal (2016).

62. AGN, TR_69853 (1575). Idoate provides useful information and transcriptions in *La Brujería*, 307–48.

villages to conduct their own inquiries that in turn encouraged villagers to provide accusations. The search for witches lasted until 1576, a phenomenon noted by the villager María de Ciáurriz who reported there had been no witches "until the executions of those accused witches of Anocíbar."[63] Within weeks of María's public execution in Pamplona, Inquisitor Salvatierra wrote a forceful letter to the tribunals informing them he was aware of the large number of witches (thirty-six) they had imprisoned. He knew they had executed some (three, according to him) and had also interrogated others under torture. He reminded the jurists that these actions defied what had been decided and asserted the Inquisition's rights over the "knowledge and punishment of the crime of heresy and of those who have had a tacit or explicit pact with the devil." It was clear the imprisoned witches were "heretics and apostates of the holy Catholic faith" as they had renounced God and worshiped the devil, and as such "they pertain to the knowledge of the Holy Office of the Inquisition."[64]

Inquisitor Salvatierra tied the Inquisition's involvement to its grave concerns for the souls of delinquents. While omitting the *maleficia* present in their confessions, Inquisitor Salvatierra highlighted the presence of the diabolical pact in the testimonies he had received from the council. This key point, he argued, transcended mere legal struggles on the temporal plane; it had dire effects for the very souls of the sentenced. Echoing previous doubts about the secular authorities' competence, Salvatierra invoked the grave consequences of the council's past failures, arguing that "what is worse, the judges have condemned and executed the witches in fire, and since they were excommunicated and the secular judges do not have the power to absolve them, *they died in mortal sin and out of the brotherhood of the Roman Church*."[65] This was not the first time this concern had been raised, as the vicar general Rena had similar worries about the damnation of the unfortunate souls in 1525. Salvatierra concluded with the sarcastic admonition they follow "the form and order of the law, of which they should not be ignorant."

The royal council vigorously defended its actions, highlighting the crimes against the kingdom that placed the witches in *its* hands. Its response to the Inquisition emphasized that the accused witches had murdered "children and animals, and the women have had unnatural

63. Idoate, *La Brujería*, 113.
64. AHN, Inq., Lib. 831, fol. 100r.
65. AHN, Inq., Lib. 831, fol. 100r. Italics mine.

sex with goats and killed animals and damaged vineyards and fields with poisons and powders."[66] It focused on the secular crimes that wrought havoc on society and neighbors and concluded that "the royal council have been and will continue to be the judges." After asserting their legitimate oversight of these cases, however, the council assured the Inquisition that "in the process of the prosecution of these crimes, if one or more of the accused have committed a crime of heresy or apostasy, *then and only then*, will they be remitted to the inquisitors, *after* they have been sentenced by this tribunal."[67] The council guarded its right to prosecute the crimes of *maleficia*, while simultaneously promising to release heretics and apostates to the Inquisition—but only *after* they had judged them for their earthly crimes. The inquisitors had problematically decided on a similar order of operations with themselves taking the lead. It was therefore not so much who got the witches, but who got them first. Should heresy or *maleficia* take precedence in the judicial order of operations?

The secular magistrates wrote to the Crown in defense of their jurisdiction. The council informed King Phillip II of their hard work and conscientious attention to the present witch trials, and of their "service to God and to Your Majesty, cleaning the land of these evil people." By framing their work as a service to God in addition to a royal task, they placed their efforts on an equal plane with the assistance offered by the Inquisition. They coupled this sacred work with the term "evil people," thereby emphasizing the antisocial nature of these criminal subjects, delinquents best handled by royal authorities. They assured the king, "when we note that one of them has committed a crime of heresy or apostasy, only then will we refer it [to the Inquisition], having been first punished by us for the other crimes they have committed."[68] While agreeing to turn the witches over to the Inquisition, the council simultaneously challenged the judicial order of operations.[69]

To their justifications as guards of both social and spiritual order, the council added another, more pragmatic, reason for its authority: administrative convenience. The magistrates argued that inquisitorial

---

66. Archivo General de Simancas, Simancas (hereafter AGS), Inq., P.R. 28–65; AHN, Inq., Lib. 831, fol. 98v.

67. AGS, Inq., P.R. 28–65. Italics mine. A copy of this document exists in the AHN, Inq., Lib. 831, fol. 99r.

68. AGS, Inq., P.R. 28–65.

69. Challenges to legal definitions fueled interjurisdictional disputes far beyond Navarra and the crime of witchcraft as regional studies of witchcraft have shown time and again. For an overview of the contexts of legal conflicts, I recommend Levack, *The Witch-Hunt*, 68–94.

privilege brought great inconveniences to the Crown, as "the inquisitors are outsiders of this kingdom and the delinquents are from within and there are many of them and they do not speak the Romance language, rather a Basque tongue very insular and different from the common Basque. It is very clear, they cannot proceed against them with the brevity and quick handling that we are used to here."[70] Thus beyond the linguistic challenge laid an administrative one, as the inconveniences in translating their "strange tongue" would delay the speed of justice.[71] The council also raised the issue of finances (arguably of greater concern than indicated), bemoaning "and the other thing is, the chamber and *fiscal* of Our Majesty has lost a great amount of money and wealth, when these offenders should be condemned [but are not]." The royal treasury sought to lessen the expenditures of initiating these proceedings but failing to see them to fruition. When delinquents were later pardoned by the Inquisition, as had happened in 1540, their material goods were no longer available for the royal tribunals' confiscation.

In a second letter to the king, also from November 1575, the council of Navarra mounted another objection to inquisitorial interference. Abandoning generalities and addressing the recent deaths of María Johan and Miguel Zubiri, the *fiscal* guarded its rights to the "thirty something women and three men" that the Inquisition sought by emphasizing the accused witches' deeds of *maleficia*. He argued: "The inquisitors generally do not know much about those said crimes. And if we [turn the witches over] to them and they beg for mercy, they will never get punished with the rigor of our tribunals, the likes of which is necessary and appropriate for such ills."[72] Their concern was, again, for the crimes that affected villagers, their livelihoods, and social order.[73] If the Inquisition pardoned all witches at will, what message would that broadcast to the populace? Further, what of the secular tribunal's right to punish criminals in its midst?[74] Underlying the difference in

---

70. AGS, Inq., P.R. 28–65.

71. See Peio Monteano for a thorough discussion of the different dialects in Navarra and the roles of linguistic factors on legal and social culture. *El iceberg Navarro: Euskera y castellano en la Navarra del siglo XVI* (Pamplona: Pamiela, 2017).

72. AHN, Inq., Lib. 831, fol. 101.

73. Briggs has shown the crucial roles of communal bonds and friction among witch trials in Lorraine, suggesting even that the pattern of reporting those who struggled with their neighbors "must be functionally related to the social meaning of witchcraft." Robin Briggs, *Witches and Neighbors: The Social and Cultural Context of European Witchcraft* (New York: Penguin, 1996), 146.

74. Legal arms throughout early modern Europe wrestled for their rights to adjudicate crimes and punish delinquents. For example, Muscovy's tsarist state invested heavily

persecution was the focus of each tribunal and the porous definition of witchcraft itself.

The council's struggle for prosecutorial power reached a crescendo when it threatened to mount a court battle against the Inquisition. The royal tribunals' unmistakably titled memorandum "On the part of the judges of the Superior Court of Navarra, in the business with the inquisitors of Logroño regarding the witches" asserted nine major points of contention. The argument against the inquisitors' abilities to properly decide which cases belonged to whom emerged in the fifth article stating: "The inquisitors do not have to be judges, though it is claimed, yet they are tasked to be able to know and determine which cases pertain to them and which do not, and this is to the detriment of the jurisdiction of the judges."[75] The unfairness of inquisitorial privilege to decide who held authority over this *crimen mixti* was punctuated by the fact that an inquisitorial position did not in fact require a formal training in the law.[76] Meanwhile, as the two judicial arms wrestled, dozens of witches, including María Xandua, remained stuck between them.

Astute early modern litigants and their *procuradores* navigated legal categories and exploited competing judiciaries according to their own needs. Xandua's *procurador* strategically utilized both the battle between the tribunals and the ambiguous nature of this *crimen mixti*. Hoping to pause María's death sentence, Pedro Larramendi pushed for her remittance to Logroño, arguing immediately after Miguel's death: "It seems that my client was accused of crimes of heresy, apostasy, and idolatry. This [secular] jurisdiction is neither competent to understand nor determine these crimes. Thus, I ask this case to be remitted to the inquisitors as the competent judges."[77] After stressing the unreliable admissions produced under torture, and the children's unsubstantiated accusations, he urged the council to revoke its sentence and "refer

---

in limiting church and local powers to retain jurisdiction over witchcraft for itself: Valerie Kivelson, *Desperate Magic: The Moral Economy of Witchcraft in Seventeenth-Century Russia* (Ithaca, NY: Cornell University Press, 2013), 28–29. And while Poland's *Constitutio* from 1543 specifically assigned the ecclesiastical courts with jurisdiction over witchcraft, it shifted (with much protest by ecclesiastics) into the hands of secular courts during the sixteenth and seventeenth centuries: Michael Ostling, *Between the Devil and the Host: Imagining Witchcraft in Early Modern Poland* (Oxford: Oxford University Press, 2011), 45–48, 53–58.

75. AGS, Inq., PR 28–65, fol. 196.

76. The royal tribunals of Navarra were exceptional for all the reasons presented so far. It is worth remembering that *not all secular courts fought the Inquisition* for rights over witchcraft as research by María Tausiet on Aragon and Jonathan Seitz on Venice has shown.

77. AGN, TR_69853 (1575), fol. 118r.

this case to the Inquisition, as I have asked. Or rather, free my client or amend the sentence she has been given." He also asked the council of Castilla to intervene in any manner it saw fit. Larramendi's vehement defense, the looming threat of Castilla's intervention, and the pressure of the Inquisition's watchful eyes proved to be successful in securing Xandua's release. And, despite the aggressive posturing and letters from Navarra's council, not only Xandua, but all the remaining witch trials ended up with the Inquisition. While documentation of the specific events that led to the witches' transfer remains unknown, the council did not transfer Xandua to the inquisitors without resistance. It prolonged her case for months by reexamining all the witnesses, including the children, an anomalous level of scrutiny compared to other trials. But finally, on the March 14, 1576, María Xandua's dossier arrived at the Holy Office and her body in its secret jails.[78] After enduring torture and detrimental prison conditions for over a year, María had finally arrived in the inquisitorial arms in Logroño. And she was not alone.

Into Inquisitorial Arms, 1576–77

Along with María Xandua came dozens of brujos and brujas from the Valley of Larraun in Navarra. Though the royal council successfully meted out sentences to nearly a dozen witches, the diabolical definition of witchcraft relied upon during the chain trials unintentionally bolstered inquisitorial authority and sent dozens of witches flying its way. Now in possession of María Xandua, the inquisitors interviewed her accusers, the brothers Miguel and Martín de Olagüe. An inquisitorial *relación* related the sobering conclusion to the first case of the 1575–76 chain trials, one triggered in Anocíbar by suspicions of María Johan's bedeviling seizures. It reported:

> The boys were brought before this Holy Office and having been examined separately . . . revoked all they had deposed and admitted to raising false testimony against María Xandua and her accomplices, and that they never went to the witches' gatherings nor saw anyone there. And that all they falsely deposed was at the urging of certain people.[79]

---

78. AHN, Inq., Lib. 833, fol. 209v.
79. AHN, Inq., Lib. 833, fol. 210r.

The young boys admitted to the inquisitors they had raised false testimony against María Xandua, their aunt María Johan, and Miguel Zubiri on the advice of unnamed others, likely the abbot of Anocíbar, Pedro Esaian, who eagerly reported their allegations.[80] While their testimony finally exonerated María Xandua's soul, it did not save her life. Over a year had passed since her transfer from the royal jails into the secret jails, and she became ill, dying in inquisitorial hands. Following the boys' recantations, the Inquisition afforded her a Christian burial. And the pivotal case of Anocíbar that sent ripples of heightened witch fears and chain trials throughout Navarra ended with the Inquisition's simple conclusion: "And the boys returned to their homes."[81]

While the Inquisition's involvement in Anocíbar came too late to save María Johan, Miguel, and his wife Graciana de Iráizoz, it processed all of the accused from the Valley of Larraun. And its intervention ensured that never again would the royal tribunals execute another witch. While the Inquisition did not "relax" any witches to the secular authorities for execution, several witches tragically perished within its secret jails. Still, the Inquisition's interference in this period's witch concerns resulted in the absolution of thirty-eight accused female witches and eight male witches, with three sentences of exile handed out.[82]

The Inquisition triumphed in this event by drawing from the ambiguous nature of this *crimen mixti* and highlighting the heretical acts committed by the accused.[83] Ironically, the secular tribunals' overreliance on a diabolical definition of witchcraft used during this wave also served to carry the accused into inquisitorial arms. And following the *auto de fé* of 1577, neither the secular nor the inquisitorial tribunals engaged with "this business of the witches" for nearly two decades.[84]

80. Idoate refers to the abbot as "zealous," *La Brujería*, 90.

81. AHN, Inq., Lib. 833, fol. 210r.

82. AHN, Inq., Lib. 833, fols. 206r–210r for the *auto de fé* in 1577. See also Idoate, *La Brujería*, 126–29, and Jesús María Usunáriz Garayoa, "La caza de brujas en la Navarra moderna (siglos XVI–XVII)," in *Akelarre: La caza de brujas en el Pirineo (siglos XIII–XIX)*, ed. Jesús María Usunáriz Garayoa, RIEV Cuadernos 9 (Donostia: Sociedad de Estudios Vascos, 2012), 314–16.

83. Idoate provides an analysis of the differences between the two jurisdictions in these trials of 1575–76 in *La Brujería*, 118–21.

84. One healer accused of sorcery was tried by the secular court in 1590, and seven people total were tried under *Supersticiones* by the Logroño tribunal, but none for witchcraft.

Liminality, 1595

Almost twenty years of freedom from witch trials ended abruptly with the "discovery" of a large group of male and female witches by the alcalde Fermín Andueza from the Valley of Araiz in 1595.[85] Within his palace, Fermín Andueza and his son Pedro imprisoned villagers and extracted confessions of numerous secular and spiritual crimes. Their oddly prolific confessions ranged from using ointments to fly to the witches' gatherings to spreading poisons made from toads to having "carnal access with Belzebut."[86] Following these peculiar confessions, all seventeen villagers—including children under twelve—were referred to Navarra's royal court. They ratified their confessions in front of the council, only to retract their initial depositions soon after. Despite the tender age of many of the accused villagers and the consistent allegations of coercion and outright threats at the hands of the antagonistic Andueza, the council accepted their initial admissions and sentenced some to whippings and exile. Sadly, many of the accused began to fall ill and died within the unhealthy prison walls, including the two youngest sisters, aged nine and thirteen.

Their *procurador* argued that Andueza had forced their original depositions with threats to burn, mutilate, and kill them unless they confessed.[87] Despite their desperate condition, including starvation and death—and the unequivocal accusations of heresy and apostasy—he did not petition for a transfer to the Inquisition. His defense focused instead on the irregularities of this case. But news of these accused male and female witches attracted the attention of an inquisitorial commissary who alerted the inquisitors at Logroño.

Inquisitor Lombrera from Logroño's tribunal submitted a report to the inquisitor general on the situation of these accused witches in April 1595. He reported that "having gotten news" that the royal court had imprisoned some witches, the tribunal requested the original *procesos*, and a commissary then examined them "to discover if they have committed a crime of apostasy or other sins against the faith."[88] While the witches had confessed to diabolically fornicating, worshiping the devil, and renouncing God, crimes falling squarely within the

---

85. Idoate offers analyses and source excerpts in *La Brujería*, 131–43, 354–71.
86. AGN, TR_71319 (1595), fol. 1r.
87. AGN, TR_71319 (1595), fol. 118r–v.
88. AHN, Inq., Lib. 791, fol. 353r.

Inquisition's domain, it had no interest in the case. Following its successful acquisition of the witches in 1576, and the clear presence of heresy in this case, why would the Inquisition decline jurisdiction?

Inquisitor Lombrera's letter suggests that the witches' revocations and the overall weakness of this case informed their ambivalence. He reported that all of the accused had revoked their confessions and warned the Inquisition to proceed "with caution in this case because of its poor quality." Lombrera found the Inquisition's involvement in witchcraft to be more trouble than it was worth, lamenting that the "business with the witches has caused the Inquisition much work, waste, and grief; they yield from it little fruit, as experience has shown and as the letters and decrees of the Suprema show us."[89] While Inquisitor Lombrera emphasized that little good could come from this particular case, he acknowledged the tribunal would ultimately defer to the Suprema's directions. In a noteworthy gesture of concern, the inquisitor pushed for a swift response, informing the inquisitor general that the accused were still imprisoned and many had died.

Sadly, the accused witches from Inza remained in Pamplona. Lombrera explained to the royal council, "For the moment these cases do not belong to the Holy Office, and so we resend them to the judges," adding that if something further seemed to pertain to the Catholic faith, to send it their way at that time.[90] After eight months of harsh imprisonment, the surviving accused male and female witches of Inza were finally freed, with a single sentence handed down to a male witch. But the witches of Inza had remained in the hands of the royal tribunals. In this case, the Inquisition exploited the equivocal definition of witchcraft and chose to remain unburdened by a sketchy case produced, under duress, by an unpopular and unjust alcalde.

For more than three decades, the various tribunals of Navarra remained uninvolved with witches. From 1577 until 1610, not a single witch was processed by the Logroño tribunal nor the royal tribunals. But beneath the surface of this calm facade lay the deep caldera of witch belief, beliefs that held the potential to morph into witch fears, and even panic, given the proper conditions.

---

89. AHN, Inq., Lib. 791, fol. 353r.
90. AGN, TR_71319 (1595), fol. 113r.

The Witch Panic, 1609–1614

Four years after the Inquisition's *auto de fé* in November 1610, the Suprema issued its new protocols featuring thirty-two clauses that sought to avoid another witch panic and prevent indiscretions such as child testimonies, mass denunciations, and accusations in the absence of any proof.[91] Its first clause advocated accountability in proving whether or not a crime had even occurred and promoted thorough investigations that privileged alternate, nonpreternatural explanations. In a similar vein, the Suprema's third clause advocated confirmation of "whether they really go to the meadows and gatherings to cause the harm they confess to," which spoke both to a legitimate search for proof and harkened back to concerns from the council in 1526.[92] In addition to recommending investigations of the purported damage caused by witchcraft, the Suprema urged an education campaign. It advised inquisitors to have local preachers explain to villagers that natural misfortunes occur in the absence of witchcraft.[93] The Inquisition acknowledged "the deep regret felt by the Holy Office and in particular by the Council, for the vexations and violence which the alcaldes of the villages without judicial authority . . . have inflicted on the accused."[94] Further, they ordered that "the *sanbenitos* of the persons relaxed in the *auto de fé* of 1610 and of the rest who were reconciled . . . are never to be hung on display."[95] Interestingly, the Suprema alluded to the jurisdictional conflicts between the Inquisition and the royal tribunals in its twenty-seventh clause, declaring: "The inquisitors are to leave the [secular] court or any other justices free to prosecute and punish these offenses without impeding them judicially or extrajudicially, or by other obstructions or personal intercession."[96] Not only did the Holy Office discourage involvement in matters of witchcraft, it encouraged silence.

---

91. For the new list of instructions, see Homza, *Village Infernos*, 175–80; Gustav Henningsen, *The Witches' Advocate: Basque Witchcraft and the Spanish Inquisition, 1609–1614*, Basque Series (Reno: University of Nevada Press, 1980), 370–77.
92. AHN, Inq., Lib. 334, fol. 245v. For an analysis of these events, see Homza, *Village Infernos*, 135–41, 146–48.
93. This should not be confused, however, with the end of witchcraft beliefs or a functional understanding of witchcraft that sometimes emerged. Rather, this directive echoed the tenth-century *Canon episcopi* and reiterated the Inquisition's earlier stance of relative skepticism from which it had deviated in this witch panic.
94. AHN, Inq., Lib. 334, fol. 251r.
95. AHN, Inq., Lib. 334, fol. 249v.
96. AHN, Inq., Lib. 334, fol. 251v.

The Suprema of the Inquisition ordered: "There should be silence in these issues. Make it clear to the commissioners and confessors, so they approach this orderly. And that only in the necessity of someone making a confession should this issue be raised, and they must preserve the same secrecy as in the other cases dealt with by the Holy Office."[97] The Inquisition, the one whose tribunal in Navarra persistently voiced its interest in the witches and sorceresses of the region for nearly a century, now urged silence and privacy in matters of witchcraft. The new instructions concluded with a directive to bind together all the materials and suggestions from the Supreme Council so that it "shall always be at hand to guide the inquisitors in future cases."[98]

The Inquisition's new policies worked. Never again would Spanish soil host a witch panic, nor would another witch receive a sentence of execution by the Inquisition (nor by the royal tribunals of Navarra). These new safeguards, forged from the protocols of 1526 and informed by reforming efforts of education, ensured that another witch panic would not occur under the Inquisition's supervision. Still, throughout the remainder of the seventeenth century (from 1613 until 1694), 167 people accused of *Supersticiones* fell to Logroño's jurisdiction, though most cases treated heterodox practices and few were accused of witchcraft.[99] While the Inquisition came no closer to an unequivocal definition of witchcraft, it had decided to approach this *crimen mixti* with greater caution and skepticism. And both the inquisitorial court and royal courts of Navarra maintained this caution, for the most part, for the remainder of the century. The witch panic and its lingering effects prompted updated and concise protocols for cases of witchcraft and would dictate the Inquisition's approach to witchcraft until its final dissolution in 1834.

The Last Witches of Both Courts, 1647

María de Ollo, a sixty-year-old healer and beggar in Pamplona, reportedly possessed "good hands," and many villagers sought her effective services. But her ability to heal exposed her to accusations for the capacity to harm, and her extensive *fama* for sorcery and witchcraft led

---

97. AHN, Inq., Lib. 334, fol. 252v.
98. AHN, Inq., Lib. 334, fol. 253r.
99. Data from Henningsen's unpublished *Supersticiones*, 2016. Recall that the category of *Supersticiones* encompassed healing, superstitious prayers, and other beliefs.

to her arrest in April 1647.[100] Imprisoned alongside María de Ollo was seventy-eight-year-old María Yrisarri, another healer from Pamplona. Though she, too, was a poor, old woman engaged in unauthorized healing practices, she did not suffer from the same *mala fama* as María de Ollo and remained free from accusations of *maleficia*. María Yrisarri emphatically denied she had done wrong, arguing instead her healing gifts came from God, as a local abbot had once assured her. True, she had blessed certain sick people, but only by using the "words of the Father, Son, and Holy Spirit."[101] If she cured in the name of God, could there even be a diabolical pact? Was this even heresy?

In June 1647, the *procurador* for María de Ollo and María Yrisarri argued for his clients to be transferred to the Inquisition. He opposed the royal judges' sentence of torture and asserted these cases belonged to the Holy Tribunal as they included "some type of heresy."[102] The royal court responded there was no reason to submit the cases to the Inquisition, insisting instead "our court will continue with the justice of this case where it began and where it will stay until its conclusion."[103] Though the court refused to relinquish authority over these women, within several months the council agreed to send the *proceso* of María Yrisarri to the Inquisition's tribunal for review.[104]

This decision infuriated the court's *fiscal* who petitioned the council to reverse its decision to surrender the case to the Inquisition. Emphasizing the witches' criminality, he argued: "The accused have caused many evils in this city and to different people, causing illness and even worse. And they have the reputation of being witches, sorceresses, and for these reasons it pertains to our court and Supreme Council to punish them for the crimes they have committed against the republic."[105] He underscored the secular nature of their crimes, reinforcing the tribunals' jurisdiction over these women. But to this standard argument he added compellingly that proof of a diabolical pact or other heresy remained absent from the case, whereas "on the other hand it is *known* that they have committed crimes pertaining to our court and council."[106] No proof existed to suggest their *maleficia* was a result of

100. AGN, TR_16058 (1647), fol. 12v.
101. AGN, TR_16058 (1647), fol. 45r.
102. AGN, TR_16058 (1647), fol. 38r.
103. AGN, TR_16058 (1647), fol. 43r.
104. AGN, TR_16058 (1647), fol. 86r.
105. AGN, TR_16058 (1647), fol. 88r.
106. AGN, TR_16058 (1647), fol. 88r. Italics mine.

heresy or a diabolical pact; meanwhile reports undeniably pointed to injury of neighbors and goods.

Though physically remaining in the royal jails, the Marías appeared in the Inquisition's *relaciones* from January 1648.[107] According to its summary, the Inquisition had asked the tribunals to remit the "accused and the original trial," a request with which the *fiscal* only partially complied.[108] In September 1648, the inquisitors began to examine the witnesses from María Yrissari's original records to determine whether or not the case involved heresy. Their reports made clear that their attention was primed for heretical acts and concluded she made "an implicit pact with the devil and that she was also suspected of heretical acts."[109] But before her transfer could occur, seventy-eight-year-old María Yrisarri died in the royal jails on November 9, 1648. It had been a year and a half since her *procurador* first requested her transfer to the Inquisition.

That same month of November, María de Ollo arrived at the Inquisition's secret jail after the *calificadores* (inquisitors designated to assess whether it fell to their jurisdiction) confirmed she "had an implicit and explicit pact with the devil and was suspect of heretical acts" and formally charged María with heresy.[110] The *relación* emphasized her "superstitions," the report of her attendance at the witches' gathering, kissing the devil's backside, and the raising of toads.[111] Though María arrived in the inquisitorial jail in November 1648, the inquisitors did not grant her an audience until February 1649. There, she confessed to her healing practices but asserted they were done in conformity with God's will. Within a month of her interrogation, sixty-year-old María became very ill and was transferred to a hospital where she died on May 11, 1649.[112] More than two years had elapsed since her initial arrest.

The trials of 1647 elucidate that accused sorceresses and witches caught between these judicial struggles could at times suffer deadly results even in the absence of a formal sentence. The royal tribunals focused on reports of *maleficia* and the *fama* of the accused, while the

---

107. AHN, Inq., Lib. 838, fol. 19v. In contrast to the 222 folios of reports from the royal court, the file from the Inquisition's records on both sorceresses covers only eight folios total.

108. AHN, Inq., Lib. 838, fol. 20v.

109. AHN, Inq., Lib. 838, fol. 21r.

110. AHN, Inq., Lib. 838, fol. 21r.

111. AHN, Inq., Lib. 838, fol. 21v.

112. AHN, Inq., Lib. 838, fol. 23r.

Inquisition sought instead acts that could be deemed heretical and diabolical. The concerns of the villagers centered around the *fama* of these women who claimed to heal illnesses but also elicited fear among their neighbors. The contrast between the trials of these sorceresses processed under both tribunals reflects the ambiguous nature of witchcraft and its complicated legal categorization.

The Last Sorceress of Navarra, 1675

María Esparza, accused of infanticide, quackery, and various acts of *maleficia*, marked the conclusion of "this business of witchcraft" for the court and council of Navarra. The villagers from her town of Asiáin reported that this chronic beggar held "the public opinion, *fama*, and reputation that she is a sorceress and that her husband was too, and this has been and continues to be the public voice and common knowledge."[113] Further damning María, four medical experts reviewed the case records but examined no body and no physician's notes. Surprisingly, they declared her healing "did not come from a natural virtue nor from the strength of natural remedies nor from the natural virtues of certain words, nor from miracles; it clearly came from the hand of the devil."[114] This ruling surprises, not because the belief in preternatural powers faded from elite mindscapes, but rather the establishment that the sickness or death of the alleged victim was unnatural proved difficult, and even more so without an examination of the body.[115] But twelve witness testimonies against her, and the deafening silence of any testimony on her behalf, sufficed for the magistrates' merciless sentence of public humiliation, two hundred lashes, and ten years' exile from the kingdom.

María's *procurador* mounted a vigorous defense and sought the Inquisition's intervention. He explained that her cures centered around mere simple prayers and rightfully blasted the medical testimony as "ignorant," ridiculing their diagnoses in the absence of an examination of the body. But his defense had been shrugged off by the court;

---

113. AGN, TR_17176 (1675), fol. 11v.

114. AGN, TR_17176 (1675), fol. 28v.

115. Establishing the *corpus delicti*, or body of the crime, was no easy task. From Venetian inquisitors to German court advisers, early modern officials struggled with establishing the *corpus delicti*, as it was difficult to be certain about the true character of the illnesses in certain trials; see Seitz, *Witchcraft and Inquisition*, 9, and Thomas Robisheaux, *The Last Witch of Langenburg: Murder in a German Village* (New York: W. W. Norton, 2009), chap. 12.

thus he argued that her case belonged before the Inquisition, insisting the secular jurists "must remit this case to the tribunal of the Holy Inquisition."[116] The court did not wish to relinquish its jurisdiction and fought vigorously over its right to María's prosecution. She had, after all, committed much *maleficia* for some time and admitted her husband had been a brujo. She engendered the fear of the villagers, extorted clients, begged relentlessly, and was a bad neighbor and a bad Christian.[117]

The court did not deny the possibility that the Inquisition could have *some* jurisdictional claims over María. It argued instead for the order of operations. Echoing debates over the sequence of sentencing between the two courts from 1526 and 1575, the royal council confirmed the court's sentence, while promising the Inquisition "after its execution, we will *then* remit the case to the Inquisition."[118] Undaunted, a commissary of the Inquisition pressed the request for her case to be submitted for its review and reported there were heretical elements that fell under its purview. The council was forced to submit her case to the Holy Office in December 1675. Meanwhile, María Esparza remained imprisoned in the royal jails while her case lulled in the doldrums, awaiting the Inquisition's decision. But the Inquisition did not want her.

María Esparza—accused of sorcery and heterodox healing—appeared in its *relación* as but a passing entry, an aside:

> María de Esparza, from the town of Asiáin in the kingdom of Navarra, was denounced to the Holy Office on the twenty-fifth of November in a letter written by the commissary of the Holy Office in Pamplona. He said she had been sentenced by the council for sorcery. . . . On the thirteenth of January of 1676 . . . three *calificadores* agreed in unison that her case did not have the quality of pertaining to religion.[119]

María's last chance for a milder sentence at the hands of the Inquisition had failed. It did not want her at this late time. In the meantime, the secular authorities did not want to feed her.

---

116. AGN, TR_17176 (1675), fol. 31r.

117. Briggs elucidates the connection between seeking charity and witchcraft accusations in *Witches and Neighbors*, 155–57.

118. AGN, TR_17176 (1675), fol. 31v. Italics mine.

119. AHN, Inq., Lib. 839, fol. 240r–v.

Her *procurador* pleaded with the court to resume her daily allowance as she was starving. Once again, María was caught in the crosswinds of the two powers: The court of Navarra argued it should not have to support her, since it had paused its sentencing only at the Inquisition's request for review of her case. And the Inquisition argued since she was not in its prisons it held no responsibility toward her whatsoever. Ultimately María escaped from the royal jails, was recaptured, and received a severe sentence of two hundred lashes and exile from the kingdom of Navarra. The last witch trial before the royal tribunals of Navarra ended with a note from her warden: Juan Saturtegui reported it took six days by horseback to lead María Esparza out of Navarra. Taking her hand, he led her across the border into Aragon, and warned her to never again return home.[120]

Never again was another trial of witchcraft or sorcery held by the royal court and council of Navarra. And in the seventeen cases that came before the Inquisition's tribunal following María Esparza, only one person received sentencing; the rest were absolved or suspended.[121] At this late date, perhaps the royal court and council and the Inquisition's tribunal at Logroño could agree finally on one thing: "This business with the witches has caused the Inquisition much work, waste, and grief; they yield from it little fruit."

The presence of both the Spanish Inquisition's tribunal in Logroño and Navarra's semiautonomous royal tribunals created an entangled legal situation for trials of witchcraft and sorcery. Both jurisdictions struggled for judicial rights over these souls accused of witchcraft for 150 years, and each raised arguments as to why *its* tribunal was most appropriate. The royal tribunals argued that the Inquisition's emphasis on confession and penance was not adequate punishment for secular crimes that impacted neighbors and property, and highlighted that many inquisitors did not have adequate legal training. The Inquisition, however, relied on a definition of witchcraft and sorcery that inherently privileged heresy, therefore placing these crimes in its own hands. Further complicating matters, Navarra's specific linguistic and geographical situation, and remarkably strong secular court, tested the limits of power for the Spanish Inquisition in matters of witchcraft at the regional level, revealing that though omnipresent,

---

120. AGN, TR_17176 (1675), fol. unnumbered.
121. Henningsen, unpublished database, 2016.

the Inquisition was not omnipotent. And while following the witch panic newly implemented inquisitorial policies prevented another witch panic and mirrored a steep decline in witch trials processed in the royal tribunals, the courts of law and public opinion continued to hold extreme power over individuals, sometimes with devastating consequences.

CHAPTER 3

The Christian Crux

> María Johan of Anocíbar is a witch. . . . She gave
> and offered herself to the Devil. . . . She spat in
> the face of a crucifix . . . and did the same to the
> image of Our Lady and other saints.
>
> —Royal tribunals, September 15, 1575

Graciana de Iráizoz was considered *una
mala cristiana*, a bad Christian. In the eyes of her neighbors, she behaved
suspiciously, attended church services infrequently, and rejected the efforts of concerned neighbors encouraging her to go to Mass. The villagers of Anocíbar reported that for the last five years or so Graciana had
preferred to stay in bed with feigned sickness instead of performing her
duties as a good Christian, one who attended the divine services and
partook in the sacraments of the holy church.[1] As witch fears spread
throughout her village in 1575 following the arrest of several accused
suspects, including Graciana's husband, Miguel Zubiri, neighbors un-
leashed a flood of pent-up resentments against her, many of which
centered on her rejection of their charitable efforts. They shared accounts of paying visits to Graciana's home, dressing her as they would
a child, and even offering to carry her to church. Her response to this
Christian charity was wholly unacceptable: she wrestled from them at
the threshold, ripped off her clothes, and returned to her bed. And
one Easter, when her neighbors successfully brought her to church, she
ignored the Mass, refusing to even glance at the altar. Not only had

---

1. AGN, TR_69853 (1576), fol. 85r.

Graciana shirked her duty as a believer, but she also rejected her role in a community of believers and dashed off as soon as the service ended. This reaffirmed the villagers' view that Graciana was not only a *mala cristiana*, but also a witch.

The villagers' testimonies point to the crucial role of religious performativity in understandings of witchcraft in early modern Navarra. The vivid accounts voiced by neighbors and reflected in the royal tribunals' records reveal that many accused of witchcraft were accused also of being *malas cristianas*, a dangerous denunciation in reform-era Navarra. Accusations against *malas cristianas* ranged from gross perversions of the faith (such as inverted Masses) to more common concerns of inadequate religious performance (such as irregular church attendance). As Navarra's bishops and priests enacted efforts at Catholic renewal, parishioners became versed in the behaviors of "good" and "bad Christians." Village testimonies, official charges, demonological treatises, and arguments both for and against the accused, all point to the epistemological connections between witchcraft beliefs, a Christian cosmology, and the context of religious revival.

The impact of the Protestant and Catholic Reformations on witchcraft beliefs and prosecutions was profound. While trials of witchcraft both preceded and followed the period of the most significant reforms, a quickly changing religious landscape intensified prosecutions and persecutions of those labeled as witches. Both Catholic and Protestant confessions (religions) pursued witches with regionally specific passion.[2] And while areas with close cross-confessional contact tended to host more witch trials, religious homogeneity did not prevent worries over witchcraft.[3] Reinvigorated fears of the devil accelerated the energy for witch trials, which reciprocally furthered diabolical fears during the period of reforms.[4] No doubt this pervasive rhetoric alerted parishioners to the proximity of diabolical influences to which all— but especially *malas cristianas*—could fall prey. And as the Reformations spread across Europe, so too did pastoral work and religious education,

---

2. Catholic witch-hunting in southwest Germany, for example, differed from the Catholic response to witch fears in southern Spain. H. C. Erik Midelfort, *Witch-Hunting in Southwestern Germany, 1582–1684: The Social and Intellectual Foundations* (Stanford: Stanford University Press, 1972), 33.

3. For useful maps and charts, I recommend Wolfgang Behringer, *Witches and Witch-Hunts* (Cambridge: Polity Press, 2004), 105, 130, 136, 150.

4. See Carlos Eire, *Reformations: The Early Modern World, 1450–1650* (New Haven, CT: Yale University Press, 2016), chap. 23, 632–40.

sowing moral anxieties and diabolical vigilance among the unlettered and elite alike.

The Reforming Landscape

Spain's Inquisition, established in 1478, prevented the entrenchment of Protestant thought, while its Edict of Expulsion exiled all practicing Jews in 1492.[5] That same year further reform efforts sought to convert Moorish populations in reconquered Spanish regions. Thus, Spain had already been reforming religious practices for nearly forty years before the start of the Protestant Reformation. Efforts launched against "Lutheranism," a broad term used to define any Protestant beliefs, came from its Inquisition's tribunals, such as the one in Logroño.[6] And although two Protestant conspiracies were uncovered and squashed in Pamplona, Luther's teachings in reality exerted a limited influence in Iberia and involved mostly elites.[7] With the Inquisition leading the battle against Protestantism, Spain's reforming efforts turned to institutional improvements such as limiting corruption and improving education.

Spain's reformation sought to strengthen the church's own central authority while raising standards of orthodoxy and education. Marked by the Council of Trent (an ecumenical council assembled at the city of Trento in Italy), the Catholic Reformation focused on reforming behaviors of the clergy and laity alike. Throughout the council's meetings, from 1545 to 1563, Spanish bishops constituted the largest representations (after the Italian episcopy), taking leading roles in the push for reform.[8] Among the clergy, reforms targeted clerical abuses such as pluralism and nepotism, while encouraging improved pastoral practices.[9] Among the Spanish laity, improving Catholic education and

---

5. Henry Kamen, *The Spanish Inquisition: A Historical Revision* (London: Weidenfeld & Nicolson, 1997).

6. For example, from 1565 to 1600, the Logroño tribunal executed twenty Protestants, burned another twenty-eight in effigy, and sent some one hundred to the galleys. E. William Monter, *Frontiers of Heresy: The Spanish Inquisition from the Basque Lands to Sicily*, Cambridge Studies in Early Modern History (Cambridge: Cambridge University Press, 1990), 37, 143–46.

7. Stuart B. Schwartz, *All Can Be Saved: Religious Tolerance and Salvation in the Iberian Atlantic* (New Haven, CT: Yale University Press, 2008), 24. Helen Rawlings, *Church, Religion and Society in Early Modern Spain* (New York: Palgrave, 2002), 37–42. Monter, *Frontiers of Heresy*, 149.

8. Ronnie Po-chia Hsia, *The World of Catholic Renewal, 1540–1770*, 3rd ed. (New York: Cambridge University Press, 2010), 22.

9. According to Helen Rawlings, Pamplona had been a particularly strong seat of papal nepotism. *Church, Religion and Society in Early Modern Spain*, 52.

practices marked the Reformation's main goals. Regular attendance at Mass and observance of the sacraments of baptism, marriage, confession, and extreme unction (anointing of the sick) all became core expectations of "good Christians."[10] Following Trent, Spain's Inquisition and episcopy turned their attention toward the habits and practices of the Old Christian population and a program of Catholic renewal.[11]

The effects of the Catholic Reformation enjoyed varying levels of success depending on the diocese. Scholars of early modern Spain have demonstrated that post-Tridentine reforms (goals emerging from Trent) experienced unequal efficacy depending on regional conditions such as the character of the local population, reform-mindedness of the bishops, and the strength of its inquisitorial tribunal. The diocese of Cuenca, for example, mounted a successful, far-reaching campaign to educate and reform the lives of the clergy and laity. But, as Sara Nalle has demonstrated, these accomplishments depended largely on the flexible application of previously existent forms of religious expression.[12] Similarly, Catalonia did experience effective reforms as Kamen has shown, though these changes were slow, uneven, and modified from the original goals laid out at Trent.[13] Reform in the peripheries of Spain, as Allyson Poska has argued for the Ourense diocese in Galicia, brought official church and ecclesiastical hierarchy to local parishes, ushering in modest change to religious behaviors. Nonetheless, Orensanos "scrupulously maintained a version of Catholicism that was based in local tradition as well as a reciprocal relationship with the heavens and the corporate tradition of their parish."[14] Even in areas where the Catholic Reformation was strong, local religious practices persisted and the implementation of reform varied depending on the specific conditions of the period, place, and people.

Navarra's reform-minded bishops played leading roles throughout the sessions of Trent, actively shaping goals. Navarra's renewal efforts

---

10. For more on the various aims of Trent's reforms, see John W. O'Malley, *Trent: What Happened at the Council* (Cambridge, MA: Belknap Press of Harvard University Press, 2013).

11. Kamen, *The Spanish Inquisition*, 258.

12. Sara Nalle refers to Catholic reforms in Cuenca as "an incongruous mixture of official compulsions and popular religious enthusiasm," a description that perfectly captures the complexities of reform, witchcraft, and belief itself. *God in La Mancha: Religious Reform and the People of Cuenca, 1500–1650* (Baltimore: Johns Hopkins University Press, 1992), 209.

13. Henry Kamen, *The Phoenix and the Flame: Catalonia and the Counter Reformation* (New Haven, CT: Yale University Press, 1993), 430–34.

14. Allyson M. Poska, *Regulating the People: The Catholic Reformation in Seventeenth-Century Spain* (Leiden: Brill, 1998), 161.

aimed to curb clerical misconduct, improve religious education for the laity, and reform the religious orders.[15] The crucial roles of the delegates from Navarra ensured they took their charge to spread the decrees from Trent seriously, circulating them among parish priests and parishioners themselves.[16] For example, Bishop Cardinal Bernardo Rojas y Sandoval called a synod in Pamplona in 1590, and within a year, printed and distributed a copy of the proceedings to every parish church.[17] But, as Amanda Scott has shown in her research on Basque *seroras* (female tertiaries), reform depended also on villagers' participation in the reforming program as "decrees played out very differently when introduced to localities."[18] Reforming efforts in Navarra successfully increased awareness of religious expectations, provided opportunities to participate in religious renewal, and offered a framework with which to scan their behaviors and those of their neighbors. Still, local religious expression along with cultural and linguistic differences limited reforms, and Navarra resisted a homogeneous, orthodox expression of Spanish Catholicism.

While villagers participated in the established rituals of the church, religion as experienced and conceived of by parishioners transcended doctrinal bounds.[19] The official church centered around the sacraments, the Roman liturgy, and its calendar, while the church at the village level drew from communal patron saints, local ceremonies, and a provincial calendar informed by the region's own sacred history.[20]

---

15. The education campaign for increased frequency of attendance at Mass and confession successfully increased the demand of catechisms as demonstrated by the proliferation in religious literature coming out of Navarra's printing presses. José Goñi Gaztambide, *Los navarros en el Concilio de Trento y la reforma tridentina en la diócesis de Pamplona* (Pamplona: Imprenta Diocesana, 1947), 285, 288.

16. For a thorough analysis of the quality and reach of Tridentine reform in Navarra, see Amanda L. Scott, *The Basque Seroras: Local Religion, Gender, and Power in Northern Iberia, 1550–1800* (Ithaca, NY: Cornell University Press, 2020), chap. 3, especially pp. 55-65.

17. This same year, the *curia diocesana* was restructured according to Tridentine reform. José Goñi Gaztambide offers a comprehensive four-volume account of Pamplona's episcopacy and their activities before, during, and after Trent. For accounts of the sixteenth century, see *Historia de los Obispos de Pamplona*, vols. 3 and 4 (Pamplona: Ediciones Universidad de Navarra, 1985).

18. This was reflected in the diocese's disregard for decrees on regulating third-order religious women and cloistering professed nuns. Scott, *The Basque Seroras*, 65.

19. For a useful and example-filled framing of the overlapping spheres of magic and religion, see Stephen Wilson, *The Magical Universe: Everyday Ritual and Magic in Pre-Modern Europe* (London: Hambledon, 2000), 459-68.

20. Much of what we know of religion in early modern Spain is derived from King Phillip II's printed questionnaire that was sent to towns and villages in New Castilla from 1575 to 1580. It is unsurprising that these results reveal a religion in which the local was of primary

Local village life relied on religious experiences to provide the crucial bonds of unity and identity, and reform efforts struggled to remove long-established symbols of belief and popular expressions of religiosity.[21] The average villager in Navarra, for example, would have been loath to stop carrying effigies of the saints to the rivers to bring about rain.[22] To fail in this ritual task could bring misfortune and even famine to the community. The needs of lay people to be able to see, hear, feel, and touch the fundamental elements of their belief system could not sufficiently be addressed by a central theology alone.[23] Thus, despite reform efforts at the hands of the episcopate and the Inquisition, Spanish Catholicism resisted a uniform manifestation and retained its nuanced local and popular expressions.[24] And as with other rural European communities, the mix of official church doctrines with local religious landscapes shaped witchcraft beliefs and the definition of who a witch was in reformation-era Navarra.

Mala Cristiana = Witch?

The concept of a *mala cristiana* often informed who was crafted as a witch in Navarra. As religious performativity held together the social fabric, those who weakened it emerged among the first to be labeled witches.[25] In at least a dozen witch trials in Navarra's royal court, the

---

significance. William A. Christian's study, *Local Religion in Sixteenth-Century Spain* (Princeton, NJ: Princeton University Press, 1981), is largely based on the questionnaire's findings.

21. As Euan Cameron has shown, despite the Council of Trent's attempt at administrative uniformity, the diversity of sacramentals, unofficial saints, folk healers, and other superstitions persisted throughout early modern Europe (and into the modern period). See *Enchanted Europe: Superstition, Reason, and Religion, 1250–1750* (New York: Oxford University Press, 2010), introduction.

22. As early as 1510, Martín de Arlés y Andosilla (canon of Pamplona) sought to curb such superstitious practices; however, to this day the ritual of bearing the effigy of San Miguel to bring about rain persists. See Javier Pagola Lorente, *A Thousand Routes through Navarre* (Pamplona: Fondo de Publicaciones del Gobierno de Navarra, 2000), 65.

23. William Christian's study of local religion in sixteenth-century Spain provides a glimpse of the sphere of direct contact between communities and their saints. See Christian, *Local Religion*, 20.

24. In his work on villages in Castilla, David Vassberg shows that even following successful Tridentine reforms local communities retained their own local saints. An example was the beloved "Lady of Riansares" to which local parishioners clung, regarding her as superior to all other virgins in the peninsula. Vassberg, *The Village and the Outside World in Golden Age Castile* (New York: Cambridge University Press, 1996), 161.

25. This could range from those who held lasting *fama* for being "dissolute and immoral," such as Anna Schmieg described by Thomas Robisheaux in *The Last Witch of Langenburg: Murder in a German Village* (New York: W. W. Norton, 2009), 72, to those who, in a

term *mala cristiana* was used interchangeably with *bruja*. Similarly—and without exception—the defense attorneys' first and foremost clause argued that the accused was a *buena cristiana*, and not a witch. The terms *buena cristiana* and conversely *mala cristiana* transcended their religious parameters throughout Navarra's trial records and were used to signify whether a person might be a witch. These signifiers resist an easy translation that retains their meaning so remain therefore in their original Spanish form.

The connection between labels of *mala cristiana* and witchcraft accusations appeared throughout Navarra's trial records with consistency. These accusations did not, however, necessarily reflect long-standing *mala fama* (negative notoriety) or an actual delinquent Christian (for instance, one who never goes to Mass).[26] Accusations of being a *mala cristiana* often resulted from *mala fama* as reflected in testimony from the village of Villanueva in 1535. When asked if he knew of any witches, Pedro Etzeberena responded that María Sagardoy must be a witch because she had "the reputation of being a *mala cristiana*."[27] His primary emphasis on María's reputation as a *mala cristiana* revealed the intimate connection in this villager's mind between witchcraft and Catholic performance. It also underscored that just as early modern witchcraft was the inversion of Christianity, a witch was the inversion of a *buena cristiana*. In a world constructed of binaries (good/evil, man/woman, angel/demon, saint/witch), inversions or strict polar opposites provided an easily recognizable representation of all that witchcraft encompassed.[28] This simple duality registered a complex range of contradictions to an early modern Christian audience who was primed to search for signs of weak Christian performance. The intimate connection between a *mala cristiana* and witchcraft in the era of Catholic renewal emerged clearly in

---

general way, imposed on others in an already meager society, as explored by Robin Briggs in his analysis of beggars in *Witches and Neighbours: The Social and Cultural Context of European Witchcraft* (New York: Penguin, 1996), 155–57.

26. As Levack lays out in his discussion of triggers (individual or communal) that arose and led to denunciations, people usually drew first from those with reputations of moral or religious deviance. This does not mean, of course, that early modern Europeans with unblemished reputations did not get accused of witchcraft. See Brian Levack, *The Witch-Hunt in Early Modern Europe*, 4th ed. (New York: Routledge, 2016), 164–70 for "The Triggers" and 145–47 for "The Personality of the Witch."

27. AGN, TR_209502 (1535), fol. 3r.

28. Clark offers an exceptional analysis of inversion, the dual classification system, the language of contrarieties, and how these informed and supported demonic witchcraft beliefs. See Stuart Clark, *Thinking with Demons: The Idea of Witchcraft in Early Modern Europe* (Oxford: Clarendon Press, 1997), 31–93.

testimony from 1576. When asked who was known to be a witch in the village of Burutain, sixty-year-old Joanot Echeberri initially responded that his small village of fourteen or fifteen hearths lacked those with *fama* for witchcraft. But then he suggested: "Domingo de Echayde must be a witch because he has seldom ever gone to hear Mass and the divine services."[29] For Pedro and Joanot, witches were foremost *malas cristianas*.

As agents of evil, these *mala cristianas* were often thought to bring misfortune and suffering to their communities. When the town of Piedramillera searched for its witches in 1576, thirty-two-year-old Catalina de Artabia reported with certainty that "there are witches" and identified three reputed witches, accusing them of sorcery, infanticide, and hanging toads on their doors. Catalina's emotional deposition reveals the religious framework informing her definition of what a witch was. Catalina reported that she had lost all ten of her children: some were stillborn, and others died shortly after birth. Her relentless misfortunes left her no choice but to conclude: "From having birthed so many dead children, and from her pains and tribulations, she knows . . . that some *mala cristianas brujas* have caused this."[30] She used the words "*mala cristianas brujas*" as one term, which in essence, they were. *Malas cristianas*, witches, had caused her suffering and the deaths of all her children. Catalina's conclusion that witches induced her misery is not surprising, as it was common to look for explanations where there seemingly were none and ascribe misfortune to diabolical causes. While a functional role in witchcraft accusations was not a requirement, witch belief often provided just that.[31]

A label of *mala cristiana* exposed villagers to accusations of witchcraft, especially during the periods of chain trials. In the case of Graciana de Iráizoz mentioned at the outset, her neighbors in Anocíbar easily identified her as *mala cristiana* who did not fulfill her Catholic duties. Multiple witnesses testified that Graciana had been viewed suspiciously by her neighbors for a long time due to her delinquency from church, her odd behavior when she did attend Mass, and her defiant rejection of their interventions, transgressions that no doubt damaged her social standing. The court's charges underscored the reasons behind the

---

29. AGN, TR_11219 (1576), fol. 7v.

30. AGN, TR_11195 (1576), fol. 3v.

31. Witchcraft accusations sometimes intersected with inexplicable tragedies, such as unseasonal weather or "the accumulation of misfortune [that seemed] unnatural." But bad things were not the cause of witchcraft beliefs; rather villagers could draw from the cauldron of witch beliefs during hard times if they so chose. Behringer, *Witches and Witch-Hunts*, 85.

accusations, reporting "the neighbors saw her *mala cristianidad* [bad Christianity]" and concluded "the accused is a witch . . . and a *mala cristiana*."[32] Graciana defended herself against these accusations, maintaining she had been unable to attend Mass due to a long-term serious illness. Within a month of her incarceration, Graciana died in prison. Though she was very thin and weak, her cellmates took care to report she died with "Jesus's name on her lips."[33]

Legal reports reflected and supported connections between Christian performativity and witchcraft. In 1576, eighteen villagers of Améscoa accused Martín Lopez, Joan de Alduy, and María de Ecala of witchcraft, highlighting their weak participation at the parish church. The *fiscal's* formal charge of witchcraft underscored this religious transgression among the plentiful accusations of *maleficia*. In addition to noting that many years had passed since they last attended religious services, the *fiscal* added when they did so "it was only to comply with their neighbors." Beyond the inadequate quantity of their attendance, he noted, too, the poor quality of their religious performance, continuing "they did not drink holy water, nor pray to the sacred sacrament. And before the priest said Mass and lifted the true body of our lord Jesus Christ and consumed it, they turned their faces and looked at the floor, and never looked at the altar nor the priest."[34] The formal charges highlight the importance that religious performance held in judicial proceedings and legal proofs of witchcraft. They also reveal that villagers enforced proper behavior and that witchcraft labels were a public production influenced by Catholic reform efforts. As the local tribunal drew from the court of public opinion, the *caliber* of Christian performance emerged as a proof of witchcraft. While villagers, priests, and the royal tribunals called the accused *malas cristianas*, the accused and their *procuradores* refuted these charges with pronouncements of being *buenas cristianas*, supported by declarations of good Catholic and Christian acts and, at times, even with material proofs.

Christian Defense

In all of the royal tribunals' witch trials—without exception—*procuradores* argued first and foremost that their client was a *buena cristiana*, a

---

32. AGN, TR_69853 (1576), fol. 85r.
33. AGN, TR_69853 (1576), fol. 100r.
34. AGN, TR_69261 (1576), fol. 56r.

defense that relied on proof of religiosity as the supreme testament of innocence. While it stands to reason this would be a common line of defense, a review of other criminal trials from the same tribunals, same time period, and same villages revealed that this defense was specifically popular in trials of witchcraft. In a sampling of two dozen criminal trials including infanticide, bigamy, rape, theft, attempted murder, and homicide, not one single *procurador* invoked the defense their client was a *buena cristiana*.[35] This review privileged the same *procuradores*, such as Pedro Larramendi, who led every defense on behalf of accused witches with proclamations of his client's status as a *buena cristiana*. And though some of these crimes such as rape, theft, and bigamy would no doubt have benefitted from character validation, at no point did they invoke the first and leading defense used to defend accused witches. This examination of contemporary nonwitchcraft trials corroborates that being a *buena cristiana* was central to a witchcraft trial defense. But what was a *buena cristiana*? Early modern religion functioned as a body of believers, and proof of membership in this community was enacted through performative visible rites and rituals.[36] Public performance through attendance at Mass, participation in Communion, confession of sins, observance of the religious calendar, receipt of the sacraments, marriage at the hands of the local priest, and a Christian Mass at the hour of death all pointed visibly to a *buena cristiana*.[37] *Procuradores* drew from this sphere of visible works, highlighting tangible actions (such as giving alms and money to the church) and participation in community activities (such as pilgrimage) to prove the accused's character as a *buena cristiana*.[38]

While witchcraft accusations varied greatly in form and function, *procuradores* centered a defense of religious devotion. For example, when Graciana Oroquieta was accused of *maleficia*, night flight, and diabolism during the chain trials of 1576, her *procurador* Pedro Larramendi

---

35. I examined twenty-five criminal trials in the AGN processed by the royal tribunals from 1570 to 1595, and none argued specifically that the accused criminal was a *buena cristiana*.

36. For more on the social creation and function of religion, see Emile Durkheim, *The Elementary Forms of Religious Life*, trans. Carol Cosman (New York: Oxford University Press, 2001), 22–28.

37. And, in theory, a good Catholic would know popular prayers and the Ten Commandments. Rawlings, *Church, Religion and Society in Early Modern Spain*, 79.

38. See Cristina Larner, *Witchcraft and Religion: The Politics of Popular Belief* (New York: Blackwell, 1984), 118.

met this hearty set of accusations with a rebuttal that underscored her religious devotion:

> She is a good Catholic Christian and person of good living and reputation, she confesses and receives communion as mandated by the holy mother church, and she hears Mass and attends the holy stations. And when entering the church, she has taken the holy water and has adored the cross and given alms and acts of charity. And she is separate from acts of sorcery and witchcraft, and this is held [to be true] and commonly reputed.[39]

Larramendi intentionally argued first and foremost for the Christianity of his client. By proving Graciana was a *buena cristiana*—as measured by attendance at Mass, participation in Catholic ritual, and confession—Larramendi disproved that she was a witch. To be both was an impossibility. Defense attorneys relied also on witness testimonies about the religious practices of the accused, highlighting villagers' responses that confirmed the accused was a *buena cristiana*, attended Mass with regularity, and had good *fama*. As with modern litigation, attorneys for the accused mounted arguments that would resonate best within their legal system. And in the witch trials of Navarra during the Catholic Reformation, it was by drawing on proofs of being a *buena cristiana*.

When Miguela de Villanueva stood accused of witchcraft and infanticide in 1576, Pedro Larramendi countered the allegations by first asserting: "She is fearful of God, a good and Catholic Christian." He connected her status as a *buena cristiana* to her privileged, Old Christian (*cristiano viejo*) lineage as a "daughter and granddaughter of . . . principled, aristocratic *buenos cristianos*."[40] Larramendi laid bare her *buena cristiana* proofs: Miguela had been baptized at birth, confirmed, and received a thorough and proper religious instruction in a timely manner. These Catholic rituals would serve as prophylactics from the diabolical seductions of witchcraft. While Larramendi's arguments invoked her ancestral credentials as an Old Christian, free from the taint of Jewish or Moorish blood, it was her active role as a *buena cristiana* that Larramendi highlighted above all else.

Like witch-hood, Catholic ritual was not an occult practice, but rather public performance. So, while Miguela's defense highlighted her

---

39. AGN, TR_344109 (1576), fol. 41.
40. AGN, TR_327295 (1576), fol. 32r.

knowledge of "Catholic understandings, the Sunday prayers, the Creed and the articles of the faith and other devotions and prayers," it was her visible actions of reciting them in the presence of her community of believers and her frequent attendance at "Mass, vespers, the holy services, always and continually, and with much devotion" that could be corroborated by witnesses. He punctuated these attributes with the confirmation: "And this is public and common knowledge." Reflecting the reforming landscape, parishioners monitored one another's church activity and drew more from publicly observed rather than privately practiced transgressions to craft their witches. As such, Larramendi highlighted her frequent confession (which transcended the requisite once per year) and Miguela's material support of her community of believers, arguing that she avidly tithed, dedicated the first fruits of her harvests, and performed "other praiseworthy and voluntary acts."[41] Even the quality of her performativity deserved notice, as he noted she enacted these practices with "much devotion." Since religiosity was measured in terms of outward performances of Christian acts, *how* devotional acts were performed appeared often in witchcraft defenses. The attention Larramendi gave to Miguela's Christian defense underscores its importance.

Clerical testimony to devotional performance on behalf of the accused could further strengthen a *buena cristiana* defense. In the 1576 trial of eighty-year-old Graciana Martínez from the village of Echarri-Aranaz, both the abbot of Urdiain and the parish priest attested to her Christianity as they disputed her witchcraft accusation. Don Miguel de Iturmendi, the seventy-four-year-old abbot, declared in the forty years he had served as abbot and vicar, he had always known Graciana to be a *"buena cristiana* and almsgiver." But what stood out most in Don Miguel's mind was the quality of her gifts. Her significant offering of a silver chalice "valued as much as six or seven *ducados*" emerged as a noteworthy offering, and multiple witnesses mentioned it in their depositions.[42] Echoing the vicar's impressions, the sixty-year-old priest Gaspar de Urdiain professed: "He has seen the accused go to the [church] and hear the divine services with devotion and receive the most sacred sacrament with <u>much</u> veneration and devotion."[43] The scribe's underlining of "much" leaps from the page. The purposeful stress on the

41. AGN, TR_327295 (1576), fol. 32r.
42. AGN, TR_327215 (1576), fol. 25r.
43. AGN, TR_327215 (1576), fol. 27r.

intensity of her devotion suggests that while a tepid performance of the Christian ritual may be enacted by anyone, *her* expression of faith registered as remarkable by the priest, a strong defense against an accusation of witchcraft. Graciana's defense rested on her Christianity and acts of charity toward her neighbors. Even so, the *fiscal* disregarded the seventeen witnesses who testified on her behalf, including two clerics, and severely sentenced the elderly, bedridden, and crippled woman to perpetual exile. While a Christian defense was crucial, it did not guarantee absolution, especially in times of heightened witch prosecutions.[44]

In addition to arguing that the accused was a *buena cristiana*, defense attorneys could draw from the accused's status as a *cristiana vieja*. In early modern Spain, being a *buena cristiana* typically also meant being an Old Christian.[45] Beginning in the mid-fifteenth century, Toledo enacted statutes of *limpieza de sangre* (purity of blood) aimed to persecute those with any trace of Jewish or Moorish ancestry and, conversely, strengthen the position of those with "clean blood," that is, Old Christians with "Christian blood." By the end of the sixteenth century, the ideology of *limpieza de sangre* had spread throughout Spain (and across the Atlantic) and severely impacted the lives and opportunities of anyone with Moorish, Jewish, or "heretical" heritage.[46] The notion of *limpieza de sangre*, at first deployed as a temporary tool to ensure the "purity of faith," had been transformed into a means of exclusion, and those with "pure" or "clean" blood used this designation to their benefit.

Procuradores at times invoked the concept of *limpieza de sangre* in their defense of the accused. In 1661, fifty-three-year-old María Brigante was accused of sorcery and the murder of a magistrate from the court. Twenty-four villagers from her hometown of Lumbier testified to her *mala fama*, and various medical doctors declared that supernatural means caused the magistrate's death. Confronted with so many accusations of *mala fama*, combined with the damning medical testimony, her *procurador* José Quadrado mounted the best defense he could: he highlighted her religiosity and her purity of blood. Not only was María a *buena cristiana*, she was also an *Old* Christian. Quadrado's first

---

44. The records of this case cannot offer a specific clue as to why the court treated her so severely.

45. Conversos, that is, newly converted Jewish populations, suffered greatly under Spanish suspicions. See Jonathan Ray, *After Expulsion: 1492 and the Making of Sephardic Jewry* (New York: New York University Press, 2013).

46. For a thorough discussion of these discriminatory statutes, see Albert A. Sicroff, *Los estatutos de Limpieza de Sangre: Controversias entre los siglos XV y XVII* (Madrid: Taurus, 1985).

article argued: "She is a woman of honor and a *buena cristiana,* fearful of God. . . . Her parents were people with honor and good birth, clean from the bad race of Jews, Moors, and those punished by the Holy Office. They were *buenos cristianos.*" And as such "they were neither witches nor sorcerers."[47] It is remarkable to find the concept of *limpieza de sangre* applied beyond Jewish and Muslim blood and applied to corrupted Old Christian blood, to witches.

Beyond pointed hats and exaggerated noses, medieval antisemitic tropes contributed to the cauldron of witch beliefs.[48] Medieval impulses of "othering" (be it Jews, lepers, or *agotes,* a marginalized minority group in the Pyrenees) laid the foundation for a persecuting and intolerant society and became inherent to the idea of the witch as the diabolical "other" within the world of Christian reform.[49] Early fourteenth-century chronicles reported Jews gathering leprous populations together—along with the devil—to distribute poisons (made of blood, herbs, and the consecrated Host) and launch an attack on Christianity.[50] These medieval concerns for "a plot directed against society" morphed into fears of a diabolical witch sect within the context of an early modern Christian society of reformations.[51] And notions of Jewish blood libel, infanticide, and cannibalism easily transferred onto the inherently polluted female witch.[52] Beyond murdering unbaptized children and desecrating the Host, witches posed a greater threat than Jewish heretics as they could masquerade as good Christians while attempting to seduce the flock.[53] Even those with pure, Old Christian blood were not safe from the devil's heightened project of seduction.

The use of *limpieza de sangre* not only appeared within the secular court of Navarra, but also emerged in Pamplona's episcopal court. When Pedro Lecumberri was denounced for witchcraft and leading his

---

47. AGN, TR_59308 (1661), fol. 58r.

48. As early as 1421, those convicted of sorcery were forced to wear the conical "Jewish hat." See Naomi Lubrich, "The Wandering Hat: Iterations of the Medieval Jewish Pointed Cap," *Jewish History* 29, no. 3 (2015): 232.

49. Carlo Ginzburg, *Ecstasies: Deciphering the Witches' Sabbath* (New York: Pantheon Books, 1991), 51–52, 67–69.

50. Ginzburg, *Ecstasies,* 35–36.

51. Ginzburg, *Ecstasies,* 121.

52. See Yvonne Owens, "The Saturnine History of Jews and Witches," *Preternature: Critical and Historical Studies on the Preternatural* 3, no. 1 (2014): 56–84.

53. Richard Kieckhefer also offered connections between Jewish accusations and those of witches. See "Avenging the Blood of Children: Anxiety over Child Victims and the Origins of the European Witch Trials," in *The Devil, Heresy and Witchcraft in the Middle Ages: Essays in Honour of Jeffrey B. Russell,* ed. Alberto Ferreiro (Leiden: Brill, 1998), 92–95.

own witch sect, his *procurador* Sancho de Berrobi argued: "Pedro de Le-cumberri is a presbyter of good living, a noble *hidalgo*, and an Old Christian in his origin and ancestry, and is a good and Catholic Christian."[54] While the claim of being a *buena cristiana* was sometimes difficult to prove, the accused could draw on their ancestry as Old Christians in their defense. Neighbors and clerics could testify to the accused's heritage and outward acts of Catholic rituals. But, besides a purely Catholic genealogy, could physical evidence be introduced to the court to support claims of *buena cristianidad*?

In one particularly rich trial, the *procurador* provided five original indulgences treasured by an accused male witch as tangible proof of his being a *buena cristiana* and, therefore, not a witch. A group of villagers in Ultzama, accused of witchcraft during the chain trials of 1576, enjoyed a solid defense from their *procurador* who argued that they were *buenas cristianas* and that the false accusations had only materialized "in the last few days . . . against them by their enemies and those who hate them."[55] But to his arguments on behalf of forty-four-year-old Sancho Yraycos, the *procurador* presented an extra layer of defense: material proof of *buena cristianidad* in the form of five indulgences from Rome (see fig. 3.1). Indulgences theoretically offered tangible evidence that the owner had engaged in prayer, confession, and monetary support of the Church, all acts belonging to a *buena cristiana* in post-Tridentine Spain.[56] This collection of sixteenth-century indulgences, presented in small documents, remains neatly tucked within the trial transcripts at the Archivo General de Navarra. The presence of these slips of paper issued by the Catholic Church, residing for centuries within the dossier of a witch trial, clearly presents the crucial connection between religious performance and witch belief in Navarra.

Indulgences served as a compelling proof of *buena cristianidad* as, in addition to payment, these indulgences would theoretically accompany visible acts such as public prayer, charitable works, and attendance at Mass and confession. They would have been obtained from simple priests who brought them back from Rome, an example of how local communities adapted official church material culture for local use.[57]

---

54. ADP, Aguinaga, Cartón 13, n. 17 (1569), fol. 34r.

55. AGN, TR_69259 (1576), fol. 36r.

56. For more on indulgences, their history, use, controversy, and scriptural underpinnings, see P. F. Palmer and A. Tavardi, "Indulgences," in *New Catholic Encyclopedia*, 2nd ed. (Detroit: Gale, 2003), 7:436–41.

57. Christian, *Local Religion*, 145.

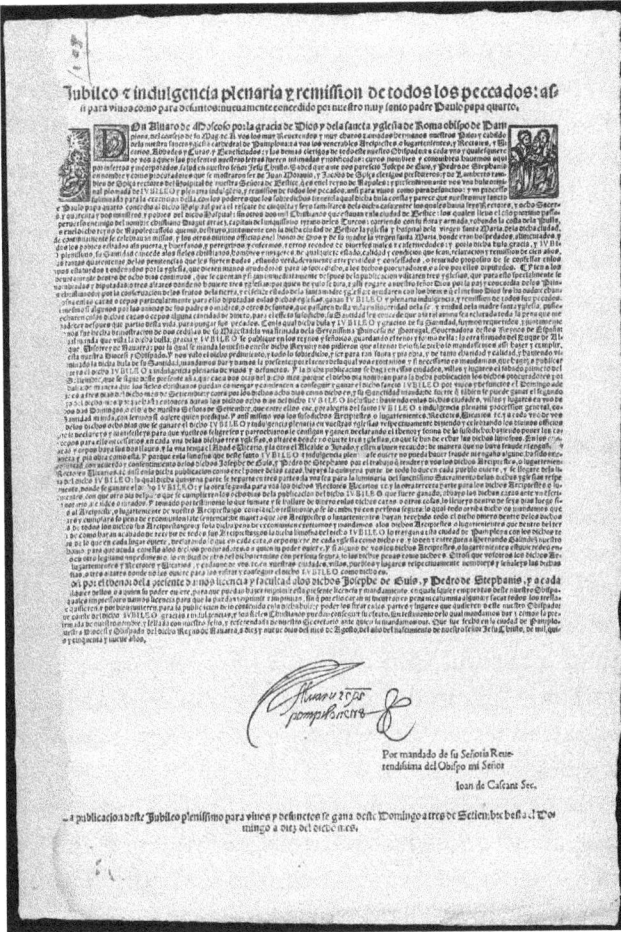

FIGURE 3.1. Plenary indulgence, ca. 1576. Used by permission of the Archivo Real y General de Navarra.

Thus when Sancho obtained these five indulgences, he tapped into official church materiality. Two of the indulgences were *bulas de la crusada*, popular indulgences in medieval and early modern Spain.[58] The granting of this indulgence would have presupposed the person had already confessed their sins and had "perfect charity," thus pointing to Sancho's financial support of the crusades against the Moors of Spain.[59]

---

58. AGN, TR_69259 (1576), fols. 103r, 104r.

59. So popular was this bull, it accounted for a large portion of the royal annual income. For more on the functions of indulgences, see Patrick J. O'Banion, *The Sacrament of Penance and*

Sancho's centenary indulgence was granted as part of the papal jubilee of 1500 and included a reprieve of temporal punishment or time in purgatory for sins committed up to that point.[60] To obtain this indulgence Sancho would have likely provided donations for pilgrimage.[61] Sancho possessed also a papal indulgence (issued by Pope Pius IV, 1559–65), a common indulgence regularly issued by popes.[62] But one of Sancho's indulgences stands out: he had obtained a plenary indulgence issued by Pope Paul IV (1555–59).[63]

The requirements for a plenary indulgence were among the most rigorous as it removed *all* temporal punishments due for the sins committed up to that time. Early Catholics would theoretically have had "to fulfill the following three conditions: sacramental confession, Eucharistic Communion, and prayer for the intention of the Sovereign Pontiff."[64] It was further required (in theory) to abstain from and renounce attachment to all forms of sin. Given these strict requirements for possession of a plenary indulgence, his *procurador* argued: "On behalf of Sancho de Yraycos, currently imprisoned . . . I present his four Bulls and one Jubilee to the *fiscal* so he can understand that Sancho is very Catholic, and a faithful Christian, and very religious, and devout."[65] Offering not only financial support to the church, Sancho performed Catholic rituals in return for forgiveness. To be sure, a *mala cristiana* or witch would not show concern for spiritual purity, penance, and prayer; a witch would not possess holy indulgences. The indulgences offered physical testimony to Sancho's religious performance, and though the court initially sentenced Sancho to five years' exile, within days his sentence was revoked, and Sancho was set free.[66]

Arguments and proofs made by the defense to refute witchcraft allegations centered on Catholic acts, attendance at Mass, regular confession, and charitable works, all of which pointed to being a *buena cristiana*. While not all *malas cristianas* attracted accusations of witchcraft, it was the principal perception considered by villagers when they indicted

---

Religious Life in Golden Age Spain (University Park: Pennsylvania State University Press, 2012), 92–102.

60. AGN, TR_69259 (1576), fol. 106r.

61. A special thanks to Dr. Thomas Robisheaux for his assistance in illuminating the requirements to obtain these indulgences.

62. AGN, TR_69259 (1576), fol. 107r.

63. AGN, TR_69259 (1576), fol. 108r.

64. Palmer and Tavardi, "Indulgences," 437.

65. AGN, TR_69259 (1576), fol. 109r.

66. AGN, TR_69259 (1576), fol. 137r.

their neighbors for witchcraft. But while villagers' reports in Navarra tended to focus on *fama* over witches' gatherings, the diabolical dimension of witch belief remained present in their deep cauldron of witch belief, emerging at times in Navarra's trials.

Christianity Inverted

In 1612 the French theologian Henri Montaigne stated: "God has his rites . . . the devil his. . . . God has his shrines, the devil his. . . . God his martyrs, the devil his."[67] Like Montaigne, early modern Navarrans' prevailing notions of witchcraft were informed by a Catholic *mentalité* that understood witches as *malas cristianas*, the opposite of *buenas cristianas*. Most villagers' reports did not extend their accusations to witches' gatherings complete with demonic sex, a diabolical pact, and a buffet of deceased babies. With slimmer influence by the more spectacular demonological writings, Navarra did not concentrate on the inverted rites of Christianity.[68] The concept of inversion—with witchcraft as a demonic copy of Christianity—did emerge in witch trials, as quotidian concerns for Catholic performance sometimes morphed into diabolical anxieties. As Stuart Clark comprehensively laid out in *Thinking with Demons*, a "culture highly sensitive to contrary oppositions" registered witchcraft as a religion shepherded by the devil.[69] Demonic witchcraft made sense in this world composed of inversions and oppositions with God and the devil at the forefront of the battle for souls. Just as God had his religion so did the devil, with witches as his parishioners. Witches were the ultimate Christian inversion; they were the devil's sect. And as such they represented the most extreme form of religious deviance: they renounced God and their baptism, committing to the devil their bodies and souls bound by a diabolical pact. Their inverted rites of Christian belief and worship were epitomized in descriptions of the witches' assemblies found commonly in learned treatises.[70] Though perhaps largely influenced by theologians and the elite, diabolical

---

67. Clark, *Thinking with Demons*, 83; citation of Henri Montaigne's *Daemonis mimica, in magiae progressu* (Paris, 1612).

68. The thousands of folios of witness testimony and summaries in the royal tribunals of Navarra make mention of only two demonologies.

69. Clark, *Thinking with Demons*, 70.

70. Examples of prominent demonologies that described the reality of the witches' gatherings include *De la demonomanie* (1580) by Jean Bodin, *Daemonolatria* (1595) by Nicolas Remy, and *Tableau de l'inconstance des mauvais anges et demons* (1612) by Pierre de Lancre. See Alan Kors and Edward Peters, *Witchcraft in Europe, 400–1700: A Documentary History*, 2nd ed. (Philadelphia:

tropes represented a fusion of learned and common notions that were present—though not predominant—in Navarra.

Reports of inverted Masses, iconoclasm, and diabolism pepper the witch trials of the royal tribunals. From the early trial of Lope Esparza in 1540 and throughout the trials of the sixteenth century, villagers' reports and official court accusations featured accounts of religious inversions and sometimes included the devil.[71] And while diabolism appeared in half a dozen trials, these reports peaked during the chain trials of 1575–76, and often reflected a diabolical definition offered by the royal tribunals rather than the villagers' testimonies as reflected in the scribal records.

The pivotal witch trial from Anocíbar in 1575 featured the witches' gatherings, the diabolical pact, and acts of iconoclasm. The *fiscal* charged these accused witches and those from surrounding villages of using "sorcery and diabolical arts to fly invisibly through the air, murder children, and destroy the crops and fields." He further claimed they entered churches and "spat on the crucifixes and the figures of the saints that are in them." Merging temporal concerns of sustenance loss in a meager society with reforming ideals of religious reverence, the *fiscal* emphatically declared these witches must be fully punished for something so "abominable and debased."[72] Witches registered as the exact opposite of *buenas cristianas* and their rituals as the most perverse inversions of sacred ceremonies.

The Devil's Mass

The chain of witch trials throughout Navarra's valleys in the last quarter of the sixteenth century invited diabolical tropes. As the village of Ultzama surveyed its landscape for those with *mala fama*, twenty-year-old villager Martín de Echalde testified against some villagers and included a description of the witches' gathering where they destroyed

---

University of Pennsylvania Press, 2001), 290–302, 322–29; Pierre de Lancre, *Tableau de l'inconstance des mauvais anges et demons*, trans. Gerhild Schultz (Turnhout: Brepols, 2006).

71. The first official report of a witches' gathering, in the case against many witches in Ochagavía in 1539, featured a reneging ceremony of God and the saints, as well as meeting in fields and the town square to dance, spread poisons, and use toad powders and blood to murder infants and adults. AGN, TR_63994 (1540). The devil had appeared in Spanish literature for centuries before the Reformations, as reflected in its literature, folklore, and art. For Spanish speakers, I recommend *El Diablo en la Edad Moderna*, ed. María Tausiet and James S. Amelang (Madrid: Marcial Pons Historia, 2004), especially 99–158.

72. AGN, TR_69853 (1575), fol. 1r.

crops with poisons made of "toad water" and baptized by the "arm of a baby."[73] In the ultimate inversion of the holy Mass, the witches used a dead child's arm as an aspergillum to bless the poisonous concoction, one responsible for the deaths of people and provisions. In lieu of holy water the witches fittingly used toad water, as toads were associated with witchcraft and death in early modern Europe.[74] This ritual—like witchcraft—inverted Christianity. These details, like those found in Martín's deposition, represented inversions of what was good, right, and holy, inversions of a *buena cristiana*.

One of the most detailed accounts of an inverted Mass emerged from an irregular trial that began in the hands of the alcalde Fermin Andueza in the valley of Araiz in 1595. According to the scribe recording the testimony produced at the palace, a group of accused villagers, including children, confessed to attending the witches' gathering in a field, adoring the devil, and engaging in diabolical sex. But soon after their transfer to the royal tribunals in Pamplona, they recanted their confessions, claiming the powerful Andueza had forced their confessions with false promises and violent threats. This coerced testimony problematizes whose voices are reflected but offers notions of the inverted Mass nonetheless. The report stated they went to a field where "two figures sat on golden thrones . . . a black man with two horns on his head" and a white woman dressed in green.[75] The dark man and his fair female consort reflected an inversion, emplotting her perhaps as Mother Mary's diabolical counterpart. The details of the golden chairs parodied the gilded altars and relics of the Catholic Church. It was in front of these figures that the accused villagers were said to have declared: "Belzebut and his consort are the true gods and saviors of all creation. And as such, to them we owe adoration."[76] Then they all adored Belzebut "as their god and Lord . . . and reneged their Christian faith." At this point the female witches, in an inversion of the holy kiss (a traditional brotherly sign of affection among Christians) kneeled on the ground and as Belzebut lifted their skirts with his hands, they took turns kissing "his behind." Following the anal kisses, Belzebut publicly had sexual intercourse with all the women, leaving María Hernando's

---

73. AGN, TR_69259 (1576), fol. 14r.

74. The biochemical properties of toads largely influenced this association. See Rochelle Rojas, "The Witches' Accomplice: Toads in Early Modern Navarre," *Sixteenth Century Journal* 51, no. 3 (2020): 693–714.

75. AGN, TR_71319 (1595), fols. 116v–117r.

76. AGN, TR_71319 (1595), fol. 117r.

white undergarments "very bloodied."[77] Not only did the devil engage in illicit sexual intercourse with multiple women, but he also left at least one covered with blood, a most profane inversion of Christ's holy blood spilled on the cross.

The council's formal accusation reflected a Catholic theology that informed the inverted Mass. Its report concluded that the witches in attendance had renounced God and the Catholic faith. As *malas cristianas* they "recognized Belzebut as Lord," and to him alone they gave adoration and reverence.[78] Their perverted God had his own temples and required of them prayer, fasting, alms, and even "confession of all their sins." The formal charges concluded that these *malas cristianas* had turned away from their community of believers, "the holy faith, and the sacraments." To be sure, there could be no greater inversion of Catholic rites and rituals than the witches' Mass.

The flexibility of witchcraft beliefs allowed the notion of *mala cristiana* to be stretched to its extreme limits as reflected in the witches' gatherings. While the label usually implied weak Catholic performativity and infrequent attendance at Mass, it could also encompass sacrilege, the diabolical pact, and sex with the devil. Regardless of its manifestation, the Catholic cosmos in post-Tridentine Navarra informed notions of witchcraft on every level and for every person, from common villagers to court magistrates to the shepherds of the holy church.

The Priest-Witch

From parish priests to bishops, church officials participated in trials of witchcraft in a variety of capacities. They heard testimonies, relayed accusations, testified in proceedings, delivered the last rites to accused witches dying in prison, and in the case of María Johan of Anocíbar, served as exorcists during interrogations under torture.[79] While clerics instigated two witch trials, pastoral testimony within the trials usually

---

77. AGN, TR_71319 (1595), fol. 118v.

78. The name Beelzebub could apply to a lesser demon or the devil himself and as such appeared in witch trials throughout early modern Europe and North America. In France, Beelzebub possessed the Ursuline nuns in 1611, while in North America, he inspired Cotton Mather to pen *Of Beelzebub and His Plot* following the Salem witch trials. See Sarah Ferber, *Demonic Possession and Exorcism* (New York: Routledge, 2004), 31–35; and Cotton Mather, *Of Beelzebub and His Plot, Original Sources*, accessed July 31, 2023, http://www.originalsources.com/Document.aspx?DocID=5DDGZ6LDDLS5NMR.

79. The Franciscan friar Francisco de Huarte attended María Johan's first torture session in case he was needed to perform an exorcism. AGN, TR_69853 (1575), fol. 109r.

favored the accused. Clerical voices, though present in the records, were neither overly represented nor necessarily privileged over other testimonies, and some accused witches received harsh sentences despite impeccable defenses provided by religious authorities (as in the case of Graciana Belza in 1561). But what of clerics themselves? Did they ever find themselves on the receiving end of a witchcraft accusation?

A local priest from the village of Burgui in the Valley of Roncal, Don Pedro Lecumberri, was tried for witchcraft by the episcopal court of Pamplona in 1569.[80] This complex witch trial began with the local alcalde of Burgui in July, was then referred to the *curia diocesana* in Pamplona, then passed on to the curia of Zaragoza, then transferred to the Inquisition (where it was rejected), and was ultimately returned to the episcopal tribunal of Pamplona, where it finally concluded in December 1570.[81] This dramatic trial lasted over a year and a half, passed through several jurisdictions, and involved a controversial priest who was loved by some and hated by others. Lecumberri's trial reflected diabolical anxieties, moralizing concerns, and the spirit of reform within the episcopal court of post-Tridentine Navarra.

Thirty-five-year-old Pedro Lecumberri, a charismatic cleric in a village of some one hundred hearths, was denounced to the alcalde for shepherding a small sect of female witches.[82] Three other members of his alleged sect received accusations alongside him: sixty-year-old María Gracieta; her daughter María Garat; and her granddaughter, seven-year-old Gracieta. The reports against them relied heavily on child testimony, a feature found in witch trials throughout early modern Navarra and beyond.[83] The first accusations came from eight-year-old Andella Garat who alleged that she was asked to join the accused in a field while she tended to her father's sheep. In an inversion of all that is good, the witches fed her vile meat and made her renounce "God and Santa María and their mother and father and godparents."

Similar to inversions emerging from the secular trials in Navarra, the episcopal court's records included the devil, desecration of sacred

---

80. This differs from what Tausiet uncovered in Aragon's ecclesiastical court, which treated eight trials of witchcraft. Though several other trials in the ADP include *brujería*, this trial reflects the most comprehensive trial of persons fingered as witches.

81. This section draws from several sources: the original 235-folio trial dossier in the ADP, the section on this case found in Florencio Idoate Iragui, *La Brujería en Navarra y sus Documentos* (Pamplona: Institución Príncipe de Viana, 1978), 74–87, and Félix Sanz Zabalza, *Las brujas de Burgui* (Navarra: Editorial Evidencia Medica, 2013).

82. ADP, Aguinaga, Cartón 13, n. 17 (1570), fol. 27r.

83. ADP, Aguinaga, Cartón 13, n. 17 (1570), fol. 27r.

objects, and the anal kiss. One witness, sixty-year-old Sebastián Baldan, grandfather to one of the young girls deceived by Pedro, reported seeing "something black like a goat with horns" that the young Gracieta walked over to "and kissed it under its tail."[84] Seven-year-old Catalina Bront also reported the anal kiss and that María Garat instructed them: "Little girls, disavow God and our Holy Mother Santa María and all the male saints and female saints."[85] Catalina reported that on another occasion "after dancing . . . they collected manure and with some little sticks they anointed the feet of [Jesus on] the cross . . . and they made obscene gestures to all the crosses."[86] The reported activities of the perverted priest and his deceived parishioners inverted his pastoral duties and—situated within a reforming mindset—imbued this set of accusations with meaning.

Though this trial featured inversion and gross sacrilege, it remained an isolated trial. All of the accused denied any connection to witchcraft, and most of the testimonies came from young girls, an irregularity noted by the defendants' *procurador*, the bishop of Saragossa, and the vicar general of Pamplona.[87] Children seldom emerged as the sole accusers in the secular witch trials of early modern Navarra.[88] But the importance of children's roles in witchcraft proceedings was sometimes heightened, as reflected in the priest-witch case of Burgui in 1569 and the infamous witch panic.[89] Due to the young age of the key accusers, the Inquisition rejected this case. As the trial passed through various jurisdictions, the reports elicited skepticism as to the realities of the accusations and general incredulity of the entire scenario. The case concluded with absolution for the three accused witches and the

---

84. ADP, Aguinaga, Cartón 13, n. 17 (1570), fol. 42r.

85. ADP, Aguinaga, Cartón 13, n. 17 (1570), fol. 48r.

86. ADP, Aguinaga, Cartón 13, n. 17 (1570), fol. 84r.

87. Idoate, *La Brujería*, 78–82.

88. While villagers under the age of discretion (twelve for girls, fourteen for boys) served as mouthpieces for the neighborhood gossip and reflected the beliefs they heard from their parents and elders, their involvement was usually not overly represented in the testimonies before the royal tribunals. The data shifts significantly, however, if we include the witch panic, suggesting that evidence resting largely on child testimonies often held an exaggerated role in moments where witch belief became dysfunctional. While the 1575 case of Anocíbar and the two young witchfinders of 1525 and 1595 center children's roles, most witch trials in the secular court did not rely entirely on juvenile involvement.

89. Of the witch panic, Lu Ann Homza has shown the persistent and crucial roles played by children, arguing the panic "should be framed as fundamentally a children's event, given that boys and girls predominated as victims and accusers." See *Village Infernos and Witches' Advocates: Witch-Hunting in Navarre, 1608–1614* (University Park: Pennsylvania State University Press, 2022), 74–75, 102–4, 185–86.

improper priest, while Lecumberri was ordered to never again speak with any of them.[90]

The case of the priest-witch in the episcopal court offers several key points. First, it reflects Navarra's vibrant legal culture where three different jurisdictions all were interested and held the power to prosecute witches. Second, it confirms that when witches were sought, those who exhibited inappropriate behaviors could be crafted as witches, even if their behavior had been tolerated for years or decades. Finally, it illuminates the intersection between reforming efforts focused on clerical misbehavior and the religious inversions in witchcraft trials.[91] As religious reformers and other intellectuals opined on witchcraft and the devil, their demonological writings both reflected and reshaped ideas about witchcraft. And as with everything in witchcraft, the corpus of witchcraft theory ranged widely depending on local factors, personalities, and temporal context.

Religious Writings and Witchcraft

The textual world of demonologies reflected, informed, and complemented the witchcraft beliefs of the early modern world.[92] Within this large corpus of writings, theologians, clergymen, natural philosophers, jurists, and intellectuals shared their doctrines, doubts, and debates about witchcraft.[93] These demonologies reflected a common Christian theology offering invaluable insights into the world of demons, the devil, and witches. Religious reformers composed dozens of demonological treatises, often informing and informed by regional witch

---

90. The records suggest that Lecumberri was engaged in inappropriate relationships with at least one of the women, and perhaps other parishioners; see Sanz Zabalza, *Las brujas de Burgui*, 149–50. ADP, Aguinaga, Cartón 13, n. 17 (1570), fol. 234r.

91. Amanda Scott's analysis of Don Pedro de Atondo, a parish priest notorious for healing, conjuring, and even violence, shows how parishioners used the diocesan courts to reform their priest's misbehaviors. See Scott, "The Wayward Priest of Atondo: Clerical Misbehavior, Local Community, and the Limits of Tridentine Reform," *Sixteenth Century Journal* 47, no. 1 (2016): 75–98.

92. It is worth noting that there were no such things as demonologies or demonologists; it is, as Jan Machielsen put it, "an artificial creation, brought together by historians," used to designate writings that included natural philosophy, religion, and law, as well as thoughts regarding demons, witchcraft, sorcery, and so forth. These writings, therefore, range from focused and intense (such as the *Malleus maleficarum*) to general and skeptical (*Disquisitiones magicae*). Machielsen, *Martin Delrio: Demonology and Scholarship in the Counter-Reformation* (Oxford: Oxford University Press, 2015), 5–7.

93. Witchcraft theory was not written in isolation and relied upon a whole range of intellectual commitments to make sense. See Clark, *Thinking with Demons*, viii.

trials.[94] Yet only two of these works found their way into the witch-trial transcripts of the royal tribunals. Both texts, *Reprobación de las supersticiones y hechicerías* (1537) by Pedro Ciruelo and *Disquisitiones magicae* (1608) by Martín Delrío, were penned by Spanish theologians (though Delrío was born in Antwerp and traveled extensively).[95] While these ecclesiastics conceived of witchcraft within a religious framework, they did not linger on the demonological aspects featured in many other popular demonologies, such as seen in Heinrich Kramer's popular *Malleus maleficarum* (1486) or the more local *Tableau de l'inconstance des mauvais anges et demons* by Pierre de Lancre (1612). They instead pushed for deeper spiritual practices, improved religious education, and caution with regard to the occult. This lack of sensational demonological writings and thought produced by Spanish theologians informed and reinforced Navarra's understandings of witchcraft.

The two demonologies appearing in Navarra's witch trials emerged from the medical testimony of four physicians in the 1675 sorcery trial of María Esparza. Doctors Francisco de Olazagutia and Francisco de Elcarte, and the master surgeons Juan de Leiza and Juan de Anelieta, were asked to determine whether certain illnesses ascribed to María were caused by natural means. They formed their conclusions by reviewing the witnesses' depositions, not by examining the affected individuals. It is within their results that Ciruelo's *Reprobación* and Delrío's *Disquisitiones* appeared as support for their commentaries explaining why certain illnesses, like those caused by preternatural means, were resistant to natural remedies. Though the medics did not engage deeply with these texts, their citations provide clues as to which demonological writings circulated in Navarra.[96]

Pedro Ciruelo composed *Reprobación de las supersticiones y hechicerías* in 1537, warning Christians to avoid superstitions, sorcery, and things that only "God could and should know."[97] The very title of

94. For a study of the demonologists assembled at the Council of Basel, see Michael Bailey and Edward Peters, "A Sabbat of Demonologists: Basel, 1431–1440," *Historian* 65, no. 6 (Winter 2003): 1375–96.

95. See the case of María Esparza, AGN, TR_17176 (1675).

96. Lu Ann Homza analyses these two demonological writings and shows how these texts could be used to "produce different witches from different sources" thus placing demonologies as one context of the crafting of witches. See *Religious Authority in the Spanish Renaissance* (Baltimore: Johns Hopkins University Press, 2000), 182–209.

97. Pedro Ciruelo, *A Treatise Reproving All Superstitions and Forms of Witchcraft, Very Necessary and Useful for All Good Christians Zealous for their Salvation*, trans. Eugene A. Maio and D'Orsay W. Pearson (London: Associated University Press, 1977), 26.

Ciruelo's work, *A Treatise Reproving All Superstitions and Forms of Witchcraft: A Very Useful Book and Necessary for All buenos cristianos*, centered his concern for proper Christian practice. Concerned by the "vain arts" to which Spaniards had fallen victim resulting from clerical negligence, he sought to "warn all the *buenos cristianos* and God's faithful servants" to guard themselves against superstitious error.[98] The treatise was comprised of three parts: The first section treated the arts of divinations and argued that all superstitious behaviors contradicted the wisdom of the Ten Commandments and thus constituted sinfulness. The second part warned against practices of nigromancy and sorcery and even astrology.[99] He also condemned healing practices performed by unofficial healers and advised that seeking such services invited diabolic delusion.[100] The text's final section denounced spoken or written curses, charms, superstitious prayers, and the evil eye. Ciruelo's main argument encouraged proper Catholic practices and discouraged seduction by arguing that occult matters should remain occult. Ciruelo's work was not the only Spanish demonology appearing in the witch trials that warned against the practices of *malas cristianas*.

Martín Delrío's *Disquisitiones magicae* (1608) cautioned adamantly against all magic. Reprinted more than twenty times, it enjoyed great popularity rivaling that of the *Malleus maleficarum*.[101] Delrío, a Jesuit theologian, wrote his treatise inspired by the lax Christian behaviors he observed and concerns for the heretical temptation of magic and sorcery.[102] He admonished Catholics against the lure of magical studies and sought to prevent them from falling into heresy, warning that some things are occult for a reason and *buenas cristianas* would do well to keep them that way. The prologue's first sentence centered his concern with Christian behavior. He counseled: "The pride and malice of God's enemies are increasing. They have a thousand ways of doing

98. Ciruelo, *A Treatise Reproving*, 26.

99. Homza, *Religious Authority*, 182–209.

100. What constituted official versus unofficial healing remained blurry throughout the early modern period, with education being one of the only distinctions. The majority of medical interventions were performed by unofficial healers. See Larner, *Witchcraft and Religion*, for a discussion of "Official and Unofficial Healing," 141–52.

101. Jan Machielsen reveals that *Disquisitiones magicae* was reprinted more times than was the *Malleus maleficarum*. Machielsen, *Martin Delrio*, 5.

102. Delrío's research into witchcraft was inspired by Jean del Vaulx, a Benedictine monk accused of witchcraft and beheaded for the crime in 1597 in Liège. Martín Antoine Del Rio, *Investigations into Magic*, ed. and trans. P. G. Maxwell-Stuart (Manchester: Manchester University Press, 1999), 6.

harm and use innumerable weapons against humanity, of which magic is the deadliest." He then forewarned that "never have there been as many witches as there are today, and the main reason for this is the faintness of a contempt for the Catholic faith."[103] Delrío cautioned against magic in any form, calling it "the handmaid of moral turpitude," and lamented that magic's seduction was great, leaving but "a few fervent Catholics left," indicating that witches teemed throughout the Catholic world. Framing magic as Satan's weapon in a holy war against God and the Catholic faith, he offered, "this book is a weapon in that war."[104] With Catholic propriety as his focus, Delrío emphasized the hope and legitimate succor that only the church could offer. Divided into four books, Delrío paired witchcraft and magic with heresy and apostasy, sending a clear warning: if one loses the faith and becomes a *mala cristiana*, the sins of heresy, magic, and witchcraft await. Delrío believed the crimes committed by witches occurred in reality, even calling witchcraft's inversions "quasi-rituals" that mimic "the sacrifice of the mass and other similar Catholic ceremonies." While Delrío found this to be "the greatest of all [the witches'] crimes" he did not launch into sordid details of diabolism as did other writers of demonological thought, such as Kramer and De Lancre, both of whom participated actively in witch trials.[105] In fact, as Jan Machielsen has recently shown in his thorough investigation of Delrío's work, "it is likely that the author of the most popular work of demonology in the early modern period never met, let alone persecuted a witch."[106] Delrío's work concluded with advice for confessors, emphasizing the crux of Catholic piety and warning them to not turn a blind eye to witchcraft as, for Delrío, it was the devil's ultimate tool in the seduction of *buenos cristianos*. He concluded his text with the hope it would reform lay Christians and clerics.

Demonologies were, in many regards, reforming texts aimed at correcting unorthodox Christian behaviors. Ciruelo and Delrío's concern with correcting improper religious education reflected the concerns of

---

103. Del Rio, *Investigations into Magic*, 27.
104. Del Rio, *Investigations into Magic*, 29.
105. Del Rio, *Investigations into Magic*, 15.
106. In *Martin Delrío*, Machielsen turns toward this demonological piece written outside of "witch hunting." Delrío, similar to other authors of so-called demonologies, was a humanist scholar and a Catholic intellectual. Machielsen's excellent work moves away from the explosive *Malleus maleficarum* trope of overzealous demonologies and invites us to examine more of these treatises individually and within their specific contexts.

Navarra's magistrates. For instance, in 1536 the courts of Navarra wrote to the king requesting an in-residence bishop. This petition drew from concerns of witchcraft, complaining that with an absent bishop "the churches of this kingdom are poorly governed, which has resulted in various errors, such as the issue with the witches."[107] So while demonologists often learned from the courts about the possible activities of witchcraft, they simultaneously developed a rational doctrine of evil, thus reaffirming that diabolical powers were real. They influenced judicial procedures and created a learned body of witchcraft literature, one as varied and nuanced as witch beliefs themselves. Regardless of their positions of skepticism, diabolism, or reforming goals, all demonologies held one truth in common: witchcraft stood as the inversion of Christianity. The demonologies emerging from the records in Navarra, however, approached this fact with a restrained pen, one that focused on Catholic propriety and the avoidance of the seductions of the occult, and did not draw out the witches' Masses in their grotesque depictions.[108]

Witchcraft beliefs in Navarra were informed by and understood within the context of Catholic Reformation, and this spirit of reform helped craft Navarra's witches. While Spain's Catholic homogeneity limited clashes between the Catholic and Protestant faiths, Catholic and Tridentine reforms *did* permeate Navarra, educating and offering Navarra's villagers the opportunity to reform improper behaviors and participate in religious renewal. Reform-era expectations centered the public ritual practice of Catholic acts and participation in the local church—outward demonstrations of being a *buena cristiana*. Though not all *malas cristianas* were witches, all witches were *malas cristianas*. Operating under this conceptual framework, accusers sought to discredit the religiosity of the accused and pointed to their deficits in Catholic performativity and Christian responsibilities. Meanwhile, *procuradores* defended their clients with declarations of their *buena cristianidad* and turned to proofs found in their religious heritage and participation in religious rituals. As reflected in several secular trials, ideas of religious inversion, the witches' Masses, and diabolism did hold meaning in Navarra, but magistrates, villagers, and theologians did not pursue that

---

107. Idoate, *La Brujería*, 279.

108. Though Pierre de Lancre was inspired by witchcraft in the Basque region when he composed his fantastical demonology, *Tableau de l'inconstance* (1612), its publication occurred after the chain trials and the witch panic in the French Basquelands.

strand of belief with great interest. And though demonological writings were produced in, inspired by, and read in Navarra, none of them fixated on the most diabolical witchcraft tropes. These factors, reciprocal and related, shaped witchcraft understandings in Navarra, understandings that placed Christian performativity at their center.

CHAPTER 4

The Testament of Toads

> The devil gives the witches a dressed toad . . . with its face like a man's and clothes in tight-fitting velvet or fine cloth.
>
> —Inquisitors at the tribunal of Logroño, 1609

In the early spring months of 1576, villagers in Piedramillera identified three witches: María de la Peña, María de San Juan, and María de Arana. Nearly twenty villagers of this tiny town of eighteen hearths furnished the secular court of Navarra with a lengthy list of charges against the three Marías, accusing them of a total of fourteen diverse transgressions.[1] Among them, María de la Peña was accused of killing Juana Lozana following an altercation, while at the same time, suspiciously sparing the life of a grotesque toad. María de San Juan was reportedly seen in her white dressing gown in the countryside at midnight, causing neighbors to suspect she was sprinkling "poisonous venoms throughout the fields and crops."[2] And María de Arana, it was said, notoriously boasted a corpulent toad, measuring in at four fingers' width, hanging from its leg on her door. The royal tribunals formally charged the Marías with attending "witches' assemblies at night in the fields with many other male witches and female witches" where they used poisonous powders to destroy the fields and

---

1. AGN, TR_11195 (1576), fols. 1r–17r.
2. AGN, TR_11195 (1576), fol. 28r.

crops, and murder their neighbors, especially children, causing "great harm to the . . . kingdom."[3]

Over the course of the sixteenth and seventeenth centuries, toads and their toxic bodies figured prominently in Navarra's secular, episcopal, and inquisitorial witch trials. The understanding of toads as magical and malignant creatures appeared in one out of two witch trial depositions in the secular court, and in nearly all the chain trials of 1575–76. As reflected in villagers' depositions in the royal tribunal's earliest witch trial of 1525, naked, nonanthropomorphic toads served as necessary ingredients for witches' *maleficia*. The witch beliefs of Navarra drew from the understandings of the toad's toxic body. This knowledge, combined with an established folkloric tradition, cast toads in crucial roles as the witch's accessory and signifiers of witchcraft. Toads and their toxins bestowed a rationality and plausibility to witchcraft accusations and legal proceedings. Toads also reveal the metamorphosis of Navarra's witchcraft beliefs as reinterpreted through the Inquisition's lens.

Toads and Poison

Since antiquity, toads in Europe have been connected to poison and evil. From classical to medieval and early modern natural histories and bestiaries, the toad's venomous property was mentioned with regularity.[4] Naturalists, herbalists, folk healers, and physicians throughout Europe expressed interest and curiosity in the potential virtues and vices of the toad. Natural histories penned by classical authorities such as Aristotle and Pliny proclaimed its medicinal potential, while warning of its toxicity. As early as the second century BCE, the Greek physician Nicander noted the pharmaceutical potential of toads; however, he first cautioned readers to avoid ingesting "a draught of the sun-loving toad," which would cause bodily discomfort and troubled breathing.[5] And in his *Natural History* (77 CE), Pliny the Elder referred to *rubetæ* in his section on "Frogs," reporting they had two protrusions like horns, but more significantly, they were "plenæ venefociorum": full of poison.[6]

---

3. AGN, TR_11195 (1576), fol. 18r.

4. Mary E. Robbins, "The Truculent Toad in the Middle Ages," in *Animals in the Middle Ages*, ed. Nona C. Flores (New York: Routledge, 2016), 25.

5. Nicander, *The Poems and Poetical Fragments*, trans. and ed. A. S. F. Gow (Cambridge: Cambridge University Press, 1953), 133.

6. Pliny the Elder, *The Natural History of Pliny*, vol. 6, trans. and ed. John Bostock, M.D., and H. T. Riley (London: Henry G. Bohn, 1953), 21.

Reflecting its amphibious nature, the toad posed both real dangers and beneficial remedies.

For centuries, the toad's skin secretions appeared in Galenic cardiac and diuretic preparations and in traditional treatments for allergies, inflammation, infections, irritations, and hemorrhages.[7] While dozens of toad uses were proposed in medieval and early modern pharmaco-peias, they came with a warning. In her medical treatise *Physica* (1155), for instance, Hildegard of Bingen proposed the toad could be used for its curative powers even as she cautioned that "the toad . . . has some diabolic art in it . . . and is sometimes dangerous."[8] Drawing from un-derstandings of sympathetic magic, she then clarified how this could be so: "Something bad often dispels another bad thing." Similarly, seventeenth-century intellectuals and folk healers drew from the spe-cial prophylactic and healing ingredients of toads in their preparation of amulets to be worn during times of plague.[9] The amulets worked by virtue of the sympathy of the poisonous toad with the pestilential venoms, an understanding informed by the homeopathic principle of "poison drives out poison . . . evil attracts evil."[10] Thus medicines were often thought to have opposite qualities contained within them. De-spite their medicinal utility, however, ultimately it was the toad's poison that drew the most attention, making it the perfect witches' accomplice.

Modern toxicology sheds light on why medical forebears—and Navarra's villagers—regarded the common toad with suspicion. All members of the *Bufo* genus produce a sticky secretion exuded from their skin and parotoid glands, a pair of well-defined skin glands be-hind the eyes that excrete bufotoxin.[11] This milky, moderately potent poison contains several identifiable components: bufagin, which affects the heart; bufotenine, a hallucinogen; and serotonin, a vasoconstrictor. Bufotoxins can dramatically damage various body parts and functions and can be fatal in large doses. Bufagins act on the heart by slowing it,

7. Calendario Rodriguez et al., "Toxins and Pharmacologically Active Compounds from Species of the Family *Bufodinae*," *Journal of Ethnopharmacology* 198 (2017): 235–54.

8. Hildegard of Bingen, *Physica*, trans. Priscilla Throop (Vermont: Healing Arts Press, 1998), 231.

9. For more on toad preparations in amulets, see Martha R. Baldwin, "Toads and Plague: Amulet Therapy in Seventeenth-Century Medicine," *Bulletin of the History of Medicine* 67, no. 2 (Summer 1993): 227–47.

10. Walter Pagel, *Paracelsus: An Introduction to Philosophical Medicine in the Era of the Renais-sance* (New York: Karger, 1982), 147.

11. K. K. Chen and Alena Kovarikova, "Pharmacology and Toxicology of Toad Venom," *Journal of Pharmaceutical Sciences* 56 no. 12 (December 1967): 1535–42.

and laboratory experiments have shown that increased dosages stop the cardiac activity of cats.[12] Similarly, studies have isolated bufotoxins from toad venoms and tested for their inhibitory effects on guinea pig hearts, concluding that they have the biochemical capacity to stop cardiac activity entirely.

Of course, Navarra's villagers would not have known of chemical formulas or modern laboratory experiments. But the toxic effects of toad venoms on small animals and pets through skin and eye irritations, vomiting, and even cardiac failure would have been observable, and further informed early moderners' association of the toad with poison and death. If toad venoms yielded palpable results in the material world through irritations and even death to animals, why could their boiled grease not also play a role in the mysterious world of witchcraft? This knowledge of the toad's power to poison in the natural world—combined with its cultural role as a demonic helper and its generally grotesque physique—made it a natural assistant and companion to the equally reviled witch.

Toads, Sin, and Death

Toads held weight in early modern European culture as both carriers of toxicity and agents of death. The literature of the classical world paired the female witch figure with the toxic toad when Horace partnered his fictional witch Canidia with the "loathsome toad" as she worked her magic into a poisonous concoction.[13] And the Roman poet Juvenal's *Satires* (early second century) told of the evil woman who murdered her husband with "toad blood" mixed with wine, teaching other wives to "bury the blackened corpses of their husbands" with the help of toads.[14] The connection between toad blood and death as reflected by these classical works would endure as a common trope in literature, trial records, and early modern depositions of accused witches who similarly placed great importance on the power of the anuran and its bodily fluids.

Within a Christian cosmology, toads and their toxic bodies—bursting with allegorical potential—embodied sin, suffering, and death. Even in

---

12. Chen and Kovarikova, "Pharmacology and Toxicology," 1537.

13. Horace, *The Works of Horace*, "The Book of the Epodes of Horace, Ode V: "The Witches Mangling of a Boy." https://en.wikisource.org/wiki/The_works_of_Horace/Book_of_Epodes.

14. Juvenal, "Satire 1," trans. G. G. Ramsay, transcribed by Robert Pearse, *The Tertullian Project*, 2008, http://www.tertullian.org/fathers/juvenal_satires_01.htm.

the Old Testament, frogs and toads (encompassed by the single Hebrew term *tsephardea*) were symbolic markers of evil. *Tsephardea* carried out God's second plague on Egypt, as the antagonistic army of anurans infested the lands and dwellings of the people, serving as agents of punishment and death.[15] *Tsephardea* again appeared in the New Testament, where they assumed the forms of corrupt spirits and demons. In his book of Revelations, the apostle John declared: "And I saw three unclean spirits like frogs come out of the mouth of the dragon, and out of the mouth of the false prophet. For they are the spirits of devils."[16] The toad inspired biblical authors to cast them as harbingers of plague and the embodiment of demons. Medieval Christian lore, iconography, sermons, and moralizing artwork relied on the toad to evoke feelings of revulsion and horror and inspire penitence in its Christian audience.[17]

Christian artists drew heavily from toad symbolism and its power to convey shared meanings to European audiences. For example, toads bite the breasts and genitals of the female statue of *Luxuria* at the entrance of the twelfth-century St. Pierre Abbey in Moissac.[18] Likewise the cauldron at Bourges Cathedral displays a toad biting the left nipple of a sinful woman in punishment of her lust. Another toad latches onto a heretical cleric's tongue, injecting him with venom as punishment for his poisonous doctrines.[19] These grotesque toads linked lust and the dangers of feminine sexuality, warning their observers against sin and the seductiveness of the female body. Renaissance artists, such as Pieter Brueghel the Elder in *The Seven Deadly Sins*, employed a poisonous toad squatting prominently in front of the female representation of *Avaritia*, avarice, to remind his audience that the ultimate reward for

---

15. It has been suggested that the plague was likely of toads rather than frogs, as common Egyptian toads were poisonous while frogs were not, and toads metamorphose more quickly and prolifically than do frogs. Richard Wasserug, "Why Tadpoles Love Fast Food," *Natural History* 93 (April 1984): 67.

16. Revelation 16:13–14, *The Holy Bible*, https://www.vatican.va/archive/ENG0839/__P12Z.HTM.

17. The toad was not universally met with fear and loathing. Ancient Egyptians, for instance, associated toads with fertility and birth, the goddess of which was Heqet, a frog-goddess. See Elizabeth Ann St. George, *Heket: Frog and Toad Magic* (London: Spook Enterprises, 2006). Similarly, multiple Native American cultures also held the toad in a positive light, associating it with fertility and life. See Adrian Morgan, *Toads and Toadstools: The Natural History, Folklore, and Cultural Oddities of a Strange Association* (Berkeley: Celestial Arts, 1995), 123–26.

18. Thomas Dale, "The Nude at Moissac: Vision, Phantasia, and the Experience of Romanesque Sculpture," in *Current Directions in Eleventh-and Twelfth-Century Sculpture Studies*, ed. Robert Maxwell and Kirk Ambrose (Turnhout: Brepols, 2010), 60–61.

19. Adrian Tudor, *Tales of Vice and Virtue: The First Old French "Vie des Peres"* (Amsterdam: Rodopi, 2005), 368.

this sin is death. Toad-like creatures also served as chief tormentors of sinners throughout Hieronymus Bosch's renditions of purgatory and hell.[20] In *The Last Judgment* (ca. 1482), toads torment a sinner who is immersed in a cask with these creatures, while in another panel, a bishop is compelled to eat a toad as a punishment for the sin of *Gula*, gluttony; meanwhile nearby a gigantic toad appears to prepare to copulate with a person guilty of *Luxuria*, lust.[21] Toads' toxic bodies created an evil legacy that made them the ideal moralizing representations for artists. The toad's cultural currency, combined with its toxic biological properties, helped shape the witchcraft beliefs of the sixteenth and seventeenth centuries.

The Toad as the Witch's Accessory

Branded as the witches' accomplice and the purveyor of poison for their maleficent charms, toads served as a biological explanation of how witches, in Navarra and beyond, could turn diabolical intent into materially harmful deeds.[22] While toads' specific roles as agents of witchcraft were flexible and varied among witness testimonies, they emerged consistently in over half of Navarra's secular witch trial records. In the earliest extant trial from 1525, witches were accused of using flayed toads and toad blood for *maleficia* and transvection. Situated within lengthy testimony recounting the witches' gathering, Martín de Zaldaiz from the village of Burguete shared a tangible recipe for the poisonous concoction used to "waste the grains and kill people." In Martín's deposition from June 1525, he explained: "To go to the witches' gathering, they anointed themselves with an unguent using . . . dead and burned

---

20. In *The Garden of Earthly Delights*, the lecherous amphibian crouches on the breast of a woman, while in the *Haywain Triptych*, a toad prefers to squat on a woman's genitals. Another example is *The Temptation of St. Anthony* where a winged toad transports the saint through the air while he is being tormented by demons. Meanwhile a demonic toad lounges in the right corner, holding a chalice being filled by a sorceress, while a toad crawls out from under a table on which poisonous food and drink are seductively displayed. See Renilde Vervoort, "The Pestilent Toad: The Significant of the Toad in the Works of Bosch," in *Hieronymus Bosch: New Insights into His Life and Work*, ed. Jos Koldeweij and Bernard Vermet (Rotterdam: Museum Boijmans Van Beuningen, NAi Publishers, 2001), 147.

21. Vervoort, "The Pestilent Toad," 147.

22. In some legal proceedings such as witch trials in Normandy, toads could even serve as tangible proof of a witch's guilt. E. William Monter, "Toads and Eucharists: The Male Witches of Normandy, 1564–1660," *French Historical Studies* 20, no. 4 (Autumn 1997): 563–95.

flayed toads."[23] Thus, according to this witness, toad grease facilitated the witches' flight.

When María de Ituren confessed to witchcraft, she, too, drew on possible uses of the amphibian's toxic body. She admitted to using toads both to commit *maleficia* and to attend the witches' gathering with "an unguent made with flayed toads."[24] In the fields she met with other witches to roast toads, mixing them with water "to make powders mixed with an herb called *usaynbelarr*. And they wasted the mountains with the powders of those roasted toads." Other villagers echoed this specific recipe in their reports, situating this nefarious concoction of roasted toads in the material world.[25] Toads at this early date were understood to provide versatile ingredients used to attend the witches' gatherings, and as the producer of their poisons.[26]

The material toxicity of the toad remained a central focus in villagers' testimony throughout the first half of the sixteenth century. María Sagardoy's witchcraft accusation in 1534 was predicated on her ability to manipulate toads for evil. Her established reputation in the village of Aezcoa as a "*mala cristiana* and poisoner" was coupled with rumors of her hunting toads to use for poisons.[27] The council charged María with being a "*malefica*" and with acts of poisoning spanning a decade, her *maleficia* assisted by the powers of the toad, which she compounded and "mixed with burned, flayed toads and big, black spiders, and the livers of children, and other deadly things. And she ground everything and made a poisonous powder."[28] María denied all charges against her, prompting the royal tribunals to order interrogation under torture in search of the "truth," an order she avoided by cleverly asserting she was four months' pregnant. At this time, in the autumn of 1534, the tribunals did not zealously pursue a conviction, nor did María's denunciation generate a search for other witches, or a hunt for every other "*mala cristiana*" in Aezcoa. The devil, night flight, and the witches' gatherings

23. Florencio Idoate Iragui, *La Brujería en Navarra y sus Documentos* (Pamplona: Institución Príncipe de Viana, 1978), 253.

24. Idoate, *La Brujería*, 264.

25. It is noteworthy that many Spanish medicinal recipes proposed using toads administered in a burned form for treatments of arthritis, cancer, and nose hemorrhages. See Rodriguez et al., "Toxins and Pharmacologically Active Compounds," table 1.

26. Ander Berrojalbiz's research shows that as early as 1370 witches in Lower Navarre were said to use cooked toads and the broth they rendered in their *maleficia*. See Ander Berrojalbiz, "The Sorcery Trial against Pes de Guoythie and Cobd," in Berrojalbiz, *Sources from the Dawn of the Great Witch Hunt in Lower Navarra, 1370* (Cham: Palgrave Macmillan, 2023), 18–19.

27. AGN, TR_209502 (1535), fol. 3r.

28. AGN, TR_209502 (1535), fol. 7r.

did not emerge. Solitary trials such as María's heavily relied on the accused's *fama* in the village and her ability to use toads for poisons but did not conform to learned diabolical ideas.

Such ideas did exist, however, and appeared in other cases handled by the royal tribunals. In 1540, the alcalde from the Valley of Salazar, Lope Esparza, was accused of witchcraft and *maleficia* enacted by the power of the evil toad. The *fiscal* charged Lope, alongside other accused witches, with assembling "many times both night and day, in their gatherings and festivities and dances of witches" to craft their poisons. They then killed using powders they made from "filth and powders and burned toads and other poisons." Witnesses also testified they killed people by "touching them all over their bodies with a toad tied by its leg . . . and with toad blood."[29] These accusations incorporated more learned, diabolical elements and included the witches' gatherings and the renunciation of God. In these trials, even though toads were situated among diabolism and heresy, they retained their roles as toxic bodies used by witches to poison their neighbors and crops. The *fiscal* officially charged the accused: "With the flayed toads they make poisonous powder, and unguents, and they anointed themselves with that and with the blood of the toads, and they anointed the people they inducted."[30] This reflected a fusion of the knowledge of bufotoxins and the heretical symbolism of its amphibious producer.

The significance of toads in Navarra transcended judicial boundaries. Like its secular counterpart, the episcopal *curia diocesana de Pamplona* reflected the toad's cultural currency in its trials.[31] In the 1569 case of the witch-priest Don Pedro Lecumberri, villagers denounced the popular thirty-five-year-old cleric in Burgui to the alcalde for witchcraft and, worse yet, leading a small sect of female witches, including children.[32] Toads served as prominent diabolical markers throughout this trial. The first accusations came from eight-year-old Andella Garat who declared that she was asked to join the accused's witch sect and was offered good food, but instead "they gave her a roasted toad with bread to eat."[33]

---

29. AGN, TR_63994 (1540), fols. 59v–60r.

30. AGN, TR_63994 (1540), fol. 2v.

31. The records also show that two inquisitors from Calahorra reported in 1540 that eleven-year-old Miguela reported it was not until she "touched a toad" that she was able to go to the witches' gathering. AGN, TR_63994 (1540), fol. 14r.

32. ADP, Aguinaga, Cartón 13, n. 17 (1569).

33. Modern experimentations conducted on humans show that bufotoxins in the bloodstream cause significant pain, disorientation, and vomiting. See Rochelle Rojas, "*Plenae veneficiorum*: Toads, Poison, and Witchcraft in Pre-Modern Europe" (forthcoming).

According to her little friend, Gracieta, her grandmother had taught her to say in a loud voice "Come here, *literna*, come here, *literna*," and out of a small pond emerged a "large toad like a puppy" with some small horns. Gracieta approached this "ox of God" and placed it in her skirt. But when another child, María Baldan, caught sight of the large black toad and uttered "Jesus!" the toad disappeared. The witches then chastised Baldan, warning her to not speak Jesus's name. Andella reported also seeing the accused witches by the river with "three toads with little bells on them, and they were shaking them with their hands."[34] As the women and girls sat there, shaking their belled toads, Andella's friend, seven-year-old Catalina Bront, and María "tried to catch live toads from the water, and they killed them with a knife to the throat."[35] They then feasted on toad flesh, which was black in color and odious in flavor. Doubting these reports, the commissary and scribe, Pedro Aguinaga, asked María Garat to demonstrate her skill in his presence along with two other officials. And so, ten-year-old María asked for a knife, and "without fear or impatience" cautiously cut the toad from its head to its bottom with deftness. She then proceeded to "skin it with great patience all over its body," expertly peeling back its skin from the neck up to its head, and around the extremities, removing its poisonous skin from its head, its torso, and its arms and legs.[36] All three men attested to their observation of her practiced toad-skinning skills.

Throughout this extensively documented trial, the prominence given to the many toads appearing in individual depositions—as well as the *curia*'s charge that groups of witches incorporated toads into inverted Mass rituals—demonstrates that toads were freighted with meaning both for the involved villagers and for the episcopal tribunal. Within this religious court, toads' spiritual significance was accentuated, and they were situated among other diabolical notions such as the anal kiss of the devil and the renunciation of God. The toads were not explicitly used to harm others in acts of *maleficia*—the likes of which would fall to the secular court's purview—but rather were invoked as a symbolic indicator of Christian transgression.

Toads were unsurprisingly a dominant feature during the chain of witch trials in 1575–76. Among the dozens of accused witches and

---

34. ADP, Aguinaga, Cartón 13, n. 17. Bell-wearing toads will reappear in the witch panic. See Gustav Henningsen, *The Salazar Documents: Inquisitor Alonso de Salazar Frías and Others on the Basque Witch Persecution* (Leiden: Brill, 2004), 152.

35. ADP, Aguinaga, Cartón 13, n. 17, fol. 48r.

36. ADP, Aguinaga, Cartón 13, n. 17, fol. 48r.

multiple trials, scores of toads appeared in the villagers' depositions beginning with María Johan in Anocíbar in 1575, and nearly all the chain trials in its wake. In his initial testimony against his aunt, ten-year-old Miguel de Olagüe reported that María Johan and her accomplices gave him and his brother "two toads in their hands and forced them to handle them." When asked what the toads were for, Miguel said he was not certain but thought "they were to make an unguent with those toads" because when they returned, they then "went to the witches' gathering."[37]

Toads emerged as protagonists in many of these trials, serving as both fantastical characters and poison providers. For example, in her accusation against Teresa de Ollo in 1576, thirteen-year-old Catalina de Ybero centered her proof on "hearing a sound like the singing of toads" and witnessing Teresa feed several toads bits of masticated bread. She also reportedly heard Teresa's daughter say "that those toads were her saints, and not the ones that were in the church."[38] This villager couched witch activity in terms of the inverse of Christianity. Here, these toads represented more than folkloric beliefs: they were grotesque manifestations of a diabolic cult.

The roles of toads varied. The villagers of Burguete, for example, claimed Graciana Loizu had *mala fama* as a witch because of her alleged intimacy with toads. Even those testifying on her behalf were familiar with the rumors of her suspect interactions with these amphibians. Burguete's shoemaker, thirty-one-year-old Juanes de Zuncarren, admitted he did not know with certainty if Graciana was a witch but confirmed that she was in the "public saying and opinion" of being a witch, adding "there was the rumor in the village of Burguete that one time Martinot de Vitoria . . . saw Graciana Loizu giving food to some toads in the field." Witness after witness echoed Martinot's story of having witnessed "Graciana Loizu giving food to two or three toads in the pastures" as he tended to his mares.[39] Though the depositions were not identical, this was a well-circulated tale that had traveled the pathways of village truth-making. So intimate was her relationship with toads, she was said to wear "the skin of a flayed toad in the hood of her coat," and to be surrounded by toads as she washed her clothes in the creek. It is noteworthy that none of the witnesses elaborated on *why* she

37. AGN, TR_69853 (1575), fol. 13v.
38. AGN, TR_327744 (1576), fol. 6r.
39. AGN, TR_98192 (1576), fol. 17r.

would be feeding toads or wearing toad leather, nor did any explicitly state that toad interactions signified witch-hood. There was no need to, since by this point the connection between toad and witch was well established in Navarra.

Based upon reports given by twenty witnesses, the tribunals formally charged Graciana with "using many spells and witchcraft, and harm and *maleficia*, and many have seen her raising toads in the countryside and solitary places."[40] The picture of an old lady breeding toads offered a powerful inversion in this farming community. Martín de Aragon, her *procurador*, offered Graciana a robust defense. He claimed that her main accuser Martinot de Vitoria was the "capital enemy" of Graciana's daughter, an argument supported by the lengthy history of legal battles between the litigants. His most striking line of defense, however, addressed her pastoral care of the clutch of toads. He argued against Martinot's testimony that he had witnessed Graciana "feeding three toads in the field," maintaining that this accusation was not credible. But it was not the plausibility of an adult feeding toads in a field he called into question; rather, it was the *weather* at the time of the alleged crime that he disputed:

> The year Martinot claims [he saw her] was the year of the big snows, the likes of which lasted until throughout March and all through Lent, when the witness says the mares were in the pasture. But they could not have been . . . nor could anyone walk in the countryside because the land was so covered with snow.[41]

This defense is telling, for it did not discount the *possibility* of the act of toad-feeding, but rather the *timing* of the act. This was not the first time a witch was accused of nurturing toads, as Graciana Martínez, a widow from the village of Urdiain, had also been charged by the royal court with "having and raising toads in her house to make poison to kill people and children and the fields" some months prior.[42] Supported by their religious and cultural contexts, toads carried weight in the legal realm as well. Throughout the 1575–76 chain trials, villager testimony tended to center toads' toxic bodies, reflecting a long-standing ingredient in the cauldron of witch beliefs (see figure 4.1).

---

40. AGN, TR_98192 (1576), fol. 44r.
41. AGN, TR_98192 (1576), fol. 158v.
42. AGN, TR_327215 (1576), fol. 10r.

FIGURE 4.1. A witch feeding her toad and animal familiars in the English witchcraft pamphlet *A Rehearsall both Straung and True, of Hainous and Horrible Actes Committed by Elizabeth Stile* (1579).

Toads emerged within the royal tribunal's torture chamber. When María Sanz's daughter accused her of witchcraft and poisoning, many of the alleged acts of *maleficia* and attendance at the witches' gatherings centered on the power of toads. Supported by thirteen witnesses' accusations of *mala fama* and witchcraft, the *fiscal* charged María with keeping toads in a pot under her bed to use for poisons and with murder and sentenced her to judicial torture.[43] In Pamplona's torture chamber in June 1576, the magistrates pressed ropes into her body in a bid to press her soul into confession. After she proclaimed her innocence, the men ordered the ropes to be tightened on María's muscles and pushed her to answer "what venom" she used to poison a neighbor's child and "what toad she put in the pot" at her neighbor's house.[44] As María cried out in pain and asked them why they "mistreated her in this way" the magistrates again tightened the ropes and inquired about the toads with which she was said to anoint her daughter and herself. She explained the cream she applied to her daughter's head was to help with the child's mental illness. But again, the judges pressed her on the toads she was said to collect in pots. In María's trial, as well with all the other cases during the chain trials of 1575–76, toads served as purveyors of

---

43. AGN, TR_327422 (1576), fol. 31r.
44. AGN, TR_327422 (1576), fol. 85v.

witches' poisons, and their presence was of great interest for the royal tribunals.

But toads metamorphosed into the witch's mark in the peculiar 1595 trial of the villagers from Inza in the Valley of Araiz. The alcalde Fermín Andueza had charged a young "witchfinder" to discover the witches in his territory, a task she did by looking for toad-shaped pupils in the villagers' eyes. As we saw earlier, the forced confessions of this group of villagers diverged significantly from the more common witchcraft concerns in Navarra and focused instead on the witches' gathering, diabolical sex, and acts of iconoclasm. As the level of diabolism escalated beyond that of any other witch trials in the secular tribunals' records, so too did the role of the toad as it metamorphosed from an accessory of witchcraft to its visible proof.

The magistrates interrogated Andueza's key witness, the twelve-year-old witchfinder Juana de Baraybar, who detected witches by looking for the devil's mark. She testified that "they are witches because they have a marking in the shape of a toad's foot in their left eye, some of them, and others in their right eyes." She admitted she had not seen these witches at any witches' gatherings but drew her conclusions exclusively from the mark in their eyes. Juana added that only those witches who have this marking, or like herself have been to the witches' gatherings, can see it. She had inherited this talent from her mother who had taken her to a gathering in the Valley of Larraun where "the witches had the mark and that is how they recognized one another."[45] She lamented that "the signs would remain for life and at no time could they be removed," even by participation in Catholic practices such as confession. Her report suggested that she was not actively seeking to denounce fellow villagers, but was persuaded by Andueza to look for witches, a task she performed by searching for a devil's mark of sorts; and in Navarra, fittingly, it was the toad. Within the narratives of this trial the toad took on a new form as learned, elite visions of the "devil's mark" came to the fore.

To be sure, villagers in Navarra believed that toads were used in witchcraft. For some, they transcended being ingredients for *maleficia* and assumed symbolic markers of witch-hood. Appearing in half of the secular trial records between 1525 and 1647, toads clearly held a central role in Navarra's witchcraft beliefs. But its invocation was not limited to

---

45. AGN, TR_71319 (1595), fol. 173v.

villagers, or secular and episcopal judges, for Spanish inquisitors, too, fell under the toad's spell.

Toads in a Panic

Toads figured prominently in the witch panic handled by the Inquisition. Elaborate descriptions of toads emerged in witness testimonies, inquisitorial reports, and even a French demonology, showing clearly the enduring influence of toads as they became embellished and anthropomorphized.[46] Even during the toad's metamorphosis, it maintained its role as the physical procurer of the witch's key ingredient within the panic's records. Eighty-year-old María de Zozaya revealed her process to make poisons: first she would cut and fillet the toads, then grate them, and finally pound them in a mortar mixed with boiled "toad liquids."[47] She had received these toads from the devil to facilitate her travel to the *akelarres*. Unlike their naked counterparts, these toads were dressed and kept securely hidden in a wooden box that had a wooden lid. She further concealed her precious toads between a chest and the wall.[48] To attend the *akelarres* on Mondays, Wednesdays, and Fridays, she pulled out her dressed toad and whipped it. And after the toad had expelled its fluid and been replaced in its box, the devil would then have vaginal and anal intercourse with her. Once María arrived at the *akelarres* there would be a "toad flock" of stabled, dressed toads "equipped with a collar hung with bells," a descriptive confession shared by several other witches from the region of Las Cinco Villas.[49] These rich details differed greatly from the toads of the sixteenth century, but still resounded within the world of witches. This world was malleable and amphibious, inviting any manner of permutations.

Unsurprisingly, dressed toads hopped into other testimonies. When nine-year-old María de Yturria from Echalar confessed to witchcraft in December 1609, she claimed Catalina de Topalda had taken her to the

---

46. Toads metamorphose during the panic. In *Invoking the Akelarre: Voices of the Accused in the Basque Witch-Craze, 1609–1614* (Brighton: Sussex Academic Press, 2019), Emma Wilby dedicated multiple chapters to presenting different "cultural and experiential matrices" (156) accused witches may have mined to arrive at such detailed toad narratives.

47. Gustav Henningsen, *The Witches' Advocate: Basque Witchcraft and the Spanish Inquisition, 1609–1614*, Basque Series (Reno: University of Nevada Press, 1980), 172.

48. She also kept a pot of toad vomit and powder made from ground toad-skin and wrapped in a piece of paper, items that the inquisitors failed to discover as the devil "must have removed them." Henningsen, *The Witches' Advocate*, 165.

49. Henningsen, *The Witches' Advocate*, 164.

akelarres where she was given a small stick and the task of guarding "the clothed toads."[50] Multiple reports of toad guardianship would emerge throughout the testimonies during the witch panic as a task relegated to the children supposedly inducted into the witch cult. While testimonies varied slightly (for example, some parishioners claimed to keep their toads hidden in a hole, under a tree, while others said they tethered their toads' legs with a cord to prevent escape), it became clear that toads were to have a central, coveted, and sometimes-clothed position within the witch panic's narratives. This was mirrored in the mental world of Beltrana de la Fargua, a forty-year-old beggar from the village of Vera. Beltrana confessed to the inquisitors that she cared for a childlike dressed toad whom she breastfed. Sometimes, as she nursed her own children (whom she supposedly also converted into witches), her dressed toad would "stretch and crane upwards from the floor until it could nurse" too.[51] And, at times, it simply metamorphosed into a child and suckled her breasts. Toads, as reflected in this inquisitorial deposition, had evolved beyond naked, poison-producing amphibians and into clothed animals, ones that would metamorphose further into anthropomorphic creatures with demonic capabilities.

The Toad as the Witch's Familiar

The Spanish inquisitors reported on toads as crucial actors in Navarra's witchcraft practices. In their twelve-page account sent to the Suprema, the inquisitors in Logroño related the acts of the accused witches to be sentenced at the *auto de fé*.[52] This formal decree (*Relación de las causas*, hereafter *Relación*), was intended for a wide audience, including the Suprema, the king of Spain (at least, the inquisitors hoped it would attract his attention), and the thousands of spectators who would witness the sentencing of these witches at the widely advertised *auto de fé* held that year.[53] Curiously, this official and authoritative text focused much of its attention on the rituals conspicuously featuring the herd of dressed toads. The prominence of the decree underscored the fact that

---

50. Henningsen, *The Witches' Advocate*, 138.

51. Henningsen, *The Witches' Advocate*, 155.

52. AHN, Inq., Lib. 835, fol. 340v. This decree begins with: "A Relation of the people who are to appear in the *auto de fé* celebrated by the Inquisition of Logroño, Sunday, the seventh day of November in the year 1610, of the acts and offenses they have committed, and the punishments they are to receive for them."

53. Lu Ann Homza, *Village Infernos and Witches' Advocates: Witch-Hunting in Navarre, 1608–1614* (University Park: Pennsylvania State University Press, 2022), 98.

lore surrounding toads had become part of legal evidence at the highest levels. The inquisitors reported on the vital function of the toads as protectors, companions, and mentors to new witches at their initiation ceremonies where the devil gifted them a prized toad, explaining:

> The dressed toad serves as a guardian angel to the new witch from then on, accompanying him and instructing him in the evil deeds that are to be done. . . .
>
> And [the witches] nourish, give gifts, and feed the toad giving it food every day, and they talk with it, and communicate their business, and [the toads] advise [the witch] when it is time to go to the *akelarre*.[54]

The dressed toads instructed them "in the wrongs to be committed" and when it was time to attend the *akelarres*. In exchange for their assistance, the witches fed their dressed toads human flesh, which they devoured eagerly amid "snarling and growling."[55] Together the witches and their dressed toads participated in vulgar orgies, destroyed crops and livestock, and even killed their neighbors. No longer mere accessories for *maleficia*, the dressed toads had become its organizers.[56]

Within the witch panic, the toad metamorphosed into the witch's servant, or familiar. The dressed toads of the *Relación* served as "guardian angels" providing companionship for the new witch and tutoring her in the art of *maleficia*. These were demons who assumed the grotesque form of half toad and half man and were costumed in velvet (*terciopelo*) and other luxurious cloth (*paño*), as a show of their importance in the church of the devil. In an inversion of the Catholic clergy, they displayed their special station through their sartorial distinctions. These toads, dressed in tailored and form-fitting fine linens

---

54. AHN, Inq., Lib. 835, fol. 346r.

55. AHN, Inq., Lib. 835, fol. 348v.

56. While normal toads were a common animal connected to witchcraft practices, these dressed toads of the Basque congregation are the only familiars I have encountered anywhere in the corpus of witchcraft literature to be adorned in fine apparel. Thus far, I have encountered only two instances of the dressing of animals in nonfictional, early modern scholarship (doubtless there may be others), and neither appears in the context of witchcraft. Robert Darnton gives an account of a costumed cat who was "shaved to look like a priest, dressed in mock vestments," and then "hanged on the gallows" in *The Great Cat Massacre and Other Episodes in French Cultural History* (New York: Vintage Books, 1984), 12. Monkeys, too, were on occasion dressed in imitation of humans both in courts and in public, a practice dating back to antiquity. See Erasmus's gloss of the adage "An Ape in Purple" (*Adagia* I.vii.10).

by the inquisitors' imaginations, at times even sported "a ribbon of bells."[57]

Familiars were lowly demons given by the devil as presents to his followers, and their role was to serve the witch. Although they are hardly unfamiliar to scholars of the early modern period, familiars have generally been assumed to be a feature of English witch beliefs. The importance and developed notion of witches' familiars have been considered "exclusive to English witchcraft," and thus far British familiars have dominated the historiography of this aspect of witch lore.[58] One expert has noted that familiars "seem to constitute the one great peculiarity in English witchcraft beliefs, secondary literature at least suggesting that equivalent beings figured very rarely in the ideas about witchcraft held in other parts of Europe."[59] English familiars took multiple forms, often as nonhuman animals, and sometimes as toads.[60] But as reflected in these trial records, familiars also served the witch-mistresses of Navarra.

As the inquisitors fashioned Navarra's toads into familiars, they drew from local lore and traditional conceptions of toads as creatures who provided the pivotal ingredient for attendance at the witches' gatherings. The Logroño tribunal reported: "They make use of these dressed toads to extract a dark and green foul-smelling liquid with which they anoint themselves to go to the *akelarres*." Pressing down on dressed toads with their hands or feet, the witches extracted the potent magical fluid, the necessary ingredients for night flight and poisonous concoctions. The witches "make them vomit from above and from the bottom the liquid they collect in an earthen pot . . . and the witches take the remainder of the liquid extracted from the toads and pour it into a huge cauldron . . . to make powders and poisons from this

---

57. AHN, Inq., Lib. 835, fol. 346r. Recall that in 1569 the toads of the priest-witch of Burgui also donned bells.

58. James Sharpe, "The Witch's Familiar in Elizabethan England," in *Authority and Consent in Tudor England*, ed. G. Bernard and S. Gunn (Aldershot: Ashgate, 2002), 209.

59. James Sharpe, *Witchcraft in Early Modern England* (New York: Routledge, 2013), 63–64. Sharpe's observation that the study of familiars is "currently one of the most urgent items on the agenda for future research into English witchcraft history" can usefully be broadened to continental inquiry.

60. A scholarly examination of witch trials from 1530 to 1705 has revealed the recurrence of various manifestations of the familiar, most of which were "nondescript" representations (such as imps), followed in prominence by mice, cats, dogs, and toads. James A. Serpell, "Guardian Spirits or Demonic Pets: The Concept of the Witch's Familiar in Early Modern England, 1530–1712," in *The Animal/Human Boundary*, ed. A. N. H. Creager and W. C. Jordan (Rochester: University of Rochester Press, 2002), 169, 171–73.

FIGURE 4.2. Toads used as ingredients for *maleficia* at the witches' gatherings. Detail from an engraving by Jan Ziarnko depicting a witches' Sabbath in *Tableau de l'inconstance des mauvais anges et demons* by Pierre de Lancre (1612).

brew" (see fig. 4.2).[61] Thus in the minds of the inquisitors, local lore and learned demonological literature fused, yielding the distinguished toads.

A final role bestowed upon the toad was its appearance in the witches' mark. The inquisitors reported: "And then the devil finally marks [the new witch] sticking a nail of his left hand into whatever part of his body he chooses and draws blood, and the pain lasts for many days, and the mark forever. And he also makes other marks in the eyes, inside, on the pupils."[62] The witches' marks, taking the shape of a toad's "paw," served as a tangible bond between the devil and the witches, physical reminders of the diabolical pact they had made. This witch's mark reminds us of the toad noted by the young witchfinder in 1525. Thus, the

---

61. AHN, Inq., Lib. 835, fol. 346r.
62. AHN, Inq., Lib. 835, fol. 346r.

Inquisition's tribunal drew substantially from the local traditions and learned lore as they conceptualized toads as infernal familiars.[63]

The Toad as a Demonological Actor

This learned tradition of witchcraft was reflected in the writings of early modern European theologians, clergymen, natural philosophers, jurists, and other literati who codified witch beliefs within their demonological literature. Early demonological writings, such as the *Errores gazariorium* (ca. 1437) and the *Malleus maleficarum* (1486) positioned the toad as a significant ingredient for witches' *maleficia*, reporting toad venom in the activities of diabolical heretics.[64] Though there is no indication whether the secular magistrates in Pamplona encountered either of these texts, the dressed toads of Navarra appeared in a widely circulated demonology during the witch panic.[65]

Toads assumed an important role in the demonological treatise composed by the French magistrate Pierre de Lancre, a judge from Bordeaux dispatched to the Basque witch trials.[66] In his *Tableau de l'inconstance des mauvais anges et demons* (1612), de Lancre reported on the horrors of demons and witches plaguing the early modern world, especially the diabolical witch sect coursing throughout the French Basque lands in 1608-9.[67] During his investigations of witchcraft in the region, de Lancre encountered toads within the cauldron of witch beliefs. For example, in 1608 twenty-eight-year-old Marie de la Ralde reported to him that she had gone to the "sabbath," and there she observed women witches taking toads in their teeth, then skinning them and crushing

---

63. In a meeting in March 1611, Bishop Venegas convened a meeting in Pamplona to which he summoned various investigators, and the Franciscans arrived with their report. In it they claimed to have proof of witchcraft in the form of four jars of unguents and a dressed toad. Supposedly these were delivered to the tribunal at Logroño, though no further information appeared. Henningsen, *The Witches' Advocate*, 219.

64. Alan Kors and Edward Peters, *Witchcraft in Europe, 400–1700: A Documentary History*, 2nd ed. (Philadelphia: University of Pennsylvania Press, 2001), 161; Heinrich Kramer, *Malleus Maleficarum*, trans. Christopher Mackay (Cambridge: Cambridge University Press, 2009), 116-17.

65. The secular witch trials do mention two demonological writings: *Reprobación de las supersticiones y hechicerías* (1537) by Pedro Ciruelo, a theologian from Aragon, and *Disquisitiones magicae* (1608), by the Jesuit theologian Martin Delrío; neither mentions toads.

66. Pierre de Lancre, *Tableau de l'inconstance des mauvais anges et demons*, trans. Gerhild Schultz (Turnhout: Brepols, 2006).

67. Jan Machielsen, *The Science of Demons: Early Modern Authors Facing Witchcraft and the Devil* (New York: Routledge, 2020), 284.

them.[68] Similarly, Marie d'Aspilcouette mentioned that witches at these "sabbaths" decapitated and roasted toads to craft the ointments and toad powders. Like her Spanish counterparts, Marie reported that "the great female witches are assisted by some demon in the form of a toad," adding that the toad perched prominently on their left shoulders and had two small horns on its head.[69]

The dressed toads of the witch panic emerged in testimony from the French side of the Basque lands. According to de Lancre's reports, sixteen-year-old Jeanette d'Abadie from Cibourne reported dressed toads in September 1609, claiming that the treasured toads were taken to a cemetery where a great party was held "to have toads baptized."[70] Dressed for this momentous occasion, the toads wore "red velvet and sometimes black velvet, with a little bell around their necks and another one around their feet." As with Christian baptism, godparents were present "with a godfather who would hold the head of this toad and a godmother who would hold it by its feet, as one holds a child in church." Jeannette's inverted world of witchcraft included a dancing lady with four toads, with only one dressed in velvet with bells on its feet, and the others carried in her fists "like a bird." But while Jeannette dressed her toad, it never became a familiar. And as her testimony predated the Inquisition's *auto de fé* and its accompanying report, de Lancre did not pursue that line of inquiry.[71] While his interrogations did not reflect the learned visions proposed by the Spanish Inquisition's *Relación*, his demonology did.

Within de Lancre's demonology, toads served as visual markers of witchcraft and played a crucial role in proving witch-hood. De Lancre, like other demonologists, often learned from the courts about the possible activities of witchcraft while simultaneously developing a rational doctrine of evil and reaffirming that diabolical powers were real. He brings into striking relief the influence of some demonologies on judicial procedure:

> I believe that the mark that Satan puts on his disciples is of great importance to the adjudication of the crime of witchcraft. Further evidence is found among all our contemporaries who are judges,

---

68. De Lancre, *Tableau de l'inconstance*, 148.
69. De Lancre, *Tableau de l'inconstance*, 150. These toad horns remind us of Pliny's natural history and the toads in Burgui from 1569.
70. De Lancre, *Tableau de l'inconstance*, 153.
71. See Wilby's analyses of Jeannette's testimony and de Lancre's interrogations in *Invoking the Akelarre*, 163–77.

as we believe that the marks are such persuasive clues and indicate such strong presumptions of guilt against the witches that, taken together with evidence, it is lawful to proceed with their conviction. This is why it is wise to remember what we learned about them from our trials.[72]

This shows clearly not only the connection between demonologies and the importance of the witches' mark, but also their influence on judicial procedure. Drawing from reports from a young witch-finder, de Lancre reported that "all the witches from Biarritz had in their left eye a mark like that of a toad's foot, which the women of this parish who confessed also said."[73] This foot marked them as the devil's property and imbued them with mysterious gifts of seeing and recognizing "things that concern only witches, things that cannot be seen by those who do not take an oath with a toad."[74] Beyond markers of a heretical pact, these toad feet indicated that the witches had powers that could, possibly, harm their neighbors and the republic.

Demonological treatises often included the authors' eyewitness account of trials. For example, de Lancre described how in September 1610 a seventeen-year-old girl was presented to him, and he saw in her left eye "something resembling a little cloud that looked like a toad's foot." The girl confessed that "Satan had marked her with his horn in her left eye" at the witches' Mass.[75] The mark not only implicated the accused in a diabolic pact but also carried evidentiary weight in establishing guilt. To be sure, only the most succinct symbol could encapsulate such a complex concept, and the toad, with its exceptionally wide web of associations, was particularly well qualified to serve in this capacity.

Toad bodies, too, played central roles in the witches' ceremonies. Here de Lancre's narrative borrowed unequivocally from the Inquisition's version of the witch initiation ceremony in his reports of the *akelarre*, which described children under the age of nine who "guard the toads with little sticks, and these toads are those that the Devil gives to each female witch, as an angel looking out for her, dressed in

---

72. De Lancre, *Tableau de l'inconstance*, 197–98.
73. De Lancre, *Tableau de l'inconstance*, 200.
74. De Lancre, *Tableau de l'inconstance*, 201.
75. De Lancre, *Tableau de l'inconstance*, 204.

FIGURE 4.3. Children guarding toads at the witches' gathering. Detail from an engraving by Jan Ziarnko depicting a witches' Sabbath in *Tableau de l'inconstance des mauvais anges et demons* by Pierre de Lancre (1612).

green or gray."[76] So highly regarded were these toads thought to be that if a child should accidentally step on one, they would be "immediately whipped." After renouncing God and swearing allegiance to the devil, the new witch "receives a dressed toad in its hood or coat; then [the devil] orders him to adore it . . . and marks them with a mark that looks like a little toad."[77] The anuran's role far transcended being a source of toxic poisons, now serving both as a familiar *and* as a permanent marker. But it maintained its chemical contribution in "recipes for placing hexes on people." When the witches' toads were whipped and swollen, they secreted a "green liquid used to harm and fly." And at the end of the witches' initiation ceremonies, de Lancre explained, "they fly through the night like birds, together with their dressed-up toads,"

---

76. De Lancre, *Tableau de l'inconstance*, 399.
77. De Lancre, *Tableau de l'inconstance*, 400.

ready to commit *maleficia*.[78] When combined with the records from the secular court, this treatise offers a remarkable window into the fusion of common understandings (poison for *maleficia*) and learned tropes (sartorial distinctions).

De Lancre's *Tableau* offers a special glimpse into the world of the witches through an image that accompanied his written treatise. Its frontispiece, crafted by the Polish artist and printmaker Jan Ziarnko in 1612, includes in its depiction of the witches' gathering a group of children armed with switches guarding a little herd of toads. This fascinating image, complete with a lettered appendix glossing the details of the figure, visually describes that which was textually recorded (fig. 4.3). It is particularly noteworthy that the toads to which these children tend, presumably for their use in *maleficia*, are unattired. The dressed toads may thus have remained mostly in the inquisitorial imaginary of Spain. In sum, de Lancre's rich demonology reveals how learned writings incorporated established, common witch beliefs in their grand syntheses. The learned body of witchcraft literature they created was as varied and nuanced as were witch beliefs, and an innovative synthesis of the two.

Following the witch panic, toads appeared one final time before the royal tribunals as reflected in the 1647 sorcery trial of María Yrisarri. Forty-year-old Joan de Ybirizu testified that some twenty-eight or twenty-nine years before, María had taken him one night to a valley in the countryside where he was left "guarding some toads while the accused went around dancing to the beat of a drummer" while she kissed a large man.[79] This witness had guarded his secret for almost three decades out of fear María would kill him should he tell anyone about the toads at the *akelarre*.[80] Joan's testimony attests to the longevity of the toad's currency and offers clues to how tropes of witchcraft were drawn from a deep reservoir of folkloric beliefs and, sometimes, childhood fantasies. It also shows how the Inquisition's learned vision of children guarding toads at the *akelarres* had entrenched itself in this villager's understanding of toad lore.

The enduring role of toads in Navarra, as seen in this late trial of 1647, demonstrates that villagers and jurists alike drew from the cauldron of

---

78. De Lancre, *Tableau de l'inconstance*, 400.

79. AGN, TR_16058 (1647), fol. 12v.

80. The interesting genesis of the term *akelarre*, which did not come into common parlance until the witch panic, remains a fascinating and popular line of inquiry. See Mikel Azurmendi, *Las brujas de Zugarramurdi: La historia del aquelarre y la Inquisición* (Córdoba: Almuzara, 2013), 139.

belief to form their notions. Religious and cultural understandings of the toad reveal its cultural currency as artists and authors used the toad to moralize sin and represent death. The biological knowledge of the toad, too, serves to illuminate the internal logic and coherence of systems of witchcraft beliefs, as toads possessed biological powers to poison. But the metamorphoses toads underwent in the witch panic draw our attention to the changing nature of witchcraft beliefs and the negotiations between elite inquisitors and Basque-speaking villagers. Examined over the course of Navarra's sixteenth and seventeenth centuries, toads within various cultural productions and witch-trial records reveal for us how witchcraft beliefs, prosecutions, and even demonologies were an adapted, negotiated, and shared cultural production.

CHAPTER 5

The Cauldron of Witch Beliefs

> I have never believed and do not believe in these
> things of illusions and dreams and false visions
> of the devil. I know for certain that it is all a false
> and diabolical illusion.
>
> —Lope Esparza, alcalde of the Valley of Salazar, 1540

In 1561, the villagers of Vidángoz spoke in almost unanimous agreement: not only was Graciana Belza a witch, but she also single-handedly orchestrated every misfortune that befell its inhabitants. Nearly a dozen villagers testified against the sixty-eight-year-old widow. Some accused her of poisoning their crops and livestock with herbs, while others claimed she stole their chickens. Still others alleged she caused "death with sorceries." The plentiful and detailed accusations against her yielded an official list of alleged deeds that commanded over three folios, a stark contrast to the sheer quarter of one folio that usually listed charges.[1] Every kerchief missing from a drying rack, every failed crop, animal death, and even several human deaths were attributed to Graciana's *maleficia*. Drawing from the "many diverse indictments against her," the *fiscal* ordered Graciana's interrogation under torture. Graciana, already elderly and feeble, maintained her innocence despite the torments that broke her arm and left her crippled. The court nonetheless condemned the widowed Graciana to one hundred lashes and five years of exile, demonstrating clearly the devastating results possible for those accused of witchcraft.

---

1. AGN, TR_211115 (1561), fols. 21r–31r. The folios in this case measured roughly seven by eleven inches.

When Graciana's neighbors labeled her as a witch, the term registered a spectrum of belief. While beliefs ranged from basic understandings that some bad neighbors were *malas cristianas* to those that understood witches as cannibalistic baby killers, these notions were not mutually exclusive and sometimes overlapped. For example, what began as concerns over María Johan of Anocíbar's convulsions morphed into diabolical accusations and chain trials. Likening people's views of witchcraft to a cauldron of beliefs, this chapter demonstrates the plasticity of witch belief as reflected in secular, nonpanic witch trials. By conducting a thorough review of the secular court trial records, the rhetoric of witchcraft emerges as a tool for reifying social hierarchies, managing conflict, and interpreting misfortune. This rhetoric reflected a fusion between the concerns of the peasantry and the stereotypes forged by judges and clerics, and allowed villagers to draw eclectically from the cauldron of belief, if they even chose to accuse someone of witchcraft at all. Within this cauldron, five prominent themes repeatedly simmered to the top: witches as women, the central role of *fama*, the corollary of kinship, the diabolical dimension, and the role of revenge. In addition to the five themes that emerge, another belief occasionally bubbled to the top of the cauldron: skepticism. A thorough review of trials outside of witch-panic contexts reveals that witchcraft beliefs were woven into the fabric of everyday life, and villagers could and did craft witches eclectically by drawing from the cauldron of witchcraft beliefs.[2]

Gender and Witchcraft

Early modern women received the brunt of witchcraft accusations, prosecutions, and executions in western Europe, accounting for an average of 75 to 80 percent of the estimated sixty thousand executions for witchcraft, a trend reflected in Navarra's gendered rates.[3] While

---

2. This reflects Behringer's finding that "coexistence with witches had been the rule, and prosecution the exception." Wolfgang Behringer, *Witches and Witch-Hunts* (Cambridge: Polity Press, 2004), 37. It reminds us, too, that witchcraft accusations comprised but one part of an expansive, vibrant "magical universe" as Stephen Wilson has shown, *The Magical Universe: Everyday Ritual and Magic in Pre-Modern Europe* (London: Hambledon, 2000).

3. In Navarra, 80 percent of those judicially processed for witchcraft by the secular tribunals were women and girls. Jesús María Usunáriz Garayoa puts the breakdown at 26 percent men for 1525–95; "La caza de brujas en la Navarra moderna (siglos XVI–XVII)," in *Akelarre: La caza de brujas en el Pirineo (siglos XIII–XIX)*, ed. Usunáriz, RIEV Cuadernos 9 (Donostia: Sociedad de Estudios Vascos, 2012), 320. Note that this did not hold firm in all parts of Europe as shown by the prevalence of men accused of witchcraft in countries such as Russia (75 percent) and Iceland (90 percent). Lara Apps and Andrew Gow, *Male Witches in Early Modern Europe*

witchcraft was strongly viewed as a female crime, men also could be suspects, a propensity that increased during chain trials and witch panics as traditional stereotypes broke down.[4] While these figures may suggest that witchcraft was "sex-related, but not sex-specific," the vast majority of witches in early modern Navarra were crafted from women and girls.[5]

Religious, cultural, and natural philosophical understandings informed the gendered nature of witch crafting in Navarra and beyond. As the medieval concept of the sorceress morphed into the witch during the mid-fifteenth century and crafted women as witches, it drew from a Christian cosmology that paired women with weakness and sin and crafted witches as women.[6] Outside of spiritual concerns, early modern culture painted women as weaker of mind, gossipy, petty, and generally untrustworthy. Natural philosophical understandings registered women's bodies as underdeveloped, unpredictable, and fundamentally flawed. Not only did women have a cold and wet body—all crummy humoral characteristics—but their wombs wandered about, causing erratic and animalistic behaviors.[7] Demonological writings, too, supported a gendered view of witchcraft, a sentiment epitomized (somewhat dramatically) by Heinrich Kramer's infamous *Malleus maleficarum* (1486) that claimed that women were "addicted to evil superstitions" and were more likely to be discovered as witches (see fig. 5.1).[8] Nonetheless, demonological writings were part of a larger body of work and, as such, did not sustain a *focus* on witches as women.[9]

(Manchester: Manchester University Press, 2003), 45; Valerie A. Kivelson, "Male Witches and Gendered Categories in Seventeenth-Century Russia," *Comparative Studies in Society and History* 45, no. 3 (2003): 617.

4. H. C. Erik Midelfort, *Witch-Hunting in Southwestern Germany, 1582–1684: The Social and Intellectual Foundations* (Stanford: Stanford University Press, 1972), 182.

5. Christina Larner's statement goes on to elaborate that women were accused, not because they were women, but because they were witches, *Witchcraft and Religion: The Politics of Popular Belief* (New York: Blackwell, 1984), 161. See Willem de Blécourt, "The Making of the Female Witch," *Gender & History* 12, no. 2 (July 2000): 289–90, for his provocative review of gender and witchcraft studies.

6. For a study on the intersections among heresy, witches, and gender, see Tamar Herzig, "Flies, Heretics, and the Gendering of Witchcraft," *Magic, Ritual, and Witchcraft* 5, no. 1 (Summer 2010): 51–80.

7. Lin Foxhall, *Studying Gender in Classical Antiquity*, (Cambridge: Cambridge University Press, 2013), chap. 4.

8. Heinrich Kramer, *Malleus Maleficarum*, trans. Christopher Mackay (Cambridge: Cambridge University Press, 2009), 41–46.

9. Michael Bailey makes this point and reveals that Johannes Nider's *Formicarius* (ca. 1437) connected women to witchcraft decades before Kramer in "The Feminization of Magic and the Emerging Idea of the Female Witch in the Late Middle Ages," *Essays in Medieval Studies* 19 (2002): 120–34.

FIGURE 5.1.   Francisco Goya, *El conjuro*, ca. 1797

Furthermore, a legal system that privileged men above women supported the gendered nature of witchcraft.[10] Women also tended to marry away from their own village and family more than men and thus "were less able to mobilize groups of kin."[11] This put them at

---

10. Provocative regional studies of early modern women and European law abound. For an overview of general trends, see Merry Wiesner-Hanks, *Women and Gender in Early Modern Europe*, 4th ed. (New York: Cambridge University Press, 2019), 51–57, and 57–58 for a list of readings. And for women and lawsuits in early modern Spain, see Renato Barahona, *Sex Crimes, Honour, and the Law in Early Modern Spain: Vizcaya, 1528–1735* (Toronto: University of Toronto Press, 2003), 117–56.

11. Robin Briggs, *Witches and Neighbors: The Social and Cultural Context of European Witchcraft* (New York: Penguin, 1996), 273.

greater risk than men for accusations and prosecutions, as they may have had less access to a kinship network to defend them from accusers and prosecutors.[12] To be sure, this patriarchal and religiously reforming society rendered women vastly more vulnerable to accusations of witchcraft.

The royal court and council of Navarra referred to *brujos y brujas* (male witches and female witches) throughout its trials. Men partook with frequency in giving depositions both for and against the accused witches, and in several cases stood as the accused. But while male witches appeared throughout the witch trials, they accounted for only approximately 20 percent of those accused in Navarra. Male witches were often related to or associated with women with *mala fama* and noticeably disappeared from the trial records with greater frequency than female witches.[13] Men enjoyed a patriarchal protective factor not available to women. Within this reform-era context, gender expectations accompanied religious norms, offering men a defense that as ordained providers, they could not complete their duties if they were sentenced for witchcraft. Women, though often providers themselves, did not enjoy the Christian defense of patriarchal duty. It is worth noting that in Navarra, brujos were more likely to be crafted by neighbors than to receive a sentence from the tribunals. While villagers crafted twenty-one men as witches, surviving records reflect sentences (by the secular court) for only four of them.[14] Drawing from patriarchal protective factors, and supported by proofs of indulgences and harvesting responsibilities, men in Navarra did not suffer from witchcraft accusations with the same intensity as women.

While women no doubt bore the brunt of witchcraft fears, early modern women in Navarra also navigated these repressions and pursued justice for themselves. Both within and outside of judicial spaces, women demonstrated strategic actions (such as carefully cultivating

---

12. In his study of Lorraine, Briggs found that half of the women accused had no husband and many had no children. He later clarifies that this statistical trend was by no means an automatic default. Navarra's secular records reflect that in isolated trials, most of the accused were widows, while during its chain trials, more married women appeared. Briggs, *Witches and Neighbors*, 264, 356.

13. This does not mean they all received absolution; rather a case would emerge including men, but only the women would receive sentencing as per the trial records.

14. Usunáriz offers the figure of seventy "indicted" men (not necessarily sentenced) in the royal tribunals from 1525 to 1595. See Usunáriz, "La caza de brujas," 320.

buena fama) and agency.[15] Women in Navarra held land, served as heirs, and enjoyed economic independence and authority on the family farmsteads (*baserri*) that formed the nucleus of Basque life.[16] Many women married later in life (on average at twenty-six years old), even if they already had children. If they bore daughters, properties could be willed to them as equal heirs in Navarra. Widowed women understood, and fought for, their dowry compensation in courts of law as Amaia Nausia Pimoulier revealed in her research on widows and "feminine resistance."[17] And as Amanda Scott has shown, Basque women maintained religious authority within their communities, even after Tridentine reforms.[18]

Early modern women cleverly used legal systems to protect their property and inheritances, to defend their honor and *fama*, and to pursue their interests in general.[19] They also understood well the devastation a witchcraft accusation could yield.[20] Not only were women far more likely to be accused of witchcraft, the types of denunciations levied against witches often overlapped with issues central to female spheres, such as infant death and breastfeeding concerns.[21] Given their

---

15. Allyson Poska has demonstrated the wide range of female behaviors and agencies in *Women and Authority in Early Modern Spain: The Peasants of Galicia* (Oxford: Oxford University Press, 2005). See her introduction for an excellent analysis of the nuances of gender in early modern Spain.

16. Women often became the heads of households as Basque men migrated to the Americas. This was largely informed by the maritime, foundry, and shipyard economies that took men away from home, and offered independence and agency to women. See Juan Javier Pescador, *The New World Inside a Basque Village* (Reno: University of Nevada Press, 2003), 67.

17. For an excellent study of widows and gender, see Amaia Nausia Pimoulier, *Ni Casadas ni Sepultadas, las Viudas: Una Historia de Resistencia Femenina* (Navarra: Txalaparta, 2022).

18. Amanda L. Scott, *The Basque Seroras: Local Religion, Gender, and Power in Northern Iberia, 1550–1800* (Ithaca, NY: Cornell University Press, 2020), 18–36, and throughout.

19. Lu Ann Homza has argued compellingly that women not only took their accusers to court for slander during the witch panic, but their actions contributed to the Inquisition's skepticism. See *Village Infernos and Witches' Advocates: Witch-Hunting in Navarre, 1608–1614* (University Park: Pennsylvania State University Press, 2022), 14–23, 109–21.

20. One such woman from Augsburg in 1650, Anna Ebler, screamed out to her neighbors that they were sending her to "the butcher's slab" as officials led her away due to accusations by other women. Lyndal Roper, *Witch Craze: Terror and Fantasy in Baroque Germany* (New Haven, CT: Yale University Press, 2004), 202.

21. Lyndal Roper located fantasies and fears at the heart of these accusations. These fears and fantasies tended to coalesce around feminine issues, such as during childbirth and the dangerous lying-in period following it. Dangerous moments such as these heightened fears, and when coupled with the sudden death of the mother or newborn, these inexplicable tragedies sometimes led to accusations, usually of other women. Roper, *Witch Craze*, 8–12, 127. Michael Ostling also argued that witchcraft anxieties were attached to issues internal to the female sphere, such as breastmilk, in *Between the Devil and the Host: Imagining Witchcraft in Early Modern Poland* (Oxford: Oxford University Press, 2011), 18. In *The Last Witch of Langenburg:*

familiarity with and fear of an accusation, it makes sense that women went to great lengths to protect their honor.[22] The "rhetoric of honor," which served to maintain and order social statuses, provided a common strategy that early modern Iberians could use when pursuing disputes against neighbors, a strategy that women especially leaned into when taking legal actions to defend their honor.[23]

Several slander trials in the secular tribunals reflect the legal paths women could take to protect themselves from a witchcraft accusation. In 1560, one such accused witch, Juana de Azparren, brought charges against her sole accuser, Johan de Villanueva, a prominent councilman of the court. He had spread rumors that Juana had been imprisoned for witchcraft in the "the País Basco" (her native French Basquelands), a dangerous charge Juana deflected by denouncing him for harassment. Opposing the councilman's lone accusation, eight witnesses testified to her *buena fama* and her unwavering church attendance. Demonstrating the ubiquity of *fama*, one witness suggested that since he had not heard the *fama* of her being a witch, it simply could not be true, reasoning: "He has always known her to be a *buena cristiana*, and if it had been another way, [he] would know or would have heard. But he has not heard this before."[24] Asked if she had been imprisoned for witchcraft in the past, he reiterated "if she *had* been imprisoned there for that reason . . . he would have known. And this is certain since they are both natives of that town of Azparren."[25] His words illuminate the reliance on, and sophisticated pathways of, *fama*. The friar Miguel de Cubieta also argued against the allegation saying he had never heard of it, and he would have known since "he confessed Joana de Azparren just last week. . . . and as such he knows that she is a *buena cristiana* . . . and that she is not a witch or a *mala cristiana*, and if she was one, [he] would know as her confessor."[26] From confessors to neighbors, witnesses argued:

Murder in a German Village (New York: W. W. Norton, 2009), chap. 1, Tom Robisheaux captures the tension surrounding the lying-in period and the explosion of witchcraft fears when a healthy new mother suddenly dies.

22. In his research on honor and violence in Castilla, Scott Taylor has likened criminal investigations to duels as they "embodied a collection of public rituals dedicated to disputing truth and reputation." Taylor, *Honor and Violence in Golden Age Spain* (New Haven, CT: Yale University Press, 2008), 78–79.

23. Here Taylor borrows from Thomas Cohen's definition of honor as a rhetorical process as opposed to a code, quality, or intangible commodity. See Taylor, *Honor and Violence*, 8, 235 n. 18.

24. AGN, TR_66473 (1560), fol. 9v.

25. AGN, TR_66473 (1560), fol. 10r. Italics mine.

26. AGN, TR_66473 (1560), fol. 13r.

"If she was a witch, we would know." Witch-hood was not an occult practice; it was a public production. It was a truth crafted by the social body, and the transmission of this *fama* imbued it with life.

Women like Juana recognized the power of the language of witchcraft and the dangers of a witchcraft accusation, and she was one of at least a dozen other villagers who charged their accusers with slander.[27] In 1583 Graciana de Aycanoa (not be confused with Graciana Belza from our opening vignette) brought a suit against María de Gorriti for false testimony, charging: "María has intentionally damaged and offended and injured [Graciana] . . . by saying all over town that she is a witch and she has killed María's small child . . . causing great scandal."[28] Multiple witnesses testified to Graciana's good *fama*, habits, and manners, leaving María imprisoned for slander. Thus *fama*, both good and bad, shaped the results of witchcraft accusations.[29] To better understand why women sought to protect themselves from slander, let us now turn to the importance of *mala fama*, a recurring theme villagers used to craft their witches.[30]

Mala Fama

Allegations of *mala fama* emerged throughout the secular records. Witnesses commonly responded to interrogations seeking witches with the simple fact that the accused had *mala fama*, suggesting that at times, *fama* alone could craft a witch. The signifier of *mala fama* was employed to designate witches, and this stigma, in turn, reinforced its designations. Informed by behavioral norms and expectations, performativity in Catholic practice, and kinship and social ties, *mala fama* served as

---

27. The AGN holds records for thirteen trials of *injurias*, spanning between 1581 and 1714. Thirteen women in total alleged false accusations of witchcraft against them, alongside seven men.

28. AGN, TR_212327 (1583), fol. 1r.

29. As early as 1415, the word *bruja* was elevated to a category of slander, or injury (*injuria*). For more on slander, see Cristina Tabernero and Jesús María Usunáriz Garayoa, "Bruja, brujo, hechicera, hechicero, sorgin como insultos en la Navarra de los siglos XVI y XVII," in *Modelos de vida y cultura en Navarra (siglos XVI y XVII)*, ed. Mariela Insúa (Pamplona: Universidad de Navarra, 2016), 382.

30. Richard Kagan found a wealth of honor cases in the court of Castilla where litigants sought to restore their honor and reputation after receiving affronts to their *fama* by words such as *judio*, *marrano*, or *hijo de puta*. But he also cautioned that insult cases could stem from deeper grievances and could have less to do with a sense of personal honor and more to do with protracted disputes or external circumstances. Kagan, *Lawsuits and Litigants in Castile 1500–1700* (Chapel Hill: University of North Carolina Press, 1981), 90–91.

the principal identifier of the witch in one out of four witch trials in Navarra.[31]

Fama stood at the intersection of social and legal realms, commanding an enduring legacy of influence in judicial understandings.[32] It served as a recognized form of early modern legal proof and reflected legal status, social prestige, power, and wealth.[33] *Fama* also functioned as a mechanism of social control, helping establish and reify behavioral expectations, while communicating the repercussions for transgressions.[34] These expectations centered on Catholic performativity, participation in the rituals of Mass and confession, and curating a reputation as a *buena cristiana*. *Buena fama* was further supported by the possession of an honorable parentage and an Old Christian lineage, though all of Navarra's accused witches identified as Old Christians.[35] Rumors and reputations held great weight as they functioned as legal facts.

Graciana Belza's case from this chapter's opening vignette highlights the importance of *mala fama* in accusations of witchcraft. While the parish priest strongly defended the notorious witch, as he had known Graciana for more than thirty years and regarded "her as a person of good living, *fama*, dealings, and reputation," nearly a dozen neighbors pointed to her *mala fama*.[36] The crucial role of her *fama* was reported by the *fiscal* who noted "the large number who bear witness against her,"

---

31. The importance of *fama* was not unique to Navarra. In Larner's research in Scotland, the majority of witchcraft accusations "were pre-selected by reputation," whether it be due to a family association or their own actions. Larner further noted that in Scotland, *fama* extended as far as twenty miles away. Larner, *Witchcraft and Religion*, 30.

32. As early as the sixth century, the Visigothic Code in Iberia drew from the concept of *infamia*, one of its many legal concepts borrowed from Roman law. See Jeffrey Bowman, "Infamy and Proof in Medieval Spain," in *Fama: The Politics of Talk and Reputation in Medieval Europe*, ed. Thelma Fenster and Daniel L. Small (Ithaca, NY: Cornell University Press, 2003), 98–99.

33. Roman law marked *infames* (those with legally declared *mala fama*) and denied them the legal protections and privileges afforded those with good *fama*. Though the Visigothic Code dedicated more than twenty statutes to *infamia* and *mala fama*, it did not clearly define the differences between these concepts. The *Sieta Partidas*, statutory codes introduced in thirteenth-century Castilla, adopted the legal concept of *fama*, providing a legal definition of *buena fama* as the "good state of a person who lives justly according to law and good customs, having no defect or mark." Bowman, "Infamy and Proof in Medieval Spain," 103–5.

34. Alison Rowlands's work on early modern German witchcraft has shown that *fama* could provide both the circumstantial evidence to support a case and the guidance to decide whether interrogative torture would be warranted. Since cases of witchcraft lacked eyewitnesses and physical proofs, communal opinion became even more crucial in these trials. See Rowlands, *Witchcraft Narratives in Germany: Rothenburg, 1561–1652* (New York: Manchester University Press, 2003), 18.

35. Over the course of my examinations of these witch trials, I have not found any accused witches reported to be *conversas*, or "new Christians."

36. AGN, TR_211115 (1560), fol. 51v.

further remarking that her accusers were "people of good living, customs, and *fama*, and *buenos cristianos*." The *fiscal* centered his arguments not on Graciana's alleged crimes and victims, but on her *mala fama* that pointed to her wickedness. He confirmed the legitimacy of this reputation by invoking her accusers' good *fama*, which stood in stark contrast to Graciana's *mala fama*. *Fama* thus depended upon quality as well as quantity. His concluding remark ordering her torture was telling: "The accusations and witnesses are too many."[37] The intensity of Graciana's *mala fama* mirrored the intensity of the torture that left her crippled.

The weight of *mala fama* relied on its entrenchment within the social fabric. Long-lived and ubiquitous *mala fama* often surfaced first in witch-hunts, while *mala fama* lacking establishment or identifiable origins invited *procuradores* to challenge its legitimacy within the legal sphere. When the village of Ziga became involved in the chain trials of 1575–76, townsfolk provided a lengthy list of suspected witches with *mala fama*. One witness, seventy-year-old Joanot de Majaferrero, shared some insights into the origins of some of the fourteen accused witches' *fama*, saying that for forty years "María de Estermiguel the *serora* and her sister Catalina de Echeberria have had and have the *fama* that they have been and are witches." Then he clarified he had no idea why they had that *fama*, admitting he had "not seen them say or do anything having to do with witchcraft."[38] He also took care to further spell out that not all of Ziga's accused possessed such chronic *fama* as the sisters, and some *fama* had been a recent production from the priest's niece. Joanot's testimony presented a blend of established town witches alongside a clutch of emergent witches. Though these appended witches did not share the established *mala fama* of the two sisters, in times or places experiencing chain trials or a witch panic, new suspects were folded into the "roll of witches" with ease.[39]

Following the period of chain trials and the witch panic (1525–1614), *mala fama* continued to inform the secular court's final trials of witchcraft throughout the seventeenth century. In the 1647 trial of María Yrisarri, the court meticulously noted the number of witnesses who pointed to her *mala fama* as follows: "Witnesses numbers 2, 4, 5, 8, 9, and 11 [say] that throughout this city the accused is in the reputation

---

37. AGN, TR_211115 (1560), fol. 61r.

38. Only fragments of this trial survive. It was among the thirteen witch trials rediscovered by Miriam Etxeberria in 2014 in the Archivo General de Navarra. AGN, TR_344108 (1576), fol. 19r. *Seroras* were a type of religious laywomen; see Scott, *The Basque Seroras*.

39. Here I refer to the "roll of witches" (*rolde brujas*).

and common opinion of everyone that she is a witch and sorceress. . . . Witnesses 4, 7, 8 said she . . . has the opinion, *fama*, and public rep-utation in this city that she is a sorceress and a witch and has done and continues to do great harm with her spells."[40] These indictments underscored the number of witnesses and highlighted her *fama* for witchcraft and sorcery. The legal language itself rested on this *fama*, demonstrating that the language of witchcraft created in the social sphere was understood and supported within a legal one up through the royal tribunal's final trial of witchcraft and sorcery.

The tribunals' final sorcery trial of fifty-year-old healer María Esparza relied heavily on *mala fama*. While villagers blamed María for everything from insufficient breast milk to spoiled grapes, witnesses and the *fiscal* highlighted her *mala fama*. The preliminary summary stated that María was imprisoned because "the ten witnesses of this Inquest all agree that the accused is in opinion, *fama*, and reputation that she is a sorceress . . . and this has been and is the public voice and *fama* and commonplace saying." This intense *fama* informed one unlucky farmer's conclusion that "the accused and her husband were those who destroyed [my grapes] by means of spells *because* they always are and have been in the opinion, *fama*, and reputation that she is a sorceress and her husband was too."[41] María's *fama* was so palpable vil-lagers paid to prevent her *maleficia*, a situation that no doubt furthered resentment.[42] Villager Pedro de Cubeldra reported that neighbors gave María Esparza and her husband money and food to avoid their *male-ficia*, explaining "they always have had and have the opinion of being witches, sorcerers, and for that reason many people gave them what they wanted, because to do contrary would result in greater harm."[43] María's intent to harm struck fear among her neighbors, and the court punished her harshly, sentencing her to two hundred lashings and ten years' exile.

The power of *mala fama* was so great it could transcend the body of the accused. Fortuno Legaz received multiple accusations from Ocha-gavía's villagers testifying they had seen him feed salt to a group of bulls (a common practice in early modern Spain) that died soon thereafter. But it was not the eyewitness evidence that commanded the focus of

---

40. AGN, TR_16058 (1647), fol. 6v.
41. AGN, TR_17176 (1675), fol. 8r. Italics mine.
42. Briggs has shown the strain begging placed on communities. *Witches and Neighbors*, 155.
43. Unfortunately, the records do not offer more details about this supposed mafia-style extortion. AGN, TR_17176 (1675), fol. 21r.

their testimonies from 1539. Instead, it was his friendship with María Goyena and María Egybel—both imprisoned for witchcraft—that galvanized suspicions he had caused the bulls' sudden deaths. Over a dozen witnesses highlighted Fortuno's *fama* resulting from his association with the disreputable women, declaring "that in all of the town of Ochagavía it is publicly known among the neighbors that Fortuno Legaz is a witch."[44] While we do not know how long the trio's *mala fama* stood, the *fiscal* charged: "The above-said witches are known and noted in the *fama* and *vos comun* in the town of Ochagavía and in the other nearby areas."[45] Though no doubt his interactions with the suddenly dead livestock held weight, Fortuno's association with the notorious witches propelled the accusations levied against him. And his comradery with the town witches sufficed for the court to sentence him to three months' exile. The power of *mala fama* extended beyond the accused, leaving friends—and family especially—of suspected witches vulnerable to accusations.

Hereditary Witchcraft

From villagers' reports to formal indictments, witchcraft legacies informed witch crafting in Navarra. While being a witch in early modern Europe was not purely hereditary, those accused often possessed connections to a relative or a neighbor who taught them the craft.[46] The belief that witchcraft was passed on within households from the older to the younger generation had deep roots, as Alison Rowlands has shown in her research on witches in Rothenberg and surrounding villages.[47] In Navarra, it appears that villagers thought knowledge of witchcraft was transferred along maternal lines.

This link between witchcraft accusations and familial antecedents became strengthened in Navarra by the Spanish preoccupation with *limpieza de sangre*. Blood in early modern Europe transcended its life-giving

---

44. AGN, TR_36180 (1539), fol. 10r.

45. AGN, TR_36180 (1539), fol. 23v.

46. This stands in contrast to what anthropologists have seen elsewhere, such as some African communities, where witchcraft is hereditary. See E. E. Evans-Pritchard, *Witchcraft, Oracles, and Magic among the Azande* (Oxford: Clarendon Press, 1991).

47. Rowlands's analyses of the Brosam family of Wettringen in 1561 showed that villagers thought Barbara Brosam had learned witchcraft from her parents-in-law. And in the 1563 trial of Appolonia Kellner and her children Appolonia, Anna, and Georg of Finsterlohr, popular opinion disclosed that the siblings had gained their reputations as witches from their mother. Rowlands, *Witchcraft Narratives in Germany*, 23, 25.

qualities and symbolized the principles of individuals, families, and entire social groups. So much so that "groups were defined according to
the alleged nature of their blood, and, thus, it was an important matrix
through which society was built and imagined."[48] The notion of pure
blood took on new meaning in Spain with the passing of *limpieza de
sangre* statutes. The notion that blood carried traits of Judaism or Islam
was prevalent in Spain and defined much of the discussions of purity
of blood. This concept amplified the importance of hereditary bonds
in Navarra, and people crafted as witches often shared bloodlines with
other accused witches. After all, if Judaism and Islam corrupted blood,
so too could witchcraft.

The significant intersection between blood and witchcraft emerged
from the *fiscal*'s official charge in the trials of 1525 that proclaimed,
"each and every one of the accused witches have had and have the inheritance of being *brujos* and *brujas* because their fathers and moth-
ers, grandfathers and grandmothers, have also been *brujos* and *brujas*,
and some of them were burned by the justices [for it]."[49] Their tainted
blood informed the tribunal's understanding—and proof—of witch-
hood. When forty-year-old Johanicot Zubieta was interviewed, he said
he knew nothing about witchcraft, except for the *fama* that Graxi Yriate
and her husband Martín Baquero were witches because "he heard that
the ancestors that used to live in their house were witches, especially
Ochocho, Graxi's uncle."[50] Johanicot continued to emphasize that "according to the *fama* and the *voz comun* of the villagers that the succes-
sors and people living in that house are witches." Worse still, he shared
that "Graciana's (Graxi) grandmother was burned for being a witch . . .
and Graciana has had an unending *mala fama*." The *fiscal*'s official
charge pointed to Graxi's hereditary lineage that doomed Graxi (and
her partner) to accusations during this time of chain trials. Similarly,
when Lope Esparza, the alcalde of the Valley of Salazar, was fingered
as a witch in 1540, the villagers readily recalled his unsavory lineage
in their reports. Sixty-year-old Juanot Ochoa stated that Lope's *mala
fama* was the fruit of his father's legacy, and the *fiscal* highlighted in
his reports that "his father, having been a witch, was imprisoned and

48. Pablo Ortega-del-Cerro and Juan Hernández-Franco, "Debates on the Nature of
Blood and the Forging of Social Models in Early Modern Spain (1630s)," *Journal of Early
Modern History* 26, no. 4 (2022): 335–60.

49. AGN, TR_35728 (1525), fol. 26v.

50. Florencio Idoate Iragui, *La Brujería en Navarra y sus Documentos* (Pamplona: Institución
Príncipe de Viana, 1978), 261.

condemned for it by the Inquisition," and concluded that Lope must also be a witch.[51] And at Lope's sentencing, the *fiscal* punctuated his verdict of banishment with the reminder that he "has been and is from a lineage of witches." Though an unconventional witch—male, *hidalgo*, and the town alcalde—the mayor's tainted bloodline trumped his privileged position.

The power of blood ran freely during the chain trials of 1575–76. When the alcaldes of the Valley of Larraun initiated their inquests, villagers turned naturally to their local witch families. The infamous Graciana Oroquieta readily came to mind as a woman condemned from birth by her mother's *fama*. Among the serious and diverse charges against her, the *fiscal*'s formal accusation highlighted the origin of her contemptible *fama*, reporting: "Graciato de Oroquieta, mother of the accused, also has lived in common opinion, *fama*, and reputation of witchcraft and sorcery for years and for all time." So "public and notorious" was her mother's *fama*, "the neighbors of Oroquieta did not want to eat anything that her hands had touched, not even the holy bread, which they did not pass to Graciato Oroquieta nor did they did take to her daughter, the accused."[52] The tangible reinforcement of Graciana's unfortunate maternal legacy was conspicuously performed in a sacred space, and such a grave slight as denying a fellow parishioner the Host visibly perpetuated the taint of witchcraft across generations. So great was her hereditary stain she was denied the body of Christ and admittance into his body of believers.

Material culture in early modern Spain reminded neighbors of the *malas cristianas brujas* in their midst. As the 1576 search for witches in the Valley of Roncal demonstrates, multiple witnesses drew from Joana Larrimpe's *mala fama*—one inherited from her mother and grandmother who were both tried by the Inquisition for witchcraft. The court highlighted that "all the witnesses said Joana Larrimpe has *fama* of being a witch *by reason* that her mother was *sanbenitada* and her *sanbenito* is in the parish church of the said town."[53] Her grandmother was forced to wear a sanbenito, a penitential garment, as a symbolic marker of her sinfulness. Sanbenitos, shortened from *saco benito*, or blessed sack, visibly marked sinners both during their punishments and for years after (see fig. 5.2). When the convicted finished their penance or

51. AGN, TR_63994 (1540), fol. 59v.
52. AGN, TR_344109 (1576), fol. 21r.
53. AGN, TR_327775 (1576), fols. 9r–10r. Italics mine.

after their execution, all the sanbenitos were collected by the church officials and publicly displayed in parish churches, with the names of the convicted.[54] For those who received sentences of death, their sanbenitos hung in the parish church as a warning to others against heresy and to serve as a "blot on the family's honor."[55] Not only had her mother been a witch but "also her maternal grandmother was killed by a garrote as her sentence for being a notorious witch."[56] Joana's maternal predecessors left her vulnerable to witchcraft accusations, and her *fama* in turn stigmatized her own daughter, Madalena Soria. The hereditary potential of witchcraft thus condemned four generations of women to *mala fama.*[57] Witch belief in Navarra supported a hereditary tendency toward witch-hood, one that was easily transmitted from mother to daughter given its feminine and sanguine nature. Even if they did not agree with a particular witchcraft accusation, villagers volunteered reports of witch legacies. For example, while sixty-year-old Joanot Echeberri from the town of Burutain did not think that Miguelico was a witch, when asked about the town's witches in 1576, he felt compelled to mention that "he has heard that [Miguelico's] late mother and grandmother had *fama* that they were witches."[58]

Drawing from the connection between blood and witchcraft, attorneys for the accused invoked their clients' purity of blood as a witchcraft defense. When María Brigante was accused by twenty-four villagers of witchcraft, sorcery, and murder, her *procurador* countered these damning depositions by invoking her purity of blood. He argued:

Her parents were people with honor and good birth, clean from the bad race of Jews, Moors, and those punished by the Holy Office [of the Inquisition]. And *buenos cristianos*, fearful of God and

54. There were different types of sanbenitos: the colors and drawings indicated the crimes the convicted had committed and the punishments they deserved. They had the name of the accused and a set of flames. E. William Monter, *Frontiers of Heresy: The Spanish Inquisition from the Basque Lands to Sicily*, Cambridge Studies in Early Modern History (Cambridge: Cambridge University Press, 1990), 332.

55. Stuart B. Schwartz, *All Can Be Saved: Religious Tolerance and Salvation in the Iberian Atlantic* (New Haven, CT: Yale University Press, 2008), 28.

56. AGN, TR_327775 (1576), 9r.

57. As demonstrated by Lope Esparza, men too were rendered vulnerable by ancestral accusations. Larner similarly identified that most of the men accused in Scotland were related to women suspects. Larner, *Witchcraft and Religion*, 73.

58. AGN, TR_11219 (1576), fol. 8r.

FIGURE 5.2. "The Sanbenito" from *Relation de l'inquisition de Goa* by Sam Gabriel Dellon (1688)

their conscience and they were neither witches nor sorcerers, but rather very observant of God's law.[59]

With so many accusations against her, María's defense relied upon her "proofs" of being a *buena cristiana*, drawing on the notion of *limpieza de sangre*.[60] The hereditary aspect of these trials shows that early modern Navarrans could draw from the *mala fama* of their neighbors and their families to craft witches. Even if they had tolerated their reputations for

59. AGN, TR_59308 (1661), fol. 58r.
60. The documentary record leaves us with no resolution to this trial.

decades, sometimes a trigger, whether it be the death of an infant, the sudden loss of a group of bulls, or general diabolical fears, could turn witch beliefs into witchcraft accusations.

Diabolical Definitions

Systems of witchcraft belief were fluid and created by a reciprocal exchange of ideas and influences. A line between a popular and an elite culture cannot be clearly drawn at any one time, as ideas are exchanged in society among different social classes.[61] Witch trial reports in Navarra reflected a hybrid mix of villagers' concerns, scribal and translative choices, and the tribunals' understandings of what witches sometimes did. During the chain trials, the court and council frequently folded attendance at the *ayuntamiento de brujas* ("witches' gathering") into their charges despite its absence from the villagers' depositions. This does not mean, however, that the witches' gatherings occupied a central component of witchcraft as understood by the magistrates. As far as the records reveal, they encouraged villagers neither to confess to attendance at these nefarious soirees nor to denounce other villagers for participation. Further distinguishing Navarra's secular trials, the devil held a peripheral role in most of Navarra's *ayuntamientos*, unlike much of western Europe's descriptions that centered the diabolical pact.[62] The reports of the witch's Mass in Navarra reflected established common witch beliefs, fused with notions of witchcraft influenced by demonological writers.

The *ayuntamiento* appeared in the earliest witch trial of 1525, demonstrating that a composite of witches' deeds was already understood. The royal tribunals' summary included tropes often found in testimonies: acts of *maleficia*, the prominent use of toads, and the *ayuntamiento* itself. The surviving testimonies from this early case are mirrored in the legal summary, but with an added diabolical dimension.[63] Drawing from

---

61. For a helpful framework of these overlapping spheres, see Jan Machielsen, *The Science of Demons: Early Modern Authors Facing Witchcraft and the Devil* (New York: Routledge, 2020), 184–90.

62. Ronald Hutton offers a clear analysis of the role of diabolism in "the making of the early modern witch" in *The Witch: A History of Fear, from Ancient Times to the Present* (New Haven, CT: Yale University Press, 2017), 168–79.

63. This is the first reference to the witches' *ayuntamiento* in the records, and it does not use the term *akelarre*. *Akelarre* was not used until 1609, so it is anachronistic to apply it to

testimonies and elite understandings, the *fiscal* charged the accused
witches from Ituren and Lasaga as follows:

> They have been and are witches and have reneged God and given
> their obedience and reverence to the Devil. . . . They go to the *ayun-*
> *tamientos* and conventicles of the Devil, and converse and dance
> with demons and with other *brujos* and *brujas*. . . . And they have
> made pacts and unguents and sacrifices of toads and the hearts
> and blood of children. And with those pacts and unguents and
> venomous things they have killed, crippled, and injured many
> people . . . and ruined the crops and trees of the earth.[64]

This early testimony combined common understandings that witches
gather to do harm to their neighbors and their livelihoods with the notion that demons and the devil were involved with these gatherings and
actions. While the recorded testimonies are no longer available to us, it is
probable that villagers did not mention the devil or demons, as their main
anxieties pertained to food supply, childbirth, hunger, and sudden death.[65]

The court's summaries in the following trials from 1540 further
demonstrate a cohesive notion of the witches' gathering, and foreshad-
owed the diabolical definitions used in the latter half of the century.
The *fiscal* charged the witches of the Valley of Salazar with renouncing
"God and our Sacred Lady and of his holy mother and his saints," then
smothering, poisoning, and disinterring children to remove their hearts
to commit their *maleficia*.[66] This reflected an integration of witness testimony and preconceived notions of the witches' gathering culled from
both folkloric and demonological sources. These early accounts of a
diabolical definition of witchcraft in Navarra reveal that the cauldron
of witch belief was already forged and used by villagers before the wave
of witch trials in 1575 and the witch panic in the early seventeenth
century. As revealed by a close reading of each witness's deposition,
sometimes some villagers tapped into this belief, and at other times

---

gatherings before this term was inaccurately created by the language of the Spanish Inquisition. See Mikel Azurmendi, *Las brujas de Zugarramurdi: La historia del aquelarre y la Inquisición*
(Córdoba: Almuzara, 2013), 139–46.

64. Idoate, *La Brujería*, 263.

65. As scholars have found throughout their witchcraft research, the greatest concerns
were of loss and death of children and limited goods. The testimonies of villagers in Navarra
in nonpanic trials reflect this. Scholars of witchcraft have also shown that seeking misfortunes does not necessarily tidily line up with or overlap with larger disasters such as drought,
famine, or disease.

66. AGN, TR_63994 (1540), fol. 2r–v.

the magistrates injected a diabolical definition into their summaries. This inconsistency demonstrates the plasticity of witch belief, as witch tropes of diabolism emerged in some trials (such as chain trials) but remained absent in others (the devil, somewhat surprisingly, did not manifest for the vigorously denounced Graciana Belza).

The stock accusation sometimes issued by the secular court, which I refer to here as its "diabolical definition," reached its zenith during the episode of witch-hunting in 1575–76. It was also at this time that the *fiscal*'s formal indictments deviated most from the reports given by villagers. In fact, this diabolical definition was levied against accused witches in every witch trial of 1575 and 1576, revealing that when witchcraft fears were heightened—or guided by a court-led search for witches—the rhetoric of witchcraft privileged preconceived notions of witchcraft over specific accusations or commonplace witch beliefs (see fig. 5.3). The diabolical notion as presented by the royal tribunals against the accused witches of Ciordia in 1575 makes clear this phenomenon during times of chain trials. From the slim testimonies presented by a mere seven witnesses, the magistrates forged an especially lengthy three-folio-long list of accusations. This diabolical definition would be echoed in the other chain trials in both substance and wording, but one charge in its entirety will serve as representative of all. The *fiscal*'s diabolical accusations, which were applied repeatedly to witches in 1575–76, went like this:

> The *brujos* and *brujas* have, for much time and years, with little fear of Our Lord God and of royal justice, made deals with the devil and have gone from their houses many nights, though their doors and windows are closed, flying through the air. First, they anoint themselves on the head and behind the ears with certain unguents the devil makes. [Then they went] to a field where a great number of men and women assembled, gave reverence to the devil that was in the figure of a cow and they danced . . . and they got on the ground on top of one another . . . [to] know each other carnally, some from the rear parts and others from the front. And not being content with the abovementioned, they then wasted the crops of the earth and mountains every year, so that for many years there have almost been no crops . . . they also harmed children, smothering and killing them.[67]

---

67. AGN, TR_327214 (1576), fol. 33r–v.

FIGURE 5.3. A witches' *akelarre*. Engraving by Jan Ziarnko depicting a witches' Sabbath in *Tableau de l'inconstance des mauvais anges et demons* by Pierre de Lancre (1612).

This stood in stark contrast to the reports made by villagers as not one single villager of Ciordia mentioned night flight, unguents, diabolism, crop failures, or multiple infanticides. And while one witness cited the death of a baby, and another spoke of sex in an open field, most villagers simply echoed who was "in opinion and reputation of being a witch and sorceress." This illustrates that legal systems were more apt to employ a preconceived construction of witchcraft in times of heightened witch fears.[68]

Over the course of Navarra's secular witch trials, the devil seldom appeared outside of the chain trials. If and when villagers gave reports of witches' gatherings, diabolical and sexual perversions were minimal.[69]

---

68. For an interdisciplinary, edited volume on the devil and early modern (mostly) Spain, see María Tausiet and James A. Amelang, eds., *El Diablo en la Edad Moderna* (Madrid: Marcial Pons Historia, 2004).

69. Diabolical sex was only mentioned in a handful of cluster trials from 1575–76, the 1595 trial inspired by Lord Andueza (AGN, TR_71319), and the witch panic of 1609. Andueza charged these villagers with diabolical acts, including sexual relations with the devil. That is, neither the royal court nor their neighbors used heterodox sexual tropes to craft them.

Their depositions centered, instead, on the act of gathering, feasting, and causing *maleficia* with poisoned powders, not through diabolical powers. At times reflecting witness testimonies and at times drawing from the communal cauldron of beliefs, the royal tribunal's diabolical definition resulted from a synthesis of actual testimony, established witch beliefs, and anxieties surrounding the diabolical. What is particular about the witches' gatherings in Navarra is its lack of fixation on the devil, except during the witch panic, which as we have seen, reflected an anomalous break from the norm. The very plasticity of the definition of witchcraft invited its function in a variety of capacities. And never again did the royal tribunals depend on a diabolical definition following the chain trials of 1575–76, though the devil appeared under the interrogations of Lord Andueza in 1595, declarations retracted by the detained villagers. By examining witch trials outside of witch panics, the plasticity of the rhetoric of witchcraft becomes clearer and shows that different tropes emerged depending on the type of trial. We see that a focus on the dramatic tends to privilege an elite vision of diabolism. As with witch trials in England, where witch panics were not the norm, diabolism was not central to witch belief or accusations leveled by villagers in isolated trials. Still, informed by Catholic reforms, the devil appeared in their discourse and made himself available in the cauldron of witch beliefs.

Village Vengeance

Accusations of witchcraft could function as an effective tool for revenge. In an interconnected society highly dependent upon one another for goods, services, and even basic survival, opportunities for resentments and bitterness emerged. The spurned lover, the neighbor who never repaid informal debts, bad neighbors whose pigs trampled the gardens, the beggar, all these people no doubt had enemies. Scholars of medieval legal culture have shown that as judicial systems slowly replaced local forms of retribution, public justice could accomplish private vengeance.[70] And with a witchcraft accusation as their weapon, early modern villagers could and did enact retribution on the legal stage.

---

70. Daniel Smail treats "vengeance as a state of mind" and shows "vengeance and justice were closely paired in society." *The Consumption of Justice: Emotions, Publicity, and Legal Culture in Marseille, 1264–1423* (Ithaca, NY: Cornell University Press, 2003), 8, 13–20, 27, 35, 131–36, 162, 183, 200, 243, and throughout.

The various legal systems, aware of the ease and dangers of false accusations, instituted safeguards such as the right of the accused to bring up charges of previous enmity and to counter their accusers with slander.[71] It was therefore not uncommon for defendants and their *procuradores* to argue that revenge and ill will (*mal voluntud*) drove an accusation. These counter-accusations are usually difficult to confirm as written sources usually do not chronicle the ongoing squabbles of villagers detailed here, thus it is remarkable to encounter the trials of two aristocratic women in the chain trials of 1576 whose claims of vindictive motives can be documentarily confirmed by decades of litigation with their accusers. Their exceptional cases demonstrate that the belief in witchcraft could be, and sometimes was, exploited and used for vengeance at the village level.

María Perez de Olalde, a *hidalga* accused of witchcraft in 1576, stands out as a case of revenge worthy of closer examination.[72] In contrast with the usual meager material goods of the accused, María's list of goods occupied several folios of possessions including multiple houses, vineyards, and properties. Diverging further from most other witch trials, the fifteen witnesses who testified against her were all related, not only to each other but to María Perez by marriage. The San Roman family, relations through her daughter's matrimony, all accused María of murdering three small children as they slept. The witness testimony was conspicuously polarized: members of the San Roman and the de la Guerra families denounced her for infanticide, while eighteen nonrelated witnesses countered this claim, alerting the jurists to this perennial feud with the San Romans.

The *fiscal* imprisoned María and charged her with its diabolical definition of witchcraft used in the chain trials.[73] María's defense focused on the enduring animosity between María's family and her accusers, one created when her husband murdered the patriarch of the San Romans. This bad blood intensified when María allegedly sought to oust his son, Don Pedro de San Roman, from his position at the frontier's customs post (at the French-Spanish border).[74] María's *procurador* highlighted the history of legal battles between the families and the San

---

71. Briggs, *Witches and Neighbors*, 138.

72. *Hidalgos* and *hidalgas* were people of nobility and enjoyed legal and social privileges in their position. Only five *hidalgos* are accused of witchcraft in the run of documents, and most of these appear within a verifiable context of revenge.

73. Note that none of the witnesses drew from diabolism to craft María Perez as a witch.

74. AGN, TR_294640 (1576), fol. 52r.

Roman's publicly sworn promise of revenge. He argued that Don Pedro de San Roman was currently holding María's son prisoner and intended to imprison María as well. A number of witnesses corroborated that the San Romans had publicly declared revenge and sought it through their false accusations of witchcraft. The archival records in Navarra confirm decades of family feuding, most likely instigated by the 1556 murder of Juan de San Roman by María Perez's husband, Pedro de Calle.[75] Two court cases support María's defense of revenge as a motive for her denunciation: Pedro de Calle's trial in which he is found guilty for Juan de San Roman's death and sentenced to ten years' exile in 1556; and the San Roman's lawsuit against the de Calles for financial restitution for the murder of their patriarch in 1557. Also leaving behind archival evidence was the fact that Pedro de San Roman used the court to settle scores with some frequency.[76] This familiarity with legal culture emboldened him to use it for personal vengeance, and he astutely seized the opportunity in 1576 during the chain trials, a pattern of crafting that presented an effective tool for revenge.

This revenge accusation took a fatal turn when seventy-year-old María Perez perished in the royal prison within one month of her arrest. Interestingly, María's witch trial continued for many months, occupying over one hundred additional folios. Hers is the only trial that continued postmortem, suggesting that *hidalga* families could and would go to great lengths to clear their names from the taint of witchcraft. While *mala fama* was perilous for all villagers, a witch's reputation could have marked financial and social consequences and damn the *hidalgo* legacy for generations. María's family continued the case for many months after her death, paying for the reexamination of witnesses. It was through this intimate testimony that a lengthy story of murder, loss, jealousy, and revenge emerged. The court neither absolved her nor found her guilty, and her children were held responsible for court costs. This case illustrates how under opportune circumstances accusations of witchcraft could be used for personal vendettas. And during times of heightened witch concerns, they were.

---

75. AGN, TR_66043 (1556).

76. Pedro de San Roman appears in multiple court cases spanning more than twenty years. In 1569, he was accused of abuse of power in his position as custom's officer by the Valle de la Berreuza (AGN, TR_27831). In 1586, he battled family members over inheritance disputes (AGN, TR_148115). And in 1593, he accused someone of attempted murder, little surprise given his contentious relationships with neighbors and family members (AGN, TR_176366).

The trial of Teresa de Ollo from the same year mirrors that of María Perez in haunting ways. Teresa, another wealthy *hidalga* woman, had a long history of feuding with another family that was enacted in the legal sphere. And a disproportionate number of witnesses emerged from a single family, the Ubanis. Like María Perez, an extensive list of goods, boasting three houses and nine vineyards, confirmed Teresa de Ollo's *hidalga* status. Teresa was also accused of murdering her own grandchild, an accusation launched by the child's other grandmother, Graciana Labayen. And like María Perez, fifty-year-old Teresa also died in prison shortly after her arrest. Through her attorney's defense and the village testimonies, a complicated web of family secrets and contention unfolded.[77] Teresa's *procurador* argued that it was "public knowledge" that the Ubanis were "capital enemies" of Teresa and her son and pointed to multiple trials "treated in various royal audiences, both criminal and civil," as evidence. This, he argued, was proof of why "they thus have sought to have her accused of being a witch."[78] Arguments for her defense concentrated on claims of revenge and, as with María Lopez, the fact that the accusers were all related to one another. Transcending mere village quibbles, this animosity was so profound that Teresa's attorney argued the vicar "Don Martin de Subica will say anything even if it is contrary to the truth. . . . [He wants] to see her dead."[79] This wish was granted. Teresa de Ollo died in prison within two months of her arrest for witchcraft.

Like María Perez, Teresa was a wealthy *hidalga* woman and unaccustomed to the cold and crude conditions the prisons offered, and similarly she died quickly. Unlike María, Teresa was absolved by the court two months following her death in the absence of further proceedings. Much like María, the long-standing feud between Teresa and her accusers left behind a robust legal trace that testifies to the usefulness of a witchcraft accusation in enacting retribution.[80] The discursive trials

---

77. Teresa's daughter married into the Ubani family, and her son Juanes married into the Labayen family. While embroiled in litigation with the Ubani family, Juanes and his mother Teresa angered the vicar of Legassa, Martín de Subica, by exposing the sexual affair between the vicar and Juanes's mother-in-law, Graciana Labayen. AGN, TR_327744 (1576).

78. AGN, TR_327744 (1576), fol. 146r.

79. AGN, TR_327744 (1576), fol. 146r.

80. In 1563, Teresa's husband had a case against Martín de Ubani over disputed land, a fight that erupted into the destruction of a stone wall. AGN, TR_324661 (1563). In 1572, Teresa's son was accused of stabbing his wife and assaulting and attempting to murder his mother-in-law, Graciana Labayen. AGN, TR_10981 (1572). Two years later, Teresa's son was in litigation against his brother-in-law, Martín de Ubani, over an inheritance. AGN, TR_326734 (1574). The following year, he litigated with his mother-in-law, Graciana Labayen, over

of the *hidalga* women accused of witchcraft in the absence of *mala fama* illustrate the versatility of witch belief. They reveal that in the years 1575–76, the court was particularly receptive to witch trials, and astute villagers seized this moment to exact revenge. While a well-timed witchcraft accusation had the potential to be used for personal reasons, it required legal systems that would support and process these claims. And certainly, we must remember that functional uses of witchcraft were the result of ingrained witch belief, not its cause.

Skepticism

Among the dizzying understandings of witch belief, one emerges as largely absent from the trial records: voices of skepticism. To be sure, some premodern people held skeptical views that questioned the realities of witchcraft and sorcery.[81] Concerns often focused on whether these deeds occurred corporeally, in dreams or imagination, or by means of diabolical delusions. Writers often presented probing questions and doubts about certain components of witchcraft in their demonological treatises, which served to both nuance the body of witchcraft literature and also to reify witch belief, as the reality of demons went unquestioned. Writings such as the *Canon episcopi* (906 CE), Johannes Nider's *Formicarius* (ca. 1437), Gianfrancesco Picodella Mirandola's *Strix* (1523), and Johann Weyer's *De praestigiis daemonum* (1563) drew from religious and scientific arguments to probe the reality of various aspects of witch belief.[82] Similarly, the inquisitor Alonso Salazar y Frías would reach his own set of skeptical conclusions during the witch panic.[83]

The villagers' reports in Navarra did not reflect learned skepticism, though likely many villagers held skeptical opinions as to the legitimacy of specific accusations of witchcraft, the reality of the witches' gatherings, or perhaps the reality of the deeds assigned to witches.[84]

---

goods and exchanges, a case that involved nearly every person in the witchcraft case. AGN, TR_327323 (1576).

81. As Jan Machielsen notes in *The Science of Demons*, 9, skepticism and belief drew from the same font. For a helpful overview of skeptical thought as to the reality of diabolical witchcraft at the elite level, see Alan Kors and Edward Peters, *Witchcraft in Europe, 400–1700: A Documentary History*, 2nd ed. (Philadelphia: University of Pennsylvania Press, 2001), chap. 10.

82. Kors and Peters, *Witchcraft in Europe*, 155–59, 239–45, 280–89.

83. Homza, *Village Infernos*, 172–81.

84. Perhaps these statements stood in for doubts or skepticism. It is quite certain that the written record does not fully reflect all doubts, and witnesses were likely not asked about their skepticism, or perhaps were uninterested in voicing their apprehensions. Similarly, the

Indeed, villagers responded frequently that "they know nothing" about witches, while others defaulted by responding with "what they have heard" and nothing more. No doubt a variety of reasons contributed to the exclusion of skeptical responses. Nonetheless, this absence is noteworthy, especially given the extensiveness of the surviving records.[85] This reinforces that witch beliefs comprised an integral piece of early modern thought, even in a region without convulsive witch persecutions.

Only two trials featured skeptical thought, and both emerged from the chain trials of 1539–40 and involved men with connections to the royal court. The first voice of skepticism came from the guard of the royal prisons, Juanes de Zubiri. The court charged him for dereliction of duty by failing to apprehend accused witches from the village of Ochagavía and even facilitating their flight. While the *fiscal* suggested that bribery by the accused alcalde, Lope Esparza, motivated his dereliction of duty, villager Iñigo Ladronde Cegema dismissed the whole witch project, proposing: "The porter in Ochagavía says . . . that all regarding the witches is a joke and dreams, and other things." Iñigo himself admitted: "I think it is true what the porter says."[86] This skepticism was not confined to the porter and this villager of Ochagavía at this time, as a member of the tribunals shared his own doubts.

The jurist, Bachiller Lope Camus, opined in the case of the insubordinate jailer. He recalled seeing Juanes in the company of Doctor Goñi, who had previously disputed "that of the witches" with the royal council, and recounted a conversation he had with Goñi:

> [Juanes de Zubiri] asked Doctor Goñi if he had faith in what the witnesses had said about having seen the alcalde dance and join in the congregations of other witches, and the doctor responded that he did not have sufficient faith . . . to charge them with it. The doctor said that the devil can transport your body and mine. . . . In fact if God permitted it, the devil could transport the city of Pamplona to the hill of San Cristobal.[87]

---

scribes may have chosen to omit testimonies that spoke to neither the guilt nor the innocence of the accused.

85. Valerie Kivelson noted the lack of "trenchant critiques of the entire enterprise of witch-hunting." *Desperate Magic: The Moral Economy of Witchcraft in Seventeenth-Century Russia* (Ithaca, NY: Cornell University Press, 2013), 10.

86. AGN, TR_63196 (1539), 79v.

87. Idoate, *La Brujería*, 281.

The doctor couched his skepticism in terms of religious belief, arguing that the devil can cause things to appear in a certain way. If it was all illusions made by the devil, a legal penalty would not serve justice. His concern was the legal ramifications of such belief. He also reinforced his skepticism by allying his belief with the Inquisition's, sharing "that he had seen certain inquisitors . . . and that they had spoken about witches, and they had come to conclude that it was more fiction of dreams than truth."[88] The skeptical thoughts of Doctor Goñi paralleled learned discussions debating the reality of witches' deeds and the role of diabolical delusions. Goñi was perhaps drawing from conclusions the Spanish Inquisition had reached after the fierce witch trials in Navarra under Judge Balanza in 1525.[89]

Both Doctor Goñi and Bachiller Camus represent lettered elites voicing their skepticism. Perhaps less educated villagers shared these sentiments, but their testimonies were not as articulate as the *bachiller*'s and simply not noted by disinterested scribes.[90] This is suggested by the one elite accused witch, Lope Esparza, a *hidalgo* and the town alcalde, who emphatically denied the accusations by asserting "those who speak of the dances and gatherings are false. And those people cannot nor should not be believed because to believe in what such people say is an error and against the Catholic faith." He then paraphrased the *Canon* by arguing, "the people who say and confess they go to dances riding . . . it is all a joke and diabolical illusion that the devil gives them in dreams and they think in their imagination." Lope couched his bold skepticism as to the reality of witchcraft in Christian terms and argued it was heretical to believe that people held preternatural powers. He even framed his skepticism as proof of being a *buena cristiana* saying, "I believe in all the articles of the Catholic Faith and in all that the holy mother church maintains."[91] While Lope implied that the Catholic Church's official policy privileged diabolical delusion over corporeal reality, the reforming

88. Idoate, *La Brujería*, 281.
89. The Inquisition's conclusions considered the difficulty in determining whether witches actually committed the crimes to which they confessed or only imagined them. This mirrors the postpanic instructions where inquisitors were also advised to work with rigorous diligence in confirming the truth, and encouraged improved sophistication in investigations, such as an inspection of the unguents witches claimed to use for their *maleficia*. See Homza, *Village Infernos*, 175–77, for a summary of the new instructions.
90. In medieval and early modern Spain, the term *bachiller* referred to the lower grades of university studies as opposed to the higher levels of coursework needed to be a *licenciado* or *doctorado*.
91. AGN, TR_63994 (1540), fol. 65r.

church in Spain possessed variable witchcraft ideas as it, too, drew from the cauldron of witch belief.[92]

The voices of skepticism in such specific terms are limited to these trials from 1539–40 demonstrating that the magical universe and the existence of witches (not necessarily legal witchcraft accusations) inhabited part of everyday life and were not "believed in" but simply known to exist. While small instances of skeptical thoughts peppered the arguments of the defense, never again do judgments as to the reality of witch belief and deeds appear. And never again did the court's interrogation questions probe the reality of witchcraft. These few skeptical voices, situated within dozens of reports in this trial (which testified to everything from Lope's usage of toads to his hereditary witch-hood), serve to illustrate the assortment of beliefs used to craft a witch in early modern Navarra. The silence on doubts about the reality of witchcraft, however, loudly conveys the fact that witches in Navarra were real to the villagers who crafted, feared, and lived with them. Finally, the complexity of human belief invites us to acknowledge what scholar Stuart Schwartz noted from his research on local religious beliefs: "The simultaneous existence of credulity and incredulity among people drawn from the same social backgrounds and who shared the same cultural understandings speaks to the potential independence of mind and thought that was always possible to individuals."[93] Indeed, all drew from the cauldron in diverse ways.

Conducting a deep analysis of every extant, nonpanic witch trial from the secular tribunal's first in 1525 to its last in 1675 reveals that witchcraft in Navarra defied broad generalizations. The cauldron of beliefs represented the intersection between a magical universe and specific qualities of witch beliefs that allows us to pinpoint five tropes and functions that emerged in witch trials. A key learning from a regional study such as this is that much can be gleaned from the mundane: witchcraft beliefs remained plastic and variable and reflected a complicated bundle of contradictions practical for those seeking revenge. It was incredibly rare to be accused of being a witch, but if one did find themselves judicially processed for an accusation, the results were often catastrophic. Even if a witch was not executed, their lives were certainly ruined, given the vast majority lacked financial resources to recover

---

92. This is reflected in the Spanish demonologies and official church doctrine toward witchcraft.

93. Schwartz, *All Can be Saved*, 169.

from the ordeal and modern science was centuries away. From *mala fama* to disfigurement by torture, a person bore the marks of being accused of being a witch for life. This even transcended the accused's body and extended to associates and descendants. While witches tended to be crafted by their neighbors, the magistrates did infuse diabolical definitions into their charges during chain trials. Fortunately, witchcraft prosecutions remained rare even as witch beliefs permeated throughout early modern Navarra.

Epilogue
Witch Crafting in Modern Spain

> [The witch-hunt] was a femicide and a
> persecution that has had great consequences and
> repercussions for many years.
>
> —Podemos (leftist political party), Navarra, 2019

Four centuries after the Inquisition burned eleven people for witchcraft in its days-long *auto de fé*, some two hundred people gathered in Zugarramurdi, a tiny village in Navarra. Over the course of three days, hundreds of Spanish and Basque-identified people alike gathered to recognize this infamous event, and to socialize, eat, drink, dance, and ponder their past. The main event, unfolding under the somber new moon, saw a dozen women paraded in front of men dressed in clerical cloaks to reenact the dramatic *auto de fé*. They were then ceremoniously led to a burning stake. But paired with this melancholy performance, thirty other activities offered attendees food, entertainment, and artisanal wares. While these reenactments occur every year, in celebration of the witch panic's 411th anniversary in 2021, multiple local agencies came together to provide "representative performances that will remind us of a part of our history," as noted by the head of the local Citizen Participation Organization.[1]

While witches continue to bewitch us, three and a half centuries have elapsed since the royal tribunals last adjudicated a trial of

---

1. Diego Sacristán, "Las brujas de Zugarramurdi vuelven a Logroño en 'Todos los Santos,'" Radio Rioja, October 28, 2019, https://cadenaser.com/emisora/2019/10/28/radio_rioja/1572270873_756708.html.

witchcraft and sorcery. Following the final trial of María Esparza in 1675, the royal tribunals handled only four cases related to witchcraft: three slander trials due to witchcraft accusations (1681, 1691, 1714) and one trial of a witchcraft accusation coupled with attempted murder (1748).[2] Yet despite the lack of witch trials in Navarra, sorcery and witchcraft narratives continued to resonate with Basque speakers, as scholars such as José Miguel de Barandaian, Julio Caro Baroja, and Florencio Idoate demonstrated in their robust compilations of nineteenth- and twentieth-century local folklore, myths, and fairy tales. Today, in twenty-first-century Navarra and the Basque country, representations of witches, devil-goats, herbalists, and other aspects of local lore and the collective imagination consistently materialize at public holiday celebrations, carnivals, and local festivals (see fig. E.1). Their presence at these events confirms that these characters hold meaning for local populations and the power of attraction for tourists. Recently, a travel site advertising yet another witch-themed attraction in the region opened with the seductive "Reality and legend have gone hand in hand since time immemorial in Navarra, where the histories of spells and sorcery have given rise to the Route of Witchcraft."[3] Drawing from its witchy past as the site of the witch panic, Zugarramurdi has emerged as a quirky tourist destination boasting a witchcraft museum, tours of caves where the *akelarres* were rumored to be held, historical architecture and mills, and a new "Route of Witchcraft." Like academic scholarship, popular artistic creations have focused on the witch panic of Zugarramurdi, even crafting two new movies inspired by the event.[4] Both of these films reflect the horrors a witchcraft accusation often brought to vulnerable women and girls.

Modern feminist movements in Spain have found connection with those, mostly women, executed as witches. Crafting themselves as witches or the descendants of witches, these contemporary women seek to subvert patriarchal and Christian systems of power that have

---

2. AGN, TR_290606 (1748). The inquisitorial tribunal at Logroño, however, continued to process hundreds of people for *Supersticiones*, though few were tried for witchcraft specifically, and none were executed for it. Henningsen, unpublished database, 2016.

3. Just as the singular witch panic of Navarra has commanded academic attention, so has its main locus, Zugarramurdi, "a locality famous for its relationship to witchcraft and *aquelarres*," become identified with witchcraft. "Navarra, tierra de brujas: Conoce su historia y leyenda," *Binter* (blog), https://elblog.bintercanarias.com/blog/navarra-tierra-de-brujas-conoce-su-historia-y-leyenda.

4. *Las brujas de Zugarramurdi* by Álex de la Iglesia, 2013; *Akelarre* by Pablo Agüero, 2020.

FIGURE E.1. Tourist signage for the Witch Caves of Zugarramurdi. Source: TurismoVasco.com, 2022.

oppressed women for millennia throughout the Spanish world and beyond. While some scholars may find this adoption inaccurate, anachronistic, or even offensive to those conforming, Catholic women crafted as witches, the trial records used throughout this book do not uphold a singular, definitive identity that would preclude such modern applications. The lack of any clear, concise, and stable definition of what a witch *could be* in the secular trial records makes it tricky to declare what a witch *cannot be*. I do not suggest that the witches in these records held developed notions of gender equity. But, despite the discursive trials and my close readings, the precise reasons why certain women were accused and persecuted by their neighbors and the courts simply remain unknown. This allows for a legitimate possibility that some of these women did indeed threaten (in reality or the imagination), wrinkle, or even rip asunder social and gender norms. Further, most modern feminists and self-identifying witches do not claim that their maternal ancestors practiced pagan rituals or stole away male genitals. As Laurel Zwissler reported on her focus group of practitioners, one self-identifying Witch shared: "If you look at the ways that the victims were presented—Pagans and Jews and Witches and anybody else—it was a stamp. They were created as Other and destroyed as Other and when that Other was gone, a new Other was more or less found."[5] This woman, a practitioner of Witchcraft as a religion, crafted her identity from the modern cauldron of witch belief—the idea of witches as scapegoats—and did not rely solely on an imagined identity of powerful or pagan women. As was the case with early modern witches, identity is crafted from narratives and stories, not just some documentations of the "truth" of the past and present. As such, the identity of modern feminist witches or Witches who practice witchcraft as a religion should be free to draw from the mythos of the past, just as every other cultural, national, ethnic, and collective identity has done.

Modern feminist groups do not necessarily invoke a nondocumentary past in their connections to witches. One modern feminist collective in Spain, the Memoria de las Brujas, does not draw from the vision of the witch as inspiration for their own identity but instead explains, "as feminists, we must deconstruct the myth of the witch and eliminate the role women have been subjected to in the long history of patriarchy." The invocation of the past is crucial in their efforts toward present gender equality, and their members center witches in their objectives, meetings, and conferences. They argue that there is presently "a struggle for memory, this struggle is based on historical work. The rewriting of the witch-hunt has to do with providing dignity and making another story about the mass murder of those women." No timidness or equivocation emerges from this goal, nor should it. They provide an interpretation, a framing of the past, just as I have done. They center the moralizing tales of bygone days for social justice today, hoping it will avoid further repetition in the future. They also remind us that people "continue to persecute and kill women accused of witchcraft in some regions of Africa and India and Latin America," bringing the very real witch-hunts occurring today to our contemporary consciousness.[6]

In addition to practitioners and feminists, some modern nations of the West have also addressed their witchcraft pasts, even issuing legal or ceremonial mea culpas to long-departed people who suffered from

---

5. Laurel Zwissler, "*In Memorium Maleficarum*: Feminist and Pagan Mobilizations of the Burning Times," in *Emotions in the History of Witchcraft*, ed. Laura Kounine and Michael Ostling (London: Palgrave Macmillan, 2016), 255. I draw here from Zwissler's use of the capitalized "Witches" for those women who identify as such.

6. Members of Memoria de las Brujas (http://memoriadelasbrujas.net/) are found throughout Spain, in Ecuador, and in New York City. Wolfgang Behringer similarly connected early modern witchcraft to those who have suffered from prosecutions in modernity in *Witches and Witch-Hunts* (Cambridge: Polity Press, 2004), 196–228.

a witchcraft accusation centuries years ago. The United States was the first to do so in 1957 when Salem, Massachusetts, formally apologized for the two hundred accusations and nineteen executions in the 1690s. And in Germany, more than fifty towns have apologized for the witch burnings, with some extending official pardons to those executed. One of the activists behind this, a retired pastor who for over a decade has urged German cities to pardon the witches, feels his campaign is relevant today because "witch persecution is still rife in parts of the world and xenophobia is rising in the west." He noted that in addition to deserving exoneration, they serve as moralizing tales against the "search for scapegoats, such as 'immigrants' that are ultimately based on fear."[7] Similarly, the first minister of Scotland Nicola Sturgeon announced in 2022 that "she was choosing to acknowledge an egregious historic injustice" and offered a formal apology to the 2,500 witches executed in early modern Scotland, mostly women.[8] As do others, the first minister understood witchcraft persecutions as an issue of justice and gender, lamenting "they were accused and killed because they were poor, different, vulnerable or in many cases, just because they were women."[9] While the witch-trial records of Navarra do not always specifically support such a claim, they certainly do not contradict the glaring gender bias among most early modern victims.

Spain has recently joined the witch-pardoning project of the modern West. The Catalan Parliament has passed a resolution to exonerate up to one thousand accused witches, following the creation of the No Eren Bruixes (They Were Not Witches) project. Compiled by the local history journal *Sapiens*, a database of more than seven hundred accused witches (mostly women) tried throughout the sixteenth and seventeenth centuries in Catalunya and Andorra provides the most

---

7. David Crossland, "German Church Finally Says Sorry for 'Bleeding Wound of Witch Burning,'" *The Times*, December 23, 2020, https://www.thetimes.co.uk/article/after-400-years-the-church-in-germany-apologises-for-burning-witches-fw6blbzf2.

8. She also signaled that parliament could choose to legislate to pardon those convicted under the law. "Nicola Sturgeon Apologises to People Accused of Witchcraft," BBC, March 8, 2022, https://www.bbc.com/news/uk-scotland-scotland-politics-60667533. Yet, as Jan Machielsen has rightfully pointed out, modern nations' apologies do not adequately address the fact that witches were created, not just by early modern judiciaries, but by fellow neighbors who, sometimes, truly felt they intended harm to their families and livelihoods. See Machielsen, "As a Historian, I Worry that Scotland's Witchcraft Apology Was a Mistake," *The Scotsman*, April 5, 2022, https://www.scotsman.com/news/opinion/columnists/as-a-historian-i-worry-that-scotlands-witchcraft-apology-was-a-mistake-dr-jan-machielsen-3640568.

9. "Nicola Sturgeon Apologises to People Accused of Witchcraft."

exhaustive documentation of accused Catalan witches so far.[10] In addition to listing names, dates, tribunals, and sentences, the project has created an interactive map. The mission of No Eren Bruixes is to "recover the memory of all these innocent women, without prejudice or falsehoods. To repair their reputations and dignify them through acts of reparation throughout the territory, in the name of all women who have been oppressed throughout history."[11] The project's manifesto has gathered nearly thirteen thousand signatures including those of public and private institutions, town halls, women's associations, community cultural centers, and countless professors, historians, journalists and individuals. Even the Catalan president Pere Aragonès has opined on the project, describing the witch-hunts as "institutionalized femicide."[12] In Navarra, some politicians are urging their local government to consider an investigation into the witch-craft persecutions, and to create memorials, markers, guided tours, learning stations, and statements in honor of the women executed for witchcraft in Navarra.[13] Parliamentarians, especially those on the left, see "the witch-hunt as antecedent of repression women suffer, in historical periods and the present."[14] Ranging from government officials to Gen Z feminists, the witch not only symbolizes the injustices of the past, but is a tangible reminder for the present and a warning for the future.

As this book has argued throughout, the very nature of witchcraft is ephemeral, variable, and plastic. And as the beliefs about witchcraft varied wildly among early modern Europeans, so too does witchcraft register quite differently for contemporary audiences. While I have conducted a documentary-based analysis according to historical methods, I am well aware, as was Foucault, that all we can write are fictions, though that is

10. This project has been conducted in consultation with historian Pau Castell and specialist Agustí Alcoberro. Link to the project: "Atles de la cacera de bruixes," Sapiens, https://www.sapiens.cat/que-es-cacera-bruixes.html.

11. "Manifest," Sapiens, accessed June 8, 2024, https://www.sapiens.cat/que-es-cacera-bruixes.html.

12. "El Parlament 'repara' la memoria de las mujeres condenadas por brujas en Catalunya," *El Periódico*, January 26, 2022, https://www.elperiodico.com/es/politica/20220126/brujas-cataluna-parlament-repara-mujeres-condenadas-brujeria-13152419.

13. Beatriz Arnedo, "El Gobierno de Navarra no investigará la caza de brujas," *Diario de Navarra*, April 20, 2022, https://www.diariodenavarra.es/noticias/navarra/2022/04/20/el-gobierno-navarra-no-investigara-caza-brujas-524591-300.html.

14. Gonzalo Núñez, "Podemos y Bildu quieren que se pida perdón por la caza de brujas del siglo XVI," *La Razón*, March 29, 2019, https://www.larazon.es/cultura/podemos-y-bildu-quieren-que-se-pida-perdon-por-las-brujas-del-siglo-xvi-LF22639233/.

not to say the truth is entirely absent.[15] The trial records themselves do not hold the "truth," as many of the beliefs and injustices and fears surrounding witchcraft were not documented, and all of the records were mediated by elite men. I therefore choose to give voice and understanding to other interpretations, even if not grounded in archival documentations.[16] Because the witch has always been malleable, I believe that modern intersections of the witch and feminism, spirituality, and other identities are valid. I propose that the witch can be usefully used to explore how belief systems create and support othering, xenophobia, and cruelty against others, usually minority populations. The role of the witch label absolutely offered a means of scapegoating, enacting revenge, and punishing social transgressions. These forms of othering—in conjunction with the suspension of ordinary legal processes—helped create witches in the early modern world.[17] It is my hope that these insights invite scholars to engage more thoughtfully with modern witchcraft understandings and practitioners, and that these connections and this intersectionality continue to illuminate the extraordinary world of witchcraft.

---

15. "I am well aware that I have never written anything but fictions. I do not mean to go so far as to say fictions are beyond truth. It seems possible to make fiction work inside of truth, to induce truthful effects with a fictional discourse, and to operate in such a manner that the discourse of truth gives rise to, 'manufactures,' something that does not yet exist, that is, 'fictions.'" Foucault, "The History of Sexuality," Finas Interview, P/K, 193, as quoted by Michel Kokora, "The Mirrored Project of Foucault and Smithton," Object Territories, accessed June 8, 2024, https://object-territories.com/the-mirrored-projects-of-foucault-and-smithson.

16. That said, we all should take care to frame our understandings and to define our terms.

17. Historical writings, such as this one, reflect the world in which they were written.

Glossary

alcalde	Traditional municipal mayor or magistrate
akelarre	Basque term for the witches' gathering (ca. 1608–14)
auto de fé	Penitential ceremony of the Inquisition
bruja/o	Female witch/male witch
buena cristiana	Good Christian
fama	Reputation, fame
fiscal	Prosecutor
hidalgo/a	Person of nobility, in theory given special rights
limpieza de sangre	Cleanliness of blood
mala cristiana	Bad Christian
mala fama	Bad reputation
maleficia	Evil deeds
procesos	Trial records or dossier
procurador	Defense attorney
Relaciones de las causas	Summaries of Inquisition cases
rolde	Roll or list of
sanbenito	Penitential smock
Supersticiones	Spanish Inquisition's category of crimes including idolatry, divination, and vain observances, which include magic, witchcraft, and occult arts
Suprema	Main office of the Inquisition

BIBLIOGRAPHY

Unpublished Primary Sources

Archivo Diocesano de Pamplona, Pamplona (ADP)
    Proceso de 1569, Aguinaga, Cartón 13
Archivo General de Navarra, Pamplona (AGN)
    Cámera de Comptos
    Comptos, Papeles Sueltos, Legajo 1, n.1 (PS1.1)
    Tribunales Reales Procesos (TR)
Archivo General de Simancas, Simancas (AGS)
    Inquisición, P.R. 28–65
Archivo Histórico Nacional, Madrid (AHN)
    Consejo de Inquisición
Archivo Particular de Juan Rena
    Caja 94, N. 13

Henningsen, Gustav, et al. *Early Modern Inquisition Database* (in preparation). Outprint of *"Supersticiones"* in the *Relaciones de causas* (1538–1694) of the Logroño Tribunal, given to this author June 2012, Madrid, Spain; and an updated version in 2016, Sevilla, Spain.

Published Primary Sources

Arles y Andosilla, Martín de. *El tratado "De Superstitionibus" de Martin de Andosilla*. Translated by José Goñi Gaztambide. Gobierno de Navarra: Institution Principe de Viana, 1971.
Ciruelo, Pedro. *A Treatise Reproving All Superstitions and Forms of Witchcraft, Very Necessary and Useful for All Good Christians Zealous for their Salvation*. Translated by Eugene A. Maio and D'Orsay W. Pearson. London: Associated University Press, 1977.
Del Rio, Martín Antoine. *Investigations into Magic*. Edited and translated by P. G. Maxwell-Stuart. Manchester: Manchester University Press, 1999.
Hildegard of Bingen. *Physica*. Translated by Priscilla Throop. Vermont: Healing Arts Press, 1998.
Kramer, Heinrich. *Malleus Maleficarum*. Translated by Christopher Mackay. Cambridge: Cambridge University Press, 2009.
Lancre, Pierre de. *Tableau de l'inconstance des mauvais anges et demons*. Translated by Gerhild Schultz. Turnhout: Brepols, 2006.

Nicander. *The Poems and Poetical Fragments*. Translated and edited by A. S. F. Gow. Cambridge: Cambridge University Press, 1953.

Pliny the Elder. *The Natural History of Pliny*. Vol. 6. Translated and edited by John Bostock, M.D., and H. T. Riley. London: Henry G. Bohn, 1953.

Secondary Sources

Álcalá, Ángel, et al. *Inquisición española y mentalidad inquisitorial*. Barcelona: Editorial Ariel, 1984.

Ankarloo, Bengt, and Stuart Clark. *Witchcraft and Magic in Europe: The Period of the Witch Trials*. London: Athlone Press, 2002.

Apps, Lara, and Andrew Gow. *Male Witches in Early Modern Europe*. Manchester: Manchester University Press, 2003.

Azurmendi, Mikel. *Las brujas de Zugarramurdi: La historia del aquelarre y la Inquisición*. Córdoba: Almuzara, 2013.

Bailey, Michael. *Battling Demons: Witchcraft, Heresy, and Reform in the Late Middle Ages*. University Park: University of Pennsylvania Press, 2003.

Bailey, Michael. "The Feminization of Magic and the Emerging Idea of the Female Witch in the Late Middle Ages." *Essays in Medieval Studies* 19 (2002): 120-34.

Bailey, Michael, and Edward Peters. "A Sabbat of Demonologists: Basel, 1431-1440." *Historian* 65, no. 6 (Winter 2003): 1375-96.

Baker, Emerson. *A Storm of Witchcraft: The Salem Trials and the American Experience*. Oxford: Oxford University Press, 2014.

Baldwin, Martha R. "Toads and Plague: Amulet Therapy in Seventeenth-Century Medicine." *Bulletin of the History of Medicine* 67, no. 2 (Summer 1993): 227-47.

Barahona, Renato. *Sex Crimes, Honour, and the Law in Early Modern Spain: Vizcaya, 1528-1735*. Toronto: University of Toronto Press, 2003.

Barry, Jonathon, and Owen Davies, eds. *Witchcraft Historiography*. Basingstoke: Palgrave Macmillan, 2007.

Bazán, Iñaki, dir. *De Túbal a Aitor, Historia de Vasconia*. Madrid: La Esfera de los Libros, 2006.

Bazán, Iñaki. "Superstición y brujería en el Duranguesado a fines de la Edad Media: ¿Amboto 1507?" *Clio & Crimen* 8 (2011): 191-224

Behringer, Wolfgang. *Witches and Witch-Hunts*. Cambridge: Polity Press, 2004.

Berrojalbiz, Ander. *Sources from the Dawn of the Great Witch Hunt in Lower Navarra, 1370*. Cham: Palgrave Macmillan, 2023.

Bever, Edward. *The Realities of Witchcraft and Popular Magic in Early Modern Europe: Culture, Cognition, and Everyday Life*. New York: Palgrave Macmillan, 2008.

Blécourt, Willem de. "The Making of the Female Witch." *Gender & History* 12, no. 2 (July 2000): 289-90.

Bowman, Jeffrey. "Infamy and Proof in Medieval Spain." In *Fama: The Politics of Talk and Reputation in Medieval Europe*, edited by Thelma Fenster and Daniel L. Small, 95-117. Ithaca, NY: Cornell University Press, 2003.

Braudel, Fernand. *The Mediterranean and the Mediterranean World in the Age of Philip II*. Translated by Sian Reynolds. Vol. 1. New York: Harper & Row, 1972.

Briggs, Robin. *Witches and Neighbors: The Social and Cultural Context of European Witchcraft*. New York: Penguin, 1996.

Bujanda, Fernando. "Documentos para la historia de la diócesis de Calahorra: Constituciones o casos del obispo don Miguel." *Berceo* 1 (1946): 121–38.

Cameron, Euan. *Enchanted Europe: Superstition, Reason, and Religion, 1250–1750*. New York: Oxford University Press, 2010.

Caro Baroja, Julio. *Con letra aguda y fina: Navarra en los textos de Julio Caro Baroja*. Edited by Matias Mugica. Navarra: Gobierno de Navarra, 2014.

Caro Baroja, Julio. *The World of the Witches*. Translated by O. N. V. Glendinning. Chicago: University of Chicago Press, 1964.

Chen, K. K., and Alena Kovarikova. "Pharmacology and Toxicology of Toad Venom." *Journal of Pharmaceutical Sciences* 56, no. 12 (December 1967): 1535–42.

Christian, William A. *Local Religion in Sixteenth-Century Spain*. Princeton, NJ: Princeton University Press, 1981.

Clark, Stuart. *Thinking with Demons: The Idea of Witchcraft in Early Modern Europe*. Oxford: Clarendon Press, 1997.

Coy, Jason P. *Strangers and Misfits: Banishment, Social Control, and Authority in Early Modern Germany*. Leiden: Brill, 2008.

Dale, Thomas. "The Nude at Moissac: Vision, Phantasia, and the Experience of Romanesque Sculpture." In *Current Directions in Eleventh-and Twelfth-Century Sculpture Studies*, edited by Robert Maxwell and Kirk Ambrose, 61–67. Turnhout: Brepols, 2010.

Darnton, Robert. *The Great Cat Massacre and Other Episodes in French Cultural History*. New York: Vintage Books, 1984.

Davis, Natalie Zemon. "Les Conteurs De Montaillou" [critical review of Emmanuel LeRoy Ladurie's *Montaillou: The Promised Land of Error*]. *Annales. Histoire, Sciences Sociales* 34, no. 1 (1979): 68–70.

Durkheim, Emile. *The Elementary Forms of Religious Life*. Translated by Carol Cosman. New York: Oxford University Press, 2001.

Edwards, Michael. *Time and the Science of the Soul in Early Modern Philosophy*. Leiden: Brill, 2013.

Eire, Carlos. *Reformations: The Early Modern World, 1450–1650*. New Haven, CT: Yale University Press, 2016.

Evans-Pritchard, E. E. *Witchcraft, Oracles, and Magic among the Azande*. Oxford: Clarendon Press, 1991.

Ferber, Sarah. *Demonic Possession and Exorcism*. New York: Routledge, 2004.

Forni, Gianfranco. "Evidence for Basque as an Indo-European Language." *Journal of Indo-European Studies* 41, no. 1/2 (2013): 39–180.

Foucault, Michel. *Discipline and Punish: The Birth of the Prison*. Translated by Alan Sheridan. 2nd ed. New York: Vintage Books, 1995.

Foxhall, Lin. *Studying Gender in Classical Antiquity*. Cambridge: Cambridge University Press, 2013.

Frather, Richard M. "Conviction According to Conscience: The Medieval Jurists' Debate Concerning Judicial Discretion and the Law of Proof." *Law and History Review* 7, no. 1 (Spring 1989): 23-88.

García Bourrellier, Rocío, María Dolores Martínez, and Sergio Solbes Ferri. *Las Cortes de Navarra desde su Incorporación a la Corona de Castilla.* Vols. 1-2. Pamplona: EUNSA, 1993.

García Pérez, Rafael. *Antes Leyes que reyes: Cultura Jurídica y Constitución Política en la Edad Moderna (Navarra, 1512-1808).* Milan: Giuffrè Editores, 2008.

Geertz, Clifford. *The Interpretation of Cultures: Selected Essays.* New York: Basic Books, 1973.

Ginzburg, Carlo. *Clues, Myths, and the Historical Method.* Translated by John Tedeschi and Anne Tedeschi. Baltimore: Johns Hopkins University Press, 1989.

Ginzburg, Carlo. *Ecstasies: Deciphering the Witches' Sabbath.* New York: Pantheon Books, 1991.

Ginzburg, Carlo. *The Night Battles: Witchcraft and Agrarian Cults in the Sixteenth and Seventeenth Centuries.* Translated by John Tedeschi and Anne Tedeschi. Baltimore: Johns Hopkins University Press, 1983.

Ginzburg, Carlo, and Anna Davin. "Morelli, Freud and Sherlock Holmes: Clues and Scientific Method." *History Workshop*, no. 9 (Spring 1980): 5-36.

Goñi Gaztambide, José. *Historia de los Obispos de Pamplona.* Pamplona: Ediciones Universidad de Navarra, 1985.

Goñi Gaztambide, José. *Los navarros en el Concilio de Trento y la reforma tridentina en la diócesis de Pamplona.* Pamplona: Imprenta Diocesana, 1947.

Gorrochatequi, Joaquin, and Joseba A. Lakarra. "Why Basque Cannot Be, Unfortunately, an Indo-European Language." *Journal of Indo-European Studies* 41, no. 1/2 (2013): 203-37.

Haliczer, Stephen. *Inquisition and Society in the Kingdom of Valencia, 1478-1834.* Berkeley: University of California Press, 1990.

Halsted, Chris. " 'They Ride on the Backs of Certain Beasts': The Night Rides, the *Canon episcopi*, and Regino of Prüm's Historical Method." *Magic, Ritual, and Witchcraft* 15, no. 3 (Winter 2021): 361-85.

Henningsen, Gustav. "La Inquisición y las Brujas." *Ehumanista: Journal of Iberian Studies* 26 (2014): 133-52.

Henningsen, Gustav. *The Salazar Documents: Inquisitor Alonso de Salazar Frías and Others on the Basque Witch Persecution.* Leiden: Brill, 2004.

Henningsen, Gustav. *The Witches' Advocate: Basque Witchcraft and the Spanish Inquisition, 1609-1614.* Basque Series. Reno: University of Nevada Press, 1980.

Henningsen, Gustav, and John A. Tedeschi, eds., in association with Charles Amiel. *The Inquisition in Early Modern Europe: Studies on Sources and Methods.* Dekalb: Northern Illinois University Press, 1986.

Herzig, Tamar. "Flies, Heretics, and the Gendering of Witchcraft." *Magic, Ritual, and Witchcraft* 5, no. 1 (Summer 2010): 51-80

Homza, Lu Ann. *Religious Authority in the Spanish Renaissance.* Baltimore: Johns Hopkins University Press, 2000.

Homza, Lu Ann. *The Spanish Inquisition, 1478-1614: An Anthology of Sources.* Indianapolis: Hackett, 2006.

Homza, Lu Ann. *Village Infernos and Witches' Advocates: Witch-Hunting in Navarre, 1608–1614*. University Park: Pennsylvania State University Press, 2022.

Hsia, Ronnie Po-chia. *The World of Catholic Renewal, 1540–1770*. 3rd ed. New York: Cambridge University Press, 2010.

Hualde, Jose Ignacio, Joseba A. Lakarra, and R. L. Trask, eds. *Towards a History of the Basque Language*. Philadelphia: John Benjamins, 1995.

Huici Goñi, María Puy. *Las cortes de Navarra durante la edad moderna*. Madrid: Ediciones Rialp, 1963.

Hutton, Ronald. *The Witch: A History of Fear, from Ancient Times to the Present*. New Haven, CT: Yale University Press, 2017.

Idoate Iragui, Florencio. *La Brujería en Navarra y sus Documentos*. Pamplona: Institución Príncipe de Viana, 1978.

Imízcoz Beunza, José María. *Elites, Poder y Red Social: Las élites del País Vasco y Navarra en la Edad Moderna*. Bilbao: Universidad del País Basco, 1996.

Jorgensen, Marianne, and Louise J. Phillips. *Discourse Analysis as Theory and Method*. London: Sage, 2002.

Kagan, Richard. *Lawsuits and Litigants in Castile 1500–1700*. Chapel Hill: University of North Carolina Press, 1981.

Kamen, Henry. *The Phoenix and the Flame: Catalonia and the Counter Reformation*. New Haven, CT: Yale University Press, 1993.

Kamen, Henry. *The Spanish Inquisition: A Historical Revision*. London: Weidenfeld & Nicolson, 1997.

Kieckhefer, Richard. "Avenging the Blood of Children: Anxiety over Child Victims and the Origins of the European Witch Trials." In *The Devil, Heresy and Witchcraft in the Middle Ages: Essays in Honour of Jeffrey B. Russell*, edited by Alberto Ferreiro, 92–95. Leiden: Brill, 1998.

Kieckhefer, Richard. *Magic in the Middle Ages*. Cambridge Medieval Textbooks. Cambridge: Cambridge University Press, 1989.

Kivelson, Valerie. *Desperate Magic: The Moral Economy of Witchcraft in Seventeenth-Century Russia*. Ithaca, NY: Cornell University Press, 2013.

Kivelson, Valerie A. "Male Witches and Gendered Categories in Seventeenth-Century Russia." *Comparative Studies in Society and History* 45, no. 3 (2003): 606–31.

Knutsen, Gunnar. *Servants of Satan and Masters of Demons: The Spanish Inquisition Trials for Superstition, Valencia and Barcelona*. Turnhout: Brepols, 2009.

Kors, Alan, and Edward Peters. *Witchcraft in Europe, 400–1700: A Documentary History*. 2nd ed. Philadelphia: University of Pennsylvania Press, 2001.

Kounine, Laura, and Michael Ostling, eds. *Emotions in the History of Witchcraft*. London: Palgrave Macmillan, 2016.

Langbein, John. *Prosecuting Crime in the Renaissance*. Cambridge, MA: Harvard University Press, 1974.

Larner, Christina. *Witchcraft and Religion: The Politics of Popular Belief*. New York: Blackwell, 1984.

Lea, Henry Charles. *A History of the Inquisition of the Middle Ages*. 3 vols. New York: MacMillan, 1906.

Lea, Henry Charles. *A History of the Inquisition of Spain*. 4 vols. New York: MacMillan, 1906-7.

Levack, Brian. *The Witch-Hunt in Early Modern Europe*. 4th ed. New York: Routledge, 2016.

Lewis, Laura. *Hall of Mirrors: Power, Witchcraft, and Caste in Colonial Mexico*. Durham, NC: Duke University Press, 2003.

Lubrich, Naomi. "The Wandering Hat: Iterations of the Medieval Jewish Pointed Cap." *Jewish History* 29, no. 3 (2015): 203–44.

Machielsen, Jan. *The Basque Witch-Hunt: A Secret History*. London: Bloomsbury, forthcoming.

Machielsen, Jan. *Martin Delrio: Demonology and Scholarship in the Counter-Reformation*. Oxford: Oxford University Press, 2015.

Machielsen, Jan. *The Science of Demons: Early Modern Authors Facing Witchcraft and the Devil*. New York: Routledge, 2020.

Marshall, Peter, ed. *The Oxford Illustrated History of the Reformation*. Oxford: Oxford University Press, 2015.

Marshall-Cornwall, James. "An Expedition to Aquitaine, 1512." *History Today* 23, no. 9 (September 1973): 640–47.

Martínez Arce, María Dolores. *Aproximación a la Justicia en Navarra durante la edad moderna: Jueces del Consejo Real en el siglo XVII*. Pamplona: Ediciones Fecit, 2005.

Midelfort, H. C. Erik. *A History of Madness*. Stanford: Stanford University Press, 1999.

Midelfort, H. C. Erik. "Witch Craze? Beyond the Legends of Panic." *Magic, Ritual, and Witchcraft* 6, no. 1 (Summer 2011): 11–33.

Midelfort, H. C. Erik. *Witch-Hunting in Southwestern Germany, 1582–1684: The Social and Intellectual Foundations*. Stanford: Stanford University Press, 1972.

Monteano, Peio. *La Guerra de Navarra (1512–1529): Crónica de la conquista española*. Pamplona: Pamiela, 2010.

Monteano, Peio. *El iceberg Navarro: Euskera y castellano en la Navarra del siglo XVI*. Pamplona: Pamiela, 2017.

Monter, E. William. *Frontiers of Heresy: The Spanish Inquisition from the Basque Lands to Sicily*. Cambridge Studies in Early Modern History. Cambridge: Cambridge University Press, 1990.

Monter, E. William. "Toads and the Eucharist: The Male Witches of Normandy, 1564–1660." *French Historical Studies* 20, no. 4 (Autumn 1997): 563–95.

Monter, E. William. *Witchcraft in France and Switzerland: The Borderlands during the Reformation*. Ithaca, NY: Cornell University Press, 1976.

Morgan, Adrian. *Toads and Toadstools: The Natural History, Folklore, and Cultural Oddities of a Strange Association*. Berkeley: Celestial Arts, 1995.

Nalle, Sara. *God in La Mancha: Religious Reform and the People of Cuenca, 1500–1650*. Baltimore: Johns Hopkins University Press, 1992.

Nenonen, Marko, and Raisa María Toivo, eds. *Writing Witch-Hunt Histories: Challenging the Paradigm*. Leiden: Brill, 2013.

O'Banion, Patrick J. *The Sacrament of Penance and Religious Life in Golden Age Spain*. University Park: Pennsylvania State University Press, 2012.

Oliver Olmo, Pedro. *Cárcel y Sociedad Represora: La criminalización del desorden en Navarra (siglos XVI–XIX)*. Gipuzkoa: Universidad del País Vasco, 2001.

O'Malley, John W. *Trent: What Happened at the Council*. Cambridge, MA: Belknap Press of Harvard University Press, 2013.

Ortega-del-Cerro, Pedro, and Juan Hernández-Franco. "Debates on the Nature of Blood and the Forging of Social Models in Early Modern Spain (1630s)." *Journal of Early Modern History* 26, no. 4 (2022): 335-60.

Ostling, Michael. *Between the Devil and the Host: Imagining Witchcraft in Early Modern Poland*. Oxford: Oxford University Press, 2011.

Owens, Yvonne. "The Saturnine History of Jews and Witches." *Preternature: Critical and Historical Studies on the Preternatural* 3, no. 1 (2014): 56-84.

Pagel, Walter. *Paracelsus: An Introduction to Philosophical Medicine in the Era of the Renaissance*. New York: Karger, 1982.

Pagola Lorente, Javier. *A Thousand Routes through Navarre*. Pamplona: Fondo de Publicaciones del Gobierno de Navarra, 2000.

Palmer, P. F., and A. Tavardi. "Indulgences." In *New Catholic Encyclopedia*, 2nd ed., vol. 7. Detroit: Gale, 2003.

Pescador, Juan Javier. *The New World Inside a Basque Village*. Reno: University of Nevada Press, 2003.

Peters, Edward. *Inquisition*. New York: Free Press, 1988.

Pimoulier, Amaia Nausia. *Ni Casadas ni Sepultadas, las Viudas: Una Historia de Resistencia Femenina*. Navarra: Txalaparta, 2022.

Poska, Allyson M. *Regulating the People: The Catholic Reformation in Seventeenth-Century Spain*. Leiden: Brill, 1998.

Poska, Allyson M. *Women and Authority in Early Modern Spain: The Peasants of Galicia*. Oxford: Oxford University Press, 2005.

Rawlings, Helen. *Church, Religion and Society in Early Modern Spain*. New York: Palgrave, 2002.

Ray, Jonathan. *After Expulsion: 1492 and the Making of Sephardic Jewry*. New York: New York University Press, 2013.

Robbins, Mary E. "The Truculent Toad in the Middle Ages." In *Animals in the Middle Ages*, edited by Nona C. Flores, 25-48. New York: Routledge, 2016.

Robisheaux, Thomas. *The Last Witch of Langenburg: Murder in a German Village*. New York: W. W. Norton, 2009.

Robisheaux, Thomas. "'The Queen of Evidence': The Witchcraft Confession in the Age of Confessionalism." In *Confessionalization in Europe, 1555–1700: Essays in Honor and Memory of Bodo Nischan*, edited by John M. Headley, Hans S. Hildebrand, and Anthony J. Papalas, 175-206. Aldershot: Ashgate, 2004.

Rodriguez, Calendario, et al. "Toxins and Pharmacologically Active Compounds from Species of the Family *Bufodinae*." *Journal of Ethnopharmacology* 198 (2017): 235-54.

Rojas, Rochelle. "*Plenae veneficiorum*: Toads, Poison, and Witchcraft in Pre-Modern Europe." Forthcoming.

Rojas, Rochelle. "The Witches' Accomplice: Toads in Early Modern Navarre." *Sixteenth Century Journal* 51, no. 3 (2020): 693-714.

Roper, Lyndal. *Oedipus and the Devil: Witchcraft, Religion, and Sexuality in Early Modern Europe*. London: Routledge, 1994.

Roper, Lyndal. *Witch Craze: Terror and Fantasy in Baroque Germany*. New Haven, CT: Yale University Press, 2004.

Rowlands, Allison. *Witchcraft and Masculinities in Early Modern Europe*. New York: Palgrave/St. Martin's Press, 2009.

Rowlands, Allison. *Witchcraft Narratives in Germany: Rothenburg, 1561–1652*. New York: Manchester University Press, 2003.

Ruggiero, Guido. *Binding Passion: Tales of Magic, Marriage, and Power at the End of the Renaissance*. New York: Oxford University Press, 1993.

Sánchez Aguirreola, Daniel. *Salteadores y Picotas: Aproximación histórica al estudio de la justicia penal en la Navarra de la Edad Moderna el caso del bandolerismo*. Pamplona: Gobierno de Navarra, 2008.

Sanz Zabalza, Félix. *Las brujas de Burgui*. Navarra: Editorial Evidencia Medica, 2013.

Schwartz, Stuart B. *All Can Be Saved: Religious Tolerance and Salvation in the Iberian Atlantic*. New Haven, CT: Yale University Press, 2008.

Scott, Amanda L. *The Basque Seroras: Local Religion, Gender, and Power in Northern Iberia, 1550–1800*. Ithaca, NY: Cornell University Press, 2020.

Scott, Amanda L. "The Wayward Priest of Atondo: Clerical Misbehavior, Local Community, and the Limits of Tridentine Reform." *Sixteenth Century Journal* 47, no. 1 (2016): 75–98.

Segura Urra, Félix. "Hechicería y brujería en la Navarra medieval: De la superstición al castigo." In *Akelarre: La caza de brujas en el Pirineo (siglos XIII–XIX)*, edited by Jesús María Usunáriz Garayoa, RIEV Cuadernos 9, 284–304. Donostia: Sociedad de Estudios Vascos, 2012.

Seitz, Jonathan. *Witchcraft and Inquisition in Early Modern Venice*. Cambridge: Cambridge University Press, 2011.

Serjeantson, Richard. "The Soul." Chap. 6 in *The Oxford Handbook of Philosophy in Early Modern Europe*, edited by Desmond M. Clarke and Catherine Wilson, online edition (Oxford Academic, May 2, 2011), https://doi.org/10.1093/oxfordhb/9780199556137.003.0007.

Serpell, James A. "Guardian Spirits or Demonic Pets: The Concept of the Witch's Familiar in Early Modern England, 1530-1712." In *The Animal/Human Boundary*, edited by A. N. H. Creager and W. C. Jordan, 157–90. Rochester: University of Rochester Press, 2002.

Shapin, Steven. *A Social History of Truth: Civility and Science in Seventeenth-Century England*. Chicago: University of Chicago Press, 1994.

Sharpe, James. *Witchcraft in Early Modern England*. New York: Routledge, 2013.

Sharpe, James. "The Witch's Familiar in Elizabethan England." In *Authority and Consent in Tudor England*, edited by G. Bernard and S. Gunn, 209–32. Aldershot: Ashgate, 2002.

Sicroff, Albert A. *Los estatutos de Limpieza de Sangre: Controversias entre los siglos XV y XVII*. Madrid: Taurus, 1985.

Smail, Daniel. *The Consumption of Justice: Emotions, Publicity, and Legal Culture in Marseille, 1264–1423*. Ithaca, NY: Cornell University Press, 2003.

St. George, Elizabeth Ann. *Heket: Frog and Toad Magic*. London: Spook Enterprises, 2006.

Tabernero, Cristina, and Jesús María Usunáriz Garayoa. "Bruja, brujo, hechicera, hechicero, sorgin como insultos en la Navarra de los siglos XVI y XVII." In *Modelos de vida y cultura en Navarra (siglos XVI y XVII)*, edited by Mariela Insúa, 381–429. Pamplona: Universidad de Navarra, 2016.

Tausiet, María. *Ponzoña en los ojos: Brujería y superstición en Aragón en el sigo XVI.* Madrid: Turner, 2004.

Tausiet, María. *Urban Magic in Early Modern Spain: Abracadabra Omnipotens.* New York: Palgrave Macmillan, 2014.

Tausiet, María, and James S. Amelang, eds. *El Diablo en la Edad Moderna.* Madrid: Marcial Pons Historia, 2004.

Taylor, Scott. *Honor and Violence in Golden Age Spain.* New Haven, CT: Yale University Press, 2008.

Tudor, Adrian. *Tales of Vice and Virtue: The First Old French "Vie des Peres."* Amsterdam: Rodopi, 2005.

Usunáriz Garayoa, Jesús María, ed. *Akelarre: La caza de brujas en el Pirineo (siglos XIII–XIX).* RIEV Cuadernos 9. Donostia: Sociedad de Estudios Vascos, 2012.

Usunáriz Garayoa, Jesús María. "La caza de brujas en la Navarra moderna (siglos XVI–XVII)." In *Akelarre: La caza de brujas en el Pirineo (siglos XIII–XIX)*, edited by Jesús María Usunáriz Garayoa, RIEV Cuadernos 9, 306–50. Donostia: Sociedad de Estudios Vascos, 2012.

Usunáriz Garayoa, Jesús María. *Historia breve de Navarra.* Madrid: Silex S.L., 2007.

Usunáriz Garayoa, Jesús María. "Las instituciones del reino de Navarra durante la Edad Moderna (1512–1808)." *Revista Internacional Estudios Vascos* 46, no. 2 (2001): 684–744.

Usunáriz Garayoa, Jesús María. *Nobleza y señoríos en la Navarra Moderna: Entre la solvencia y las crisis económica.* Navarra: EUNSA, 1997.

Vassberg, David. *The Village and the Outside World in Golden Age Castile.* New York: Cambridge University Press, 1996.

Vervoort, Renilde. "The Pestilent Toad: The Significant of the Toad in the Works of Bosch." In *Hieronymus Bosch: New Insights into His Life and Work*, edited by Jos Koldeweij and Bernard Vermet, 145–52. Rotterdam: Museum Boijmans Van Beuningen, NAi Publishers, 2001.

Voltmer, Rita. "The Witch in the Courtroom: Torture and the Representations of Emotion." In *Emotions in the History of Witchcraft*, edited by Laura Kounine and Michael Ostling, 97–116. London: Palgrave Macmillan, 2016.

Wasserug, Richard. "Why Tadpoles Love Fast Food." *Natural History* 93 (April 1984): 60–69.

Wiesner-Hanks, Merry. *Women and Gender in Early Modern Europe.* 4th ed. New York: Cambridge University Press, 2019.

Wilby, Emma. *Invoking the Akelarre: Voices of the Accused in the Basque Witch-Craze, 1609–1614.* Brighton: Sussex Academic Press, 2019.

Willumsen, Liv Helene. *Witches of the North: Scotland and Finnmark.* Brill: Leiden, 2013.

Wilson, Stephen. *The Magical Universe: Everyday Ritual and Magic in Pre-Modern Europe*. London: Hambledon, 2000.

Zwissler, Laurel. "*In Memorium Maleficarum*: Feminist and Pagan Mobilizations of the Burning Times." In *Emotions in the History of Witchcraft*, edited by Laura Kounine and Michael Ostling, 249–63. London: Palgrave Macmillan, 2016.

INDEX

Page numbers in *italics* indicate figures or tables.

www.ingramcontent.com/pod-product-compliance
Lightning Source LLC
Chambersburg PA
CBHW020443100426

42812CB00036B/3428/J